GENERAL SYSTEMS THEORY
AND
HUMAN COMMUNICATION

GENERAL SYSTEMS THEORY
AND
HUMAN COMMUNICATION

Edited By

Brent D. Ruben, Ph.D.

Director, Institute of Communication Studies

Rutgers University

New Jersey

and

John Y. Kim, Ph.D.

Assistant Professor

Department of Human Communication

Rutgers University

New Jersey

HAYDEN BOOK COMPANY, INC.

Rochelle Park, New Jersey

For
Malcolm S. MacLean, Jr.
Teacher, Colleague, Friend

Library of Congress Cataloging in Publication Data
Main entry under title:

General systems theory and human communication.

　　Bibliography: p.
　　Includes index.
　　1. Communication.　2.　System theory.
I.　Ruben, Brent D.　II.　Kim, John Y.
P91.G38　　　　001.5'1　　　　75-8981
ISBN 0-8104-5941-8

Printed in the United States of America

1　2　3　4　5　6　7　8　9　PRINTING

75 76 77 78 79 80 81 82 83　YEAR

Acknowledgments

Grateful acknowledgment is made for permission to use the following material:

Chapter 1: From the *General Systems Yearbook,* Vol. I, February 1956. Reprinted by permission of the Society for General Systems Research, publishers of *General Systems Yearbook.* This paper was originally printed in *Main Currents in Modern Thought,* 71, 75, 1955.

Chapter 2: Reprinted from *Management Science,* Volume 2, No. 3, April 1956, pp. 197-208.

Chapter 3: From the *General Systems Yearbook,* Vol. XV, 1970. Reprinted by permission of the Society for General Systems Research, publishers of *General Systems Yearbook.*

Chapter 4: From the *General Systems Yearbook,* Vol. I, February 1956, pp. 18-28. Reprinted by permission of the Society for General Systems Research, publishers of *General Systems Yearbook.* This paper was originally printed by Bell Telephone Laboratories.

Chapter 5: Reprinted by permission from *Systematics,* Vol. 10, No. 1, 1972, pages 40-54. *Systematics* is the Quarterly Journal of the Institute for Comparative Study of History, Philosophy and the Sciences, Sherborne House, Sherborne nr. Cheltenham, Glos. England GL54 3D2.

Chapter 6: From the *General Systems Yearbook,* Vol. VIII, 1963, pp. 107-114. Reprinted by permission of the Society for General Systems Research, publishers of *General Systems Yearbook.* This paper was originally published by the Department of Natural Science, Michigan State University.

Chapter 7: From *Human Information Processing: Individuals and Groups Functioning in Complex Social Situations* by Harold M. Schroder, Michael J. Driver, and Siegfried Streufert. Copyright © 1967 by Holt, Rinehart and Winston, Inc. Reprinted by permission of Holt, Rinehart and Winston, Inc.

Chapter 8: Reprinted from *Man in Systems,* edited by Milton D. Rubin by permission of Gordon & Breach, New York. Copyright © 1971 by Gordon and Breach.

Chapter 9: Reprinted from pages 201-209 from Chapter 16 of *Toward a Unified Theory of Behavior,* edited by Roy R. Grinker, Sr. © 1966 by Basic Books, Inc., Publishers, New York.

Editors' Preface

In preparing this volume we have been reminded of our huge debt to all of our colleagues and students, too numerous to mention by name, who over the past years have stimulated and broadened our thinking about general systems and human communication. To each we are truly appreciative.

We are of course grateful to the contributors to this volume, many of whom have given generously of their time and advice as the project progressed. The suggestions of both Dick Budd and Erv Bettinghaus, have been especially helpful to us at critical stages in the development of the book, and we are appreciative of their concern.

Special thanks also to Greg Andriate, Kathi Teichman and Kyle Kurtz. Their interest, commitment, and competency have been essential at every step in the preparation of this manuscript. Finally, it is appropriate to acknowledge the support for study in general systems theory and human communication made possible by a research grant from the Graduate College of Rutgers University, during the 1973–1974 academic year.

BRENT D. RUBEN
JOHN Y. KIM

New Brunswick, New Jersey

Contents

GENERAL SYSTEMS THEORY
AND
HUMAN COMMUNICATION

INTRODUCTION

The goal of this volume is to acquaint the reader with the philosophy, theory, and basic concepts of general systems, and to explore their applicability to human communication theory. General systems theory today is receiving increasing attention and application in sociology, psychiatry, philosophy, biology, administration, economics, and international relations, yet formal traces of contemporary systems theory were virtually non-existent little more than two decades ago. It should, of course, be noted that some of the foundation concepts of systems thinking are rooted deeply in classical thoughts in philosophy, sociology, and physics and are neither unique to general systems theory nor to these times. Still, in the past twenty years, drawing especially on work in cybernetics and information theory, scholars such as Ludwig von Bertalanffy, Anatol Rapoport, Kenneth Boulding, James G. Miller, Roy Grinker, Walter Buckley, Magorah Maruyama, Ervin Laszlo, and numerous others, have provided impetus and the basic foundation for the formalized study of organization, systems, and their relationship to one another and to their environments.

Their resulting framework is an attempt to develop an integrated and unified paradigm for approaching phenomena of study in any one of a number of different disciplines, and points to some rather different ways of thinking. As a consequence, a number of prominent scholars suggest that general systems provides more than just a theory, but indeed is an alternative *Weltanschauung*—a new and unique world view.

It is primarily with regard to its focus on the nature, function, and consequence of human organization that we find a particular relevance of the systems perspective for human communication study. Four notions are critical in this regard:

1) The recognition that a multi-individual unit is something other than the simple sum of the individual parts, has dramatic consequence for the manner in which one understands the dynamic processes of intrapersonal, interpersonal, and socio-cultural communication.

2) Of no less importance, is the focus on multi-lateral causality among parts of a system, among systems, and among systems and their environments. The implications of this for understanding human communication are far-reaching, and underscore the inadequateness of uni-lateral formulations of information processing phenomena.

3) A third focus of general systems theory is upon the relation between antecedent and consequent conditions in human systems, leading to the recognition that one set of initial conditions can give rise to different final states, and conversely, differing initial conditions may result in a single outcome. This understanding raises serious questions about stimulus-response models and research paradigms for the study of human communication processes.

4) General systems theory directs attention also to the distinction between what might be termed *information systems*, which are concerned with networks and the movement of data from one place to another, and *communication systems*, which concern themselves with the functional utilities the data have for people, a distinction which seems to us absent in much of current communication study proceeding under the rubric of "systems research" at the present time.

Beyond this, human communication theory may also benefit significantly from the consideration of the major problem for which general systems theory was perceived as a solution. In "General System Theory" von Bertalanffy noted:

> "Modern science is characterized by its ever-increasing specialization, necessitated by the enormous amount of data, the complexity of techniques and of theoretical structures within every field. This, however has led to a breakdown of science as an integrated realm: The physicist, the biologist, the psychologist and the social scientist are, so to speak, encapsulated in a private universe, and it is difficult to get word from one cocoon to the other."[1]

We believe that the state of affairs outlined by von Bertalanffy, for which he proposed a general system theory as a solution, is precisely the same set of conditions which now faces the serious scholar of human communication. Human communication theory has often, we think, been stunted in its growth by provincial, sometimes incestuous, and often disciplinary-specific traditions. In areas ranging from anthropology, art, and biology to neurophysiology, psychology, and zoology, scholars have for years concerned themselves with communication, and yet extensive cross-disciplinary fertilization and integration has simply not yet occurred. Journalism, speech communication, mass communication, semiotics, and information sciences have all too frequently been victimized by a similar intellectual isolationism. For this set of problems, general systems seems to provide a potential solution.

Whether or not general systems is a way of thinking, a set of concepts, a theory, a meta-theory, a philosophy, truly a new world view, or a combination, is a question with which we have wrestled since our earliest acquaintance with the area. And while we have yet to resolve this dilemma, we are convinced of the value of the thinking of scholars who have contributed to the writings on general systems theory. It is the belief that the student of human communication and the behavioral sciences will find the ideas of general systems as insightful, provocative and intellectually expansive as we have, which has prompted us to prepare this volume.

Organization of the Volume

We have divided the book into three rather distinct sections. In Section I, we present several of the classic works in the field of general systems theory. They summarize basic theoretical and philosophical issues and introduce the basic concepts which continue to undergird systems thinking, suggesting a variety of concerns we think central to an integration of human communication and systems theory.

Section II is devoted to four approaches to communication and information processes which suggest various levels of analysis at which communication may be conceived in systems terms. They also provide specifics at each level indicating the basis upon which more systematic and internally consistent frameworks for conceiving of communication may be developed.

In Section III, we present the work of a number of writers in communication, each of which, in its manner, is reflective of a particular kind of integration and synthesis of the notions of general systems theory with those of human communication.

In all this, our goal is to provide for those interested in human communication study, a basic reference source on general systems theory, its philosophy, basic concepts, and the nature and range of possible applications of general systems thinking to communication. For those individuals who are already familiar with the literature of general systems theory, the volume will provide insights into the nature of human communication and its critical role in the existence of living systems which we hope will prove equally valuable.

References and Notes

1. Bertalanffy, Ludwig von, "General System Theory," in *General Systems Textbook,* Vol. 1, 1956, p. 1 and p. 2 of this volume.

SECTION I
General Systems:
Philosophy, Theory, and Basic Concepts

In this section of the volume we have included cornerstone theoretical and philosophical works. Except for the pieces by Ervin Laszlo and Anatol Rapoport, all of the articles were first published in the 1950s, and appeared in *General Systems,* the yearbook of the Society for General Systems Research, after first having been printed in other journals.

The work by von Bertalanffy is one of the first and probably the single most widely referenced theoretical statement on general systems. In it, Von Bertalanffy considers the problems of wholeness of organisms, organizations, and organized complexities. Particular focus is placed upon "living organisms," and the concept of open systems. Von Bertalanffy later more fully develops the systems framework in his several books, including *General System Theory* (1968) and *Robots, Men and Minds* (1967), and in a number of journal articles published before his death in 1972. Often termed "the father of general system theory," his works have laid the foundation for the set of approaches, theories, applications, and methodologies which are collectively called general systems theory.

Boulding was one of the first among social scientists to recognize the trend of convergence of traditionally distant disciplines in a general theory of systems. In "General Systems Theory—The Skeleton of Science," one of Boulding's main concerns is the increasing specialization of disciplines understood to correspond to a segment of the "empirical world," as with physics, chemistry, biology, psychology, sociology, economics, and so on. He suggests as one solution that we "look over the empirical universe and pick out certain general *phenomena* which are found in many different disciplines, and to seek to build up general theoretical models relevant to these phenomena." Some examples, universally found in many different disciplines, are the dynamics of population aggregates; the interaction of an "individual" of some kind with its environment; the phenomenon of growth; the theory of information and communication,

4

and so on. Boulding suggests that the resulting formulation could serve as the basis for a general theory of systems void of some difficulties of present classification.

In "Modern Systems Theory—An Outlook for Coping with Change," Rapoport provides a discussion on the various meanings of "theory." He posits that there are three different aspects of theory: the logical or *deductive* component of a theory (as in mathematics); the *predictive* content of a theory (as in natural science); and the *heuristic* aspect of a theory—"its ability to provide intellectual points of leverage for investigation." He suggests that for the behavioral sciences at this point in time, the heuristic aspect is the most important element of general systems theory, noting that "the value of heuristic theories is in the opportunity they offer to look at things in a new way and so to gain a measure of 'understanding.'"

A well-documented and detailed answer to the question what is a system, is provided by Hall and Fagen, in "Definition of System." In this piece, extensively referenced by many systems scientists, the authors develop rigorous and detailed definitions not only of *system*, but *objects*, *relationships*, and *attributes*, and other systems structures and processes as well. Other concepts defined in this work include: physical systems, environment, the relationship between system and environment, subsystems, man-made systems, and open and closed systems.

Lastly, we include in this section one of the most recent articles by Ervin Laszlo, who it might be said belongs to the second generation of systems scholars. He has been a highly productive contributor to the literature of systems theory, his most recent works including *Introduction to Systems Philosophy* (1972) and *The Systems View of the World* (1972). In "Basic Constructs of Systems Philosophy" Laszlo provides a discussion of "ordered wholeness," "self-stabilization," "self-organization," and "hierarchization" providing a framework that has clear utility, we believe, for systems-oriented scientists in the behavioral and social sciences, in general, and communication in particular.

1
General System Theory

LUDWIG VON BERTALANFFY

Modern science is characterized by its ever-increasing specialization. This has been necessitated by the enormous amount of data and the complexity of techniques and theoretical structures within every field. Unfortunately, this specialization has led to a breakdown of science as an integrated realm: The physicist, the biologist, the psychologist, and the social scientist are, so to speak, encapsulated in a private universe, and it is difficult to get word from one cocoon to the other.

There is, however, another remarkable aspect of modern science. If we survey the more recent evolution of science, as compared to that of a few decades ago, we are impressed by the fact that similar general viewpoints and conceptions have appeared in very diverse fields. Problems of organization, of wholeness, and of dynamic interaction, are encountered in modern physics, chemistry, physical chemistry, and technology. Problems of an organismic sort are also prevalent throughout biology. As a consequent it is not sufficient to study isolated parts and processes since the essential problems are the organizing relations that result from dynamic interaction of those parts. The same trend is evident in *gestalt* theory and other modern conceptions of the social sciences as distinguished from classical conceptions in psychology, for example. These parallel developments in the various fields are even more dramatic considering the fact that they are mutually independent and have been developing largely in ignorance of one another.

Until recent times, the corpus of laws of nature was almost identical with theoretical physics; few attempts to state exact laws in non-physical fields have gained universal recognition. However, given the development and the impact of the biological, behavioral, and social sciences, it has become necessary to expand our conceptual schemes to accommodate those phenomena in fields where the laws of physics are not usefully applicable.

Such trends toward generalized theories are taking place in many fields and in a variety of ways. For example, an elaborate theory regarding the dynamics of biological populations, the struggle for existence, and biological equilibria has developed out of the pioneering work of Lotka and Volterra.[1] The theory operates with biological notions such as individuals, species, coefficients of competition, and the like. A similar procedure is applied in quantitative economics and econometrics.[2]

Consider another example: living organisms are essentially open systems, that is, systems exchanging matter with their environment. Conventional physics and physical chemistry deal with closed systems, and only in recent years has theory been expanded to include irreversible processes, open systems, and states of non-equilibrium. If, however, we want to apply the model of open systems to, say, the phenomena of animal growth, we automatically come to a generalization of theory referring not to physical but to biological units.[3] In other words, we are dealing with generalized systems. The same is true of the fields of cybernetics and the theory of information which have gained so much interest in the past few years.

Thus we can conclude that there are models, principles, and laws that apply to generalized systems or their subclasses, irrespective of their particular kind, the nature of their component elements, or the relations of "forces" between them. It seems legitimate, therefore, to postulate a theory, not of systems of a more or less special kind, but of universal principles applying to systems in general.

Major Factors

This is the basis for the development of a new discipline, called general system theory. It is directed toward the formulation and derivation of those principles which are valid for "systems" in general.

1) A first consequence of the existence of general system properties is the appearance of structural similarities or isomorphies in different fields. There are correspondences in the principles which govern the behavior of widely different entities. This correspondence is due to the fact that these distinct entities all can be considered, in certain respects, as "systems," that is, complexes of elements standing in interaction. The fact that these fields are concerned with "systems," leads to a correspondence in general principles, and may even reveal special laws when the conditions of the phenomena under consideration correspond. In fact, similar concepts, models, and laws have often appeared in widely different fields, independently and based upon totally different facts.

System isomorphies also appear in problems which are not readily amenable to quantitative analysis but are nevertheless of great intrinsic interest. That there are, for example, isomorphies between biological systems and social entities like animal communities and human societies which raise some interesting questions. One must ask, which principles are common to the several levels of organization and so may legitimately be transferred from one level to another, and which are specific so that transfer leads to dangerous fallacies? Can civilizations and cultures usefully be considered as systems?

It would seem that a general theory of systems would be a useful tool providing, on the one hand, models that can be used in, and transferred to, different fields, and safeguarding, on the other hand, from vague analogies which often have marred the progress in these fields.[4]

(2) There is, however, another and possibly more important aspect of general system theory. To use an expression of W. Weaver,[5] classical science was highly successful in developing the theory of unorganized or disorganized complexity which stems from statistics, the laws of chance, and, in the last resort, the second law of thermodynamics. But today our main problem is that of organized complexity. Concepts like those of organization, wholeness, directiveness, teleology, control, self-regulation, differentiation, and the like, which are alien to conventional physics, pop up often in the biological, behavioral, and social sciences, and are indispensable for dealing with living organisms and social groups. General system theory is in principle capable of giving exact definitions for such concepts and, in suitable cases, of putting them to quantitative analysis.

(3) If we have briefly indicated what general system theory means, it will avoid misunderstanding also to state what it is not. It is not pure mathematics. Further, general system theory is not a search for vague and superficial analogies between physical, biological, and social systems. Analogies as such are of little value, since dissimilarities as well as similarities between phenomena, can always be found. The point is not that physical systems, organisms, and societies are all the same. In principle, it is the same sort of situation as where the law of gravitation applies to Newton's apple, the planetary system, and the phenomenon of tide. This means that in some rather limited aspects a certain theoretical system is common. It does not mean that there is a particular resemblance between apples, planets, and oceans in a great number of other aspects.

Framework of General System Theory

The framework of general system theory[6] can be summarized as follows:

(1) There is a general tendency towards integration in the various sciences, natural and social.

(2) Such integration seems to be centered in a general theory of systems.

(3) Such theory may be an important means for aiming at exact theory in the non-physical fields of science.

(4) Developing unifying principles running "vertically" through the universes of the individual sciences, this theory brings us nearer to the goal of the unity of science.

(5) This can lead to a much-needed integration in scientific education.

Limitations of Conventional Physics

One major impetus for the development of a general system theory is as a result of the limitations of classical physics: Conventional physics deals only with closed systems, that is, systems which are considered to be isolated from their environment. Thus, physical chemistry tells us about the reactions, their rates, and the chemical equilibria eventually established in a closed vessel where a number of reactants are brought together. Thermodynamics expressly declares that its laws only apply to closed systems. In particular, the second principle of thermodynamics states that, in a closed system, a certain quantity, called entropy, must increase to a maximum, and eventually the process comes to a stop at a state of equilibrium. The second principle can be formulated in different ways, one being that entropy is a measure of probability, and so a closed system tends toward a state of most probable distribution. The most probable distribution, however, of a mixture, say, of red and blue glass beads, or of molecules having different velocities, is a state of complete disorder. Having separated all red beads on one hand, and all blue ones on the other, or having, in a closed space, all fast molecules, that is, a high temperature on the right side, and all slow ones, a low temperature, at the left, is a highly improbable state of affairs. So the tendency towards maximum entropy or the most probable distribution is the tendency to maximum disorder.

However, we find systems which by their very nature and definition are not closed systems. Every living organism is essentially an open system. It maintains itself in a continuous inflow and outflow, building up and breaking down of components, never being, so long as it is alive, in a state of chemical and thermodynamic equilibrium, but maintained rather in a so-called steady state. This is the very essence of that fundamental phenomenon of life which is called metabolism, the chemical processes within living cells. What now? Obviously, the conventional formulations of physics are, in principle, inapplicable to the living organism *qua* open system and steady state, and we may well suspect that many characteristics of living systems which are paradoxical in view of the laws of physics, are precisely a consequence of this fact.

It is only in recent years that an expansion of physics, in order to include open systems, has taken place.[7] This theory has shed light on many obscure phenomena in physics and biology, and has also led to important general conclusions of which I will mention only two.

The first is the principle of equifinality.[8] In any closed system, the final state is unequivocally determined by the initial conditions: for example, the motion in a planetary system where the positions of the planets at a time t are unequivocally determined by their positions at a time t_0. Or in a chemical equilibrium,.the final concentrations of the reactants naturally depend on the initial concentrations. If either the initial conditions or the process is altered, the final state will also be changed. This is not so in open systems. Here, the same final state may be reached from different initial conditions and in different ways. This is what is called equifinality, and it has a significant meaning for the phenomena of biological regulation.

Those familiar with the history of biology will remember that it was equifinality that led the German biologist Driesch to embrace vitalism, that is, the doctrine that vital phenomena are inexplicable in terms of natural science. Driesch's argument was based on experiments on embryos in early development. The same final result, a normal individual of the sea urchin, can develop from a complete ovum, from each half of a divided ovum, or from the fusion product of two whole ova. The same applies to embryos of many other species, including man, where identical twins are the product of the splitting of one ovum.

Equifinality, according to Driesch, contradicts the laws of physics, and can be accomplished only by a soul-like vitalistic factor which governs the processes in foresight of the goal—the normal organism to be established. It can be shown, however, that open systems, insofar as they attain a steady state, must show equifinality, so the supposed violation of physical laws disappears.[9]

Another apparent contrast between inanimate and animate nature is what sometimes was called the violent contradiction between Lord Kelvin's degradation and Darwin's evolution, between the law of dissipation in physics and the law of evolution in biology. According to the second principle of thermodynamics, the general trend of events in physical nature is toward states of maximum disorder and levelling down of differences, with the socalled heat death of the universe as the final outlook when all energy is degraded into evenly distributed heat of low temperature and the world process comes to a stop. In contrast, the living world shows, in embryonic development and in evolution, a transition towards higher order, heterogeniety, and organization.[10]

In consideration of the theory of open systems, the apparent contradiction between entropy and evolution disappears. In all irreversible processes, entropy must increase. Therefore, the change of entropy in closed systems is always positive, order is continually destroyed. In open systems, however, we have not only production of entropy due to irreversible processes, but also import of the entropy which may well be negative. This is the case in the living organism which imports complex molecules high in free energy. Thus, living systems, maintaining themselves in a steady state, can avoid the increase of entropy, and may even develop towards states of increased order and organization.

From these examples, you may guess the bearing of the theory of open systems. Among other things, it shows that many supposed violations of physical laws in living nature disappear with the generalized version of the concept of systems to include open as well as closed systems. Examples of the use of the concepts of open systems are provided in ecology and the evolution towards a climax formation (Whitacker),[11] in psychology where "neurological systems" were considered as "open dynamic systems" (Krech), [12] in philosophy where the trend toward "trans-actional" as opposed to "self-actional" and "inter-actional" viewpoints closely corresponds to the open-system model (Bentley).[13]

Information Theory and Feedback

Another development which is closely connected with system theory is that of the mathematical theory of communication. It has often been said that energy is the currency of physics, just as economic values can be expressed in dollars or pounds. There are, however, certain fields of physics and technology where this currency is not readily acceptable. This is the case in the field of communication which, due to the development of telephones, radio, radar, calculating machines, servo-mechanisms, and other devices, has led to the rise of a new mathematical field.[14]

The general notion in mathematical communication theory is that of information. Information is measured in terms of decisions. Take the game of *Twenty Questions*, where we are supposed to find out an object by having questions answered about it by *yes* or *no*. The amount of information conveyed in one answer is a decision between two alternatives, such as animal or non-animal. With two questions, it is possible to decide for one out of four possibilities, for example, mammal — non-mammal, or flowering plant — non-flowering plant. With three questions it is a decision out of eight, and so forth.

Thus, the logarithm at the basis 2 of the possible answers can be used as a measure of information, the unit being the so-called binary unit or bit. The information contained in two answered questions is $\log_2 4 = 2$ bits, of three answers, $\log_2 8 = 3$ bits, and so forth. This measure of information happens to be similar to that of entropy or rather negative entropy, since entropy also is defined as a logarithm of probability. But entropy, as we have already heard, is a measure of disorder; hence negative entropy or information is a measure of order or of organization since the latter, compared to distribution at random, is an improbable state. In this way information theory comes close to the theory of open systems, which may increase in order and organization, or show negative entropy. But negative entropy can be considered a measure of decisions, taken out of equally probable ones, a measure of improbability or information.

Another central concept of communication theory is *feedback*. A simple scheme for feedback is the following. In the classical case of stimulus-response, a stimulus affects a receptor; the message of the receptor is transmitted to some controlling apparatus, and from this to an effector which gives the response. In feedback, the result of the effector's activity is monitored back to the receptor so that the system is self-regulating.

Feedback arrangements are used in modern technology to a wide extent for the stabilization of a certain action, as in thermostats or in radio receivers; or for the direction of actions towards a goal where the aberration from that goal is fed back, as information, till the goal or target is reached. This is the case in self-propelled missiles which seek their target, anti-aircraft fire control systems, ship-steering systems, and other so-called servo-mechanisms.

There are also a large number of biological phenomena which correspond to the feedback scheme. First, there are the phenomena of so-called homeostasis[15] or maintenance of balance in the living organism, the prototype of which is thermo-regulation in warm-blooded animals. Cooling of the blood stimulates certain centers in the brain which "turn on" heat producing mechanisms of the body, and the body temperature is monitored back to the center so that temperature is maintained at a constant level. Similar homeostatic mechanisms exist in the body for maintaining the constancy of a great number of physico-chemical variables. Furthermore, feedback systems comparable to the servo-mechanisms of technology exist in the animal and human body for the regulation of actions. If we want to pick up a pencil, report is made to the central nervous system of the amount of which we have failed the pencil in the first instance; this information then is fed back to the central nervous system so that the motion is controlled till it reaches its aim.

A great variety of systems in technology and in living nature follow the feedback scheme. Cybernetics was introduced by Norbert Wiener to deal centrally with such systems. The theory tries to show that

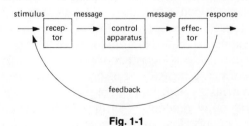

Fig. 1-1

mechanisms of a feedback nature are at the basis of teleological or purposeful behavior in man-made machines as well as in living organisms, and in social systems.

It should be kept in mind, however, that the feedback scheme is of a rather special nature. It presupposes structural arrangements of the type mentioned. There are, however, many regulations in the living organism which are of an essentially different nature, namely, those where the order is effectuated by a dynamic interplay of processes.

Remember the classical example of embryonic regulation where the whole is re-established from the parts in an equifinal process. It can be shown that the *primary* regulations in organic systems, that is, those which are most fundamental and primitive in embryonic development as well as in evolution operate through dynamic interaction. They are based upon the fact that the living organism is an open system, maintaining itself in, or approaching a steady state. Superimposed are those regulations which we may call *secondary,* and which are controlled by fixed arrangements, especially of the feedback type.

This state of affairs is a consequence of a general principle of organization which may be called progressive mechanization. At first, systems—biological, neurological, psychological, or social—are governed by dynamic interaction of their components; later on, fixed arrangements and conditions of constraint are established which render the system and its parts more efficient, but also gradually diminish and eventually abolish its equipotentiality.[16]

Causality and Teleology

Another development refleted in the concepts of general system theory relates to modes of scientific explanation in general. It has to do with a major change in the scientific world-picture in the past few decades.[17] In the world view called mechanistic, born of classical physics of the 19th century, the aimless play of the atoms, governed by the inexorable laws of mechanical causality, produced all phenomena in the world, inanimate, living, and mental. No room was left for any directiveness, order, or telos. The world of the organisms appeared a mere product of chance, accumulated by the senseless play of mutation at random and selection; the mental world as a curious and rather inconsequential epiphenomenon of material events.

The only goal of science appeared to be the analytical, that is, the splitting-up of reality into ever smaller units and the isolation of individual causal trains. Thus, physical reality was split up into mass points or atoms, the living organism into cells, behavior into reflexes, perception into punctual sensations, and so forth. Correspondingly, causality was essentially one-way: one sun attracts just one planet, one gene in the fertilized ovum produces such and such inherited character, one sort of bacterium produces this or that disease, mental elements are lined up, like the beads in a string of pearls, by the law of association.

Now we may state as characteristic of modern science that this scheme of isolable units acting in one-way causality has proved to be insufficient. Hence the appearance, in all fields of science, of notions like wholeness, holistic, organismic, *gestalt,* and so forth which all signify that in the last resort, we must think in terms of systems of elements in mutual interaction.

Similarly, notions of teleology and directiveness appeared to be outside the scope of science and the playground of mysterious, super-natural or anthropomorphic agencies; or else, a pseudo-problem, intrinsically alien to science, and merely a misplaced projection of the observer's mind into a nature governed by purposeless laws. Nevertheless, these aspects exist, and you cannot conceive of a living organism, not to speak of behavior and human society, without taking into account what variously and rather loosely is called adaptiveness, purposiveness, goal-seeking, and the like.

It is characteristic of the present view that these aspects are taken seriously as a legitimate problem for science; moreover, we can well indicate models showing such behavior.

Two such models we have already mentioned. One is equifinality, the tendency towards a characteristic final state from different initial states and in different ways, based upon dynamic interaction in an open system attaining a steady state. The second is feedback and involves the homeostatic maintenance of a characteristic state or the seeking of a goal, based on circular causal chains and mechanisms monitoring back information on deviations from the state to be attained or goal to be reached.

A third model for adaptive behavior, a *Design for a Brain,* was developed by Ashby, who incidentally starts with the same mathematical definitions and equations for a general system as were used by this author. Both writers have developed their systems independently and, following different lines of interest, have arrived at different theorems and conclusions. Ashby's model for adaptiveness is, roughly, that of step functions defining a system, that is, functions which, after a certain critical value is overstepped, jump into a new family of differential equations. This means that, having passed a critical state, the system starts off in a new way of behavior. Thus, by means of step functions, the system shows adaptive behavior by what the biologist would call trial and error: It tries different ways and means, and eventually settles down in a field where it does not come any more in conflict with critical values of the environment. Such a system adapting itself by trial and error was actually constructed by Ashby as an electromagnetic machine, called the homeostat.

I am not going to discuss the merits and shortcomings of these models of teleological or directed behavior. What should be stressed, however, is the fact that teleological behavior directed towards a characteristic final state or goal is not something off limits to natural science. Rather it is a form of behavior which can well be defined in scientific terms and for which the necessary conditions and possible mechanisms can be indicated.

What is Organization?

Considerations of *organization* are the core of general system theory. The notion of organization was alien to the mechanistic world. The problem did not appear in classical physics, mechanics, electrodynamics, and so forth. Even more, the second principle of thermodynamics indicated destruction of order as the general direction of events. It is true that this is different in modern physics. An atom, a crystal, or a molecule are organizations, as Whitehead never failed to emphasize. In biology, organisms, by definition, are organized things. But although we have an enormous amount of data on biological organization, from biochemistry to cytology, to histology and anatomy, we do not have a real theory of biological organizations which permits explanation of the empirical facts.

Characteristic of organization, whether a living organism or a society, are notions like those of wholeness, growth, differentiation, hierarchical order, dominance, control, competition, and so forth. Such notions do not appear in conventional physics. System theory is well capable of dealing with these matters and it is possible to define such notions within the mathematical model of a system.[18]

There are also many aspects of organizations which do not easily lend themselves to quantitative interpretation. This difficulty is not unknown in natural science. Thus, the theory of biological equilibria or that of natural selection are highly developed fields of mathematical biology, and nobody doubts that these theories are legitimate, essentially correct and an important part of the theory of evolution and of ecology. It is hard, however, to apply them in the field because the parameters chosen, such as selective value, rate of destruction and generation, and the like cannot easily be determined. So we have to content ourselves with a qualitative argument which, nonetheless, may lead to interesting consequences.

As an example of the application of general system theory to human society, I will refer to a book by Boulding, entitled *The Organizational Revolution*, in which he presents a general model of organization, stating what he calls Iron Laws holding good for any organization.[19] For example, Boulding notes the Malthusian law which states that the increase of a population is greater than that of its resources. Then there is a law of the optimum size of organizations: the larger an organization grows the longer are the paths of communication and this, depending on the particular nature of the organization, acts as a limiting factor and does not allow an organization to grow beyond a certain critical size. According to the law of instability, many organizations are not in a stable equilibrium but show cyclic fluctuations which result from the interaction of subsystems. The important law of oligopoly states that, if there are competing organizations, the instability of their relations and hence the danger of friction and conflicts increase as the number of those organizations decrease. Thus, so long as they are relatively small and numerous, they muddle through in some way to coexistence. But if only a few or a competing pair is left, as is the case with the colossal political blocks of the present day, conflicts become devastating to the point of complete mutual destruction. The number of such general theorems of organization can easily be enlarged and can be developed with precision in particular areas.[20]

General System Theory and the Unity of Science

Let me close these remarks with a few words about the general implications of interdisciplinary theory. The integrative function of general system theory can perhaps be summarized as follows. So far, the unification of science has been seen in the reduction of all sciences to physics. From our point of view, a unitary conception of the world may be based, not only upon physics, but rather on the isomorphy of laws in many different fields. This means identifying structural uniformities of the schemes we are applying. It means also that the world—the total of observable phenomena—shows structural uniformities, manifesting themselves by isomorphic traces of order in its different levels.

We come, then, to a conception which, in contrast to reductionism, we may call perspectivism.[12] We cannot reduce the biological, behavioral, and social levels to the lowest level, that of the constructs and laws of physics. We can, however, find constructs and possibly laws within the individual levels. The world is, as Aldous Huxley once put it, like a Neapolitan ice cake where the levels, the physical, the biological, the social, and the moral universe, represent the chocolate, strawberry, and vanilla layers. We cannot reduce strawberry to chocolate—the most we can say is that, possibly in the last resort, all is vanilla, all mind or spirit. The unifying principle is that we find organization on all levels.

The mechanistic world view, taking the play of physical particles for ultimate reality, found its expression in a civilization glorifying physical technology which eventually has led to the catastrophes of our time. Possibly the model of the world as a great organization can help to reinforce the sense of reverence for the living which we have almost lost in the last sanguinary decades of human history.

General System Theory and the Need for Scientific Generalists

After this necessarily sketchy outline of the meaning and framework of general system theory, let me try to answer the question of what it may contribute to integrative education. In order not to appear partisan, I give a few quotations from authors who were not themselves engaged in the development of general system theory.

A few years ago, a paper, entitled "The Education of Scientific Generalists," was published by a group of scientists comprising the engineer, Bode, the sociologist, Mosteller, the mathematician, Tukey, and the biologist, Winsor.[22] The authors emphasize the "need for a simpler, more unified approach to scientific problems." They write:

"We often hear that 'one man can no longer cover a broad enough field' and that 'there is too much narrow specialization' . . . We need a simpler, more unified approach to scientific problems, we need men who practice science—not a particular science, in a word, we need scientific generalists."

The authors then make clear how and why generalists are needed in various fields such as physical chemistry, biophysics, the application of chemistry, physics, and mathematics to medicine, and they continue:

"Any research group needs a generalist, whether it is an institutional group in a university or a foundation, or an industrial group . . . . In an engineering group, the generalist would naturally be concerned with system problems. These problems arise whenever parts are made into a balanced whole."

In a symposium of the Foundation for Integrated Education, Professor Mather discussed "Integrative Studies for General Education."[23] He states:

"One of the criticisms of general education is based upon the fact that it may easily degenerate into the mere presentation of information picked up in as many fields of enquiry as there is time to survey during a semester or a year . . . If you were to overhear several senior students talking, you might hear one of them say 'our professors have stuffed us full, but what does it all mean?' . . . more important is the search for basic concepts and underlying principles that may be valid throughout the entire body of knowledge."

In answer to what these basic concepts may be, Mather states:

"Very similar general concepts have been independently developed by investigators who have been working in widely different fields. These correspondences are all the more significant because they are based upon totally different facts. The men who developed them were largely unaware of each other's work. They started with conflicting philosophies and yet have reached remarkably similar conclusions . . . "Thus conceived, "Mather concludes, "Integrative studies would prove to be an essential part of the quest for an understanding of reality."

No comments seem to be necessary. Conventional education in physics, biology, psychology, or the social sciences treats them as separate domains, the general trend being that increasingly smaller sub-domains become separate sciences, and this process is repeated to the point where each speciality becomes a triflingly small field, unconnected with the rest. In contrast the educational demands of training "Scientific Generalists" and of developing interdisciplinary "basic principles" are precisely those general system theory tries to fill. They are not a mere program or a pious wish since, as we have tried to show, such theoretical structure is already in the process of development. In this sense, general system theory seems to provide an important thrust not only towards interdisciplinary synthesis but integrated education as well.[24]

References and Notes

1. *Cf.* the recent survey: D'Ancona, U., *The Struggle for Existence*, Leiden: 1954.
2. E.g., Boulding, K., *A Reconstruction of Economics*, New York: 1950; and G. Tintner, *Econometrics*, New York: 1952.
3. For a brief survey of theory, *see* L. Bertalanffy, "Problems of Organic Growth," *Nature*, Vol. 163, 1949, p. 156; "Metabolic Types and Growth Types," *American Naturalist*, Vol. 85, 1951, p. 111.
4. For a discussion of "analogy," "logical homology," and "explanation proper," *see* L. von Bertalanffy, "Problems of General System Theory," *Human Biology*, Vol. 23, 1951, p. 302.
5. Weaver, W., "Science and Complexity," *American Scientist*, Vol. 36, 1948, p. 4.
6. It seems that A. Lotka, *Elements of Physical Biology*, Baltimore: 1925, was the first to advance the idea of general system laws, introducing the simultaneous differential equations for the definition of general systems which were used by the later authors (Bertalanffy, Ashby, *see below*). The idea of a general system theory was developed by Bertalanffy in the late thirties and presented in various lectures, but this material remained unpublished until 1945 ("Zueiner allgemeinen Systemlehre," *Blaetter f. Deutsche Philosophie*, Vol. 18, 3/4). Without using the term, general system theory, but with a similar intention, the same mathematical frame has been used by W. R. Ashby, *Design for a Brain*, London: 1952.
7. Although the idea of the organism as a "dynamic equilibrium" goes back at least, to Johannes Müller and Dubois-Raymond, the concept of "open system," so far as can be ascertained, was first used in thermodynamics by R. Defay ("Introduction a la thermodynamique des systems ouverts," *Acad. Roy. de Belgique, Bull. Classe des Sciences*, 53 Serie 15, 1929, p. 678). In 1932, L. von Bertalanffy introduced the same concept in biology, emphasizing that an expansion of the theory of physical chemistry is

needed in order to deal adequately with the steady state of the organism *(Theoretische Biologie,* Erster Band. Berlin: 1932; "Untersuchungen ueber die Gesetzlichkett des Wachstums," *Roux' Archive;* Vol. 131, 1934, p. 613). Kinetic principles of open systems were first developed, concurrently by A. C. Burton "The Properties of the Steady State Compared to those of Equilibrium as Shown in Characteristic Biological Behavior," *J. Cell. Comp. Physiol.,* Vol. 14, 1939, p. 327, and L. von Bertalanffy, *Naturwissenschaften,* Vol. 28, 1940, p. 521.

8. Introduced by Bertalanffy, "Der Organismus als physikalisches System betrachtet," *Naturwissenschaften,* Vol. 28, 1940, p. 521.

9. It should perhaps be mentioned that equifinality is not a mathematical characteristic but a physical characteristic of (certain) open systems. It does not depend on the structure of the system equations but on the meaning of the parameters so that formally identical equations may apply to non-equifinal closed systems as well as to equifinal open systems. However, the equifinal case where the final state depends only on the reaction and transport parameters and not on the initial conditions, is found only in open systems.

10. The contrast between inanimate and living nature has been formulated by L. Brillouin, "Life, Thermodynamics, and Cybernetics," *American Scientist,* Vol. 37, 1949, p. 554, as follows: "How is it possible to understand life, when the whole world is ruled by such a law as the second principle of thermodynamics which points towards death and annihilation"? This apparent paradox has often been used as the basis for vitalistic or theological arguments (e.g., H. Adams, *The Degradation of the Democratic Dogma,* New York: 1920; R. Woltereck, *Ontologie des Lebendigen,* Stuttgart: 1939; E. Schroedinger, *What is Life?,* Cambridge, England: 1945; Lecomte du Noüy, *Human Destiny,* New York: 1947; R. E. D. Clark, *Darwin: Before and After,* London: 1948.

11. Whitacker, R. H., "A Consideration of Climax Theory: The Climax as a Population and Pattern," *Ecol. Monographs,* Vol. 23, 1953, p. 41.

12. Krech, D., "Dynamic Systems, Psychological Fields, and Hypothetical Constructs," *General Systems Yearbook,* Vol. 1, 1956, p. 144; cf. also L. von Bertalanffy, "Theoretical Models in Biology and Psychology," *Journal of Personality,* Vol. 20, 1951, p. 24.

13. Bentley, A. F., "Kinetic Inquiry," *Science,* Vol. 112, 1950, p. 775.

14. *See* Shannon, C. E., and W. Weaver, *The Mathematical Theory of Communication,* Urbana, Ill.: 1949, N. Wiener, *Cybernetics,* New York: 1948.

15. Cannon, W. B., "Organization for Physiological Homeostasis," *Physiol. Rev.,* Vol. 9, 1929, p. 397.

16. For a more detailed discussion of dynamic and feedback regulation, see L. von Bertalanffy, "Towards a Physical Theory of Organic Teleology," *Human Biology,* Vol. 23, 1941, p. 346; progressive mechanization: "An Outline of General System Theory," *British Journal of Philosophy of*

Science, Vol. 1, 1950, p. 139; *Problems of Life,* New York: 1952; and Hall and Fagen, "Definition of System," *General Systems Yearbook,* Vol. 1, 1956, p. 18, included in edited form as Chapter 4 of this volume.

17. *Cf.* Frank, L. K., G. E. Hutchinson, W. K. Livingstone, W. S. McCulloch, and N. Wiener, "Teleological Mechanisms," Ann N. Y. Academy Scie. 50, 1948.

18. *See* Bertalanffy, "An Outline of General System Theory," *British Journal of Philosophy of Science,* Vol. 1, 1950.

19. Boulding, K. E., *The Organizational Revolution,* New York: 1953.

20. *Cf.* McCelland, Ch. A., "Applications of General System Theory in International Relations," *Main Currents in Modern Thought,* Vol. 12, 1955, p. 27.

21. *Cf.* Bertalanffy, Ludwig von, "An Essay on the Relativity of Categories," *British Journal of Philosophy of Science,* Vol. 22, 1955, p. 243.

22. Bode, H., F. Mosteller, J. Tukey, and C. Winsor, "The Education of a Scientific Generalist," *Science,* Vol. 109, 1949, p. 553.

23. Mather, K. F., "Objectives and Nature of Integrative Studies," *Main Currents in Modern Thought,* Vol. 8, 1951, p. 11.

24. *Cf.* Bertalanffy, Ludwig von, "Philosophy of Science in Scientific Education," *Scientific Monthly,* Vol. 77, 1953, p. 233.

2
General Systems Theory— The Skeleton of Science

KENNETH E. BOULDING

General systems theory is a name which has come into use to describe a level of theoretical model-building which lies somewhere between the highly generalized constructions of pure mathematics and the specific theories of the specialized disciplines. Mathematics attempts to organize highly general relationships into a coherent system, a system however which does not have any necessary connections with the "real" world around us. It studies all thinkable relationships abstracted from any concrete situation or body of empirical knowledge. It is not even confined to "quantitative" relationships narrowly defined—indeed, the developments of a mathematics of quality and structure is already on the way, even though it is not as far advanced as the "classical" mathematics of quantity and number. Nevertheless, because in a sense mathematics contains all theories, it contains none; it is the language of theory, but it does not give us the content. At the other extreme we have the separate disciplines and sciences, with their separate bodies of theory. Each discipline corresponds to a certain segment of the empirical world, and each develops theories which have particular applicability to its own empirical segment. Physics, chemistry, biology, psychology, sociology, economics and so on all carve out for themselves certain elements of the experience of man and develop theories and patterns of activity (research) which yield satisfaction in understanding, and which are appropriate to their special segments.

In recent years increasing need has been felt for a body of systematic theoretical constructs which will discuss the general relationships of the empirical world. This is the quest of general systems theory. It does not seek, of course, to establish a single, self-contained "general theory of practically everything" which will replace all the special theories of particular disciplines. Such a theory would be almost without content, for we always pay for generality by sacrificing content, and all we can say about practically everything is almost nothing. Somewhere, however, between the specific that has no meaning and the general that has no content there must be, for each purpose and at each level of abstraction, an optimum degree of generality. It is the contention of the general systems theorists that this optimum degree of generality in theory is not always reached by the particular sciences. The objectives of general systems theory then can be set out with varying degrees of ambition and confidence. At a low level of ambition, but with a high degree of confidence, it aims to point out similarities in the theoretical constructions of different disciplines, where these exist, and to develop theoretical models having applicability to at least two different fields of study. At a higher level of ambition, but with perhaps a lower degree of confidence, it hopes to develop something like a "spectrum" of theories—a system of systems which may perform the function of a "gestalt" in theoretical construction. Such "gestalts" in special fields have been of great value in directing research towards the gaps which they reveal. Thus the periodic table of elements in chemistry directed research for many decades towards the discovery of unknown elements to fill gaps in the table until the table was completely filled. Similarly a "system of systems" might be of value in directing the attention of theorists towards gaps in theoretical models, and might even be of value in pointing towards methods of filling them.

Science, Knowledge, Systems

The need for general systems theory is accentuated by the present sociological situation in science. Knowledge is not something which exists and grows in the abstract. It is a function of human organisms and of social organization. Knowledge, that is to say, is always what somebody knows: the most perfect transcript of knowledge in writing is not knowledge if nobody knows it. Knowledge, however, grows by the receipt of meaningful information—that is, by the intake of messages by a knower which are capable of reorganizing his knowledge. We will quietly duck the question as to what reorganizations constitute "growth" of knowledge by defining "semantic growth" of knowledge as those reorganizations which can profitably be talked about, in writing of speech, by the Right People. Science, that is to say, is what can be talked about profitably by scientists in their role as scientists. The crisis of science today arises because of the increasing difficulty of such profitable talk among scientists as a whole. Specialization has outrun trade, communication between the disciplines becomes increasingly difficult, and the Republic of Learning is breaking up into isolated subcultures with only tenuous lines of communication between them—a situation which threatens intellectual civil war. The reason for this breakup in the body of knowledge is that in the course of specialization the receptors of information themselves become specialized. Hence physicists only talk to physicists, economists to economists—worse still, nuclear physicists only talk to nuclear physicists and econometricians to econometricians. One wonders sometimes if science will not grind to a stop in an assemblage of walled-in hermits, each mumbling to himself words in a private language that only he can understand. In these days the arts may have beaten the sciences to this desert of mutual unintelligibility, but that may be merely because the swift intuitions of art reach the future faster than the plodding leg work of the scientists. The more science breaks into sub-groups, and the less communication is possible among the disciplines, however, the greater chance there is that the total growth of knowledge is being slowed down by the loss of relevant communications. The spread of specialized deafness means that someone who ought to know something that someone else knows isn't able to find it out for lack of generalized ears.

It is one of the main objectives of general systems theory to develop these generalized ears, and by developing a framework of general theory to enable one specialist to catch relevant communications from others. Thus the economist who realized the strong formal similarity between utility theory in economics and field theory in physics is probably in a better position to learn from the physicists than one who does not. Similarly a specialist who works with the growth concept—whether the crystallographer, the virologist, the cytologist, the physiologist, the psychologist, the sociologist or the economist—will be more sensitive to the contributions of other fields if he is aware of the many similarities of the growth process in widely different empirical fields.

There is not much doubt about the demand for general systems theory under one brand name or another. It is a little more embarrassing to inquire into the supply. Does any of it exist, and if so where? What is the chance of getting more of it, and if so, how? The situation might be described as promising and in ferment, though it is not wholly clear what is being promised or brewed. Something which might be called an "interdisciplinary movement" has been abroad for some time. The first signs of this are usually the development of hybrid disciplines. Thus physical chemistry emerged in the third quarter of the nineteenth century, social psychology in the second quarter of the twentieth. In the physical and biological sciences the list of hybrid disciplines is now quite long— biophysics, biochemistry, astrophysics are all well established. In the social sciences social anthropology is fairly well established, economic psychology and economic sociology are just beginning. There are signs, even, that Political Economy, which died in infancy some hundred years ago, may have a re-birth.

In recent years there has been an additional development of great interest in the form of "multisexual" interdisciplines. The hybrid disciplines, as their hyphenated names indicate, come from two respectable and honest academic parents. The newer interdisciplines have a much more varied and occasionally even obscure ancestry, and result from the reorganization of material from many different fields of study.

Cybernetics, for instance, comes out of electrical engineering, neurophysiology, physics, biology, with even a dash of economics. Information theory, which originated in communications engineering, has important applications in many fields stretching from biology to the social sciences. Organization theory comes out of economics, sociology, engineering, physiology, and Management Science itself is an equally multidisciplinary product.

On the more empirical and practical side the interdisciplinary movement is reflected in the development of interdepartmental institutes of many kinds. Some of these find their basis of unity in the empirical field which they study, such as institutes of industrial relations, of public administration, of international affairs, and so on. Others are organized around the application of a common methodology to many different fields and problems, such as the Survey Research Center and the Group Dynamics Center at the University of Michigan. Even more important than these visible developments, perhaps, though harder to perceive and identify, is a growing dissatisfaction in many departments, especially at the level of graduate study, with the existing traditional theoretical backgrounds for the empirical studies which form the major part of the output of Ph.D. theses. Take but a single example from the field with which I am most familiar: It is traditional for studies of labor relations, money and banking, and foreign investment to come out of departments of economics. Many of the needed theoretical models and frameworks in these fields, however, do not come out of "economic theory" as this is usually taught, but from sociology, social psychology, and cultural anthropology. Students in the department of economics, however, rarely get a chance to become acquainted with these theoretical models, which may be relevant to their studies, and they become impatient with economic theory, much of which may not be relevant.

It is clear that there is a good deal of interdisciplinary excitement abroad. If this excitement is to be productive, however, it must operate within a certain framework of coherence. It is all too easy for the interdisciplinary to degenerate into the undisciplined. If the interdisciplinary movement, therefore, is not to lose that sense of form and structure which is the "discipline" involved in the various separate disciplines, it should develop a structure of its own. This I conceive to be the great task of general systems theory. For the rest of this paper, therefore, I propose to look at some possible ways in which general systems theory might be structured.

Organization of General Systems Theory

Two possible approaches to the organization of general systems theory suggest themselves, which are to be thought of as complementary rather than competitive, or at least as two roads each of which is worth exploring. The first approach is to look over the empirical universe and to pick out certain general phenomena which are found in many different disciplines, and to seek to build up general theoretical models relevant to these phenomena. The second approach is to arrange the empirical fields in a hierarchy of complexity of organization of their basic "individual" or unit of behavior, and to try to develop a level of abstraction appropriate to each.

Some examples of the first approach will serve to clarify it, without pretending to be exhaustive. In almost all disciplines, for instance, we find examples of populations—aggregates of individuals conforming to a common definition, to which individuals are added (born) and subtracted (die) and in which the age of the individual is a relevant and identifiable variable. These populations exhibit dynamic movements of their own, which can frequently be described by fairly simple systems of differential equations. The populations of different species also exhibit dynamic interactions among themselves, as in the theory of Volterra. Models of population change and interaction cut across a great many different fields—ecological systems in biology, capital theory in economics which deals with populations of "goods," social ecology, and even certain problems of statistical mechanics. In all these fields population change, both in absolute numbers and in structure, can be discussed in terms of birth and survival functions relating numbers of births and of deaths in specific age groups to various aspects of the system. In all these fields the interaction of population can be discussed in terms of competitive, complementary, or parasitic relationships among populations of different species, whether the species consist of animals, commodities, social classes or molecules.

Another phenomenon of almost universal significance for all disciplines is that of the interaction of an "individual" of some kind with its environment. Every discipline studies some kind of "individual"—electron, atom, molecule, crystal, virus, cell, plant, animal, man, family, tribe, state, church, firm, corporation, university, and so on. Each of these individuals exhibits "behavior," action, or change, and this behavior is considered to be related in some way to the environment of the individual—that is, with other individuals with which it comes into contact or into some relationship. Each individual is thought of as consisting of a structure or complex of individuals of the order immediately below it—atoms are an arrangement of protons and electrons, molecules of atoms, cells of molecules, plants, animals and men of cells, social organizations of men. The "behavior" of each individual is "explained" by the structure and arrangement of the lower individuals of which it is composed, or by certain principles of equilibrium or homeostasis according to which certain "states" of the individual are "preferred." Behavior is described in terms of the restoration of these preferred states when they are disturbed by changes in the environment.

but man is unique

Another phenomenon of universal significance is growth. Growth theory is in a sense a subdivision of the theory of individual "behavior," growth being one important aspect of behavior. Nevertheless there are important differences between equilibrium theory and growth theory, which perhaps warrant giving growth theory a special category. There is hardly a science in which the growth phenomenon does not have some importance, and though there is a great difference in complexity between the growth of crystals, embryos, and societies, many of the principles and concepts which are important at the lower levels are also illuminating at higher levels. Some growth phenomena can be dealt with in terms of relatively simple population models, the solution of which yields growth curves of single variables. At the more complex levels structural problems become dominant and the complex interrelationships between growth and form are the focus of interest. All growth phenomena are sufficiently alike, however, to suggest that a general theory of growth is by no means an impossibility.

Another aspect of the theory of the individual and also of interrelationships among individuals which might be singled out for special treatment is the theory of information and communication. The information concept as developed by Shannon has had interesting applications outside its original field of electrical engineering. It is not adequate, of course, to deal with problems involving the semantic level of communication. At the biological level, however, the information concept may serve to develop general notions of structuredness and abstract measures of organization which give us, as it were, a third basic dimension beyond mass and energy. Communication and information processes are found in a wide variety of empirical situations, and are unquestionably essential in the development of organization, both in the biological and the social world.

These various approaches to general systems through various aspects of the empirical world may lead ultimately to something like a general field theory of the dynamics of action and interaction. This, however, is a long way ahead.

A second possible approach to general systems theory is through the arrangement of theoretical systems and constructs in a hierarchy of complexity, roughly corresponding to the complexity of the "individuals" of the various empirical fields. This approach is more systematic than the first, leading towards a "system of systems." It may not replace the first entirely, however, as there may always be important theoretical concepts and constructs lying outside the systematic framework. I suggest below a possible arrangement of "levels" of theoretical discourse.

(1) The first level is that of the static structure. It might be called the level of *frameworks*. This is the geography and anatomy of the universe—the patterns of electrons around a nucleus, the pattern of atoms in a molecular formula, the arrangement of atoms in a crystal, the anatomy of

the gene, the cell, the plant, the animal, the mapping of the earth, the solar system, the astronomical universe. The accurate description of these frameworks is the beginning of organized theoretical knowledge in almost any field, for without accuracy in this description of static relationships no accurate functional or dynamic theory is possible. Thus the Copernican revolution was really the discovery of a new static framework for the solar system which permitted a simpler description of its dynamics.

(2) The next level of systematic analysis is that of the simple dynamic system with predetermined, necessary motion. This might be called the level of *clockworks*. The solar system itself is of course the great clock of the universe from man's point of view, and the deliciously exact predictions of the astronomers are a testimony ot the excellence of the clock which they study. Simple machines such as the lever and the pulley, even quite complicated machines like steam engines and dynamos fall mostly under this category. The greater part of the theoretical structure of physics, chemistry, and even of economics falls into this category.

(3) The next level is that of the control mechanism or cybernetic system, which might be nicknamed the level of the *thermostat*. This differs from the simple stable equilibrium system mainly in the fact that the transmission and interpretation of information is an essential part of the system. As a resutl of this the equilibrium position is not merely determined by the equations of the system, but the system will move to the maintenance of any *given* equilibrium, within limits. Thus the thermostat will maintain *any* temperature at which it can be set; the equilibrium temperature of the system is not determined solely by its equations. The trick here, of course, is that the essential variable of the dynamic system is the *difference* between an "observed" or "recorded" value of the maintained variable and its "ideal" value. If this difference is not zero the system moves so as to diminish it; thus the furnace sends up heat when the temperature as recorded is "too cold" and is turned off when the recorded temperature is "too hot." The homeostasis model, which is of such importance in physiology, is an example of a cybernetic mechanism, and such mechanisms exist through the whole empirical world of the biologist and the social scientist.

(4) The fourth level is that of the "open system," or self-maintaining structure. This is the level at which life begins to differentiate itself from not-life: it might be called the level of the *cell*. Something like an open system exists, of course, even in physico-chemical equilibrium systems; atomic structures maintain themselves in the midst of a throughput of atoms. Flames and rivers likewise are essentially open systems of a very simple kind. As we pass up the scale of complexity of organization towards living systems, however, the property of self-maintenance of structure in the midst of a throughput of material becomes of dominant importance. An atom or a molecule can presumably exist without

throughput: the existence of even the simplest living organism is inconceivable without ingestion, excretion and metabolic exchange. Closely connected with the property of self-maintenance is the property of self-reproduction. It may be, indeed, that self-reproduction is a more primitive or "lower level" system than the open system, and that the gene and the virus, for instance, may be able to reproduce themselves without being open systems. It is not perhaps an important question at what point in the scale of increasing complexity "life" begins. What is clear, however, is that by the time we have got to systems which both reproduce themselves and maintain themselves in the midst of a throughput of material and energy, we have something to which it would be hard to deny the title of "life."

(5) The fifth level might be called the genetic-societal level; it is typified by the *plant* and it dominates the empirical world of the botanist. The outstanding characteristics of these systems are first, a division of labor among cells to form a cell-society with differentiated and mutually dependent parts (roots, leaves, seeds, etc), and second, a sharp differentiation between the genotype and the phenotype, associated with the phenomenon of equifinal or "blueprinted" growth. At this level there are no highly specialized sense organs and information receptors are diffuse and incapable of much throughput of information—it is doubtful whether a tree can distinguish much more than light from dark, long days from short days, cold from hot.

(6) As we move upward from the plant world towards the animal kingdom we gradually pass over into a new level, the "animal" level, characterized by increased mobility, teleological behavior, and self-awareness. Here we have the development of specialized information-receptors (eyes, ears, etc.) leading to an enormous increase in the intake of information; we have also a great development of nervous systems, leading ultimately to the brain, as an organizer of the information intake into a knowledge structure or "image." Increasingly as we ascend the scale of animal life, behavior is response not to a specific stimulus but to an "image" or knowledge structure or view of the environment as a whole. This image is of course determined ultimately by information received into the organism; the relation between the receipt of information and the building up of an image, however, is exceedingly complex. It is not a simple piling up or accumulation of information received, although this frequently happens, but a structuring of information into something essentially different from the information itself. After the image structure is well established most information received produces very little change in the image—it goes through the loose structure, as it were, without hitting it, much as a sub-atomic particle might go through an atom without hitting anything. Sometimes, however, the information is "captured" by the image and added to it, and sometimes the information hits some kind of a "nucleus" of the image and a reorganization takes place, with far

reaching and radical changes in behavior in apparent response to what seems like a very small stimulus. The difficulties in the prediction of the behavior of these systems arises largely because of this intervention of the image between the stimulus and the response.

(7) The next level is the "human" level, that is of the individual human being considered as a system. In addition to all, or nearly all, of the characteristics of animal systems man possesses self consciousness, which is something different from mere awareness. His image, besides being much more complex than that even of the higher animals, has a self-reflexive quality—he not only knows, but knows that he knows. This property is probably bound up with the phenomenon of language and symbolism. It is the capacity for speech—the ability to produce, absorb, and interpret *symbols,* as opposed to mere signs like the warning cry of an animal—which most clearly marks man off from his humbler brethren. Man is distinguished from the animals also by a much more elaborate image of time and relationship; man is probably the only organization that knows that it dies, that contemplates in its behavior a whole life span, and more than a life span. Man exists not only in time and space but in history, and his behavior is profoundly affected by his view of the time process in which he stands.

(8) Because of the vital importance for the individual man of symbolic images and behavior based on them it is not easy to separate clearly the level of the individual human organism from the next level, that of social organizations. In spite of the occasional stories of feral children raised by animals, man isolated from his fellows is practically unknown. So essential is the symbolic image in human behavior that one suspects that a truly isolated man would not be "human" in the usually accepted sense, though he would be potentially human. Nevertheless it is convenient for some purposes to distinguish the individual human as a system from the social systems which surround him, and in this sense social organizations may be said to constitute another level of organization. The unit of such systems is not perhaps the person—the individual human as such—but the "role"—that part of the person which is concerned with the organization or situation in question, and it is tempting to define social organizations, or almost any social system, as a set of roles tied together with channels of communication. The interrelations of the role and the person, however, can never be completely neglected—a square person in a round role may become a little rounder, but he also makes the role squarer, and the perception of a role is affected by the personalities of those who have occupied it in the past. At this level we must concern ourselves with the content and meaning of messages, the nature and dimensions of value systems, the transcription of images into a historical record, the subtle symbolizations of art, music, and poetry, and the complex gamut of human emotion. The empirical universe here is human life and society in all its complexity and richness.

(9) To complete the structure of systems we should add a final turret for transcendental systems, even if we may be accused at this point of having built Babel to the clouds. There are, however, the ultimates and absolutes and the inescapable unknowables, and they also exhibit systematic structure and relationship. It will be a sad day for man when nobody is allowed to ask questions that do not have any answers.

One advantage of exhibiting a hierarchy of systems in this way is that it gives us some idea of the present gaps in both theoretical and empirical knowledge. Adequate theoretical models extend up to about the fourth level, and not much beyond. Empirical knowledge is deficient at practically all levels. Thus at the level of the static structure, fairly adequate descriptive models are available for geography, chemistry, geology, anatomy, and descriptive social science. Even at this simplest level, however, the problem of the adequate description of complex structures is still far from solved. The theory of indexing and cataloguing, for instance, is only in its infancy. Librarians are fairly good at cataloguing books, chemists have begun to catalogue structural formulae, and anthropologists have begun to catalogue culture trails. The cataloguing of events, ideas, theories, statistics, and empirical data has hardly begun. The very multiplication of records, however, as time goes on will force us into much more adequate cataloguing and reference systems than we now have. This is perhaps the major unsolved theoretical problem at the level of the static structure. In the empirical field there are still great areas where static structures are very imperfectly known, although knowledge is advancing rapidly, thanks to new probing devices such as the electron microscope. The anatomy of that part of the empirical world which lies between the large molecule and the cell, however, is still obscure at many points. It is precisely this area, however,—which includes, for instance, the gene and the virus—that holds the secret of life, and until its anatomy is made clear the nature of the functional systems which are involved will inevitably be obscure.

The level of the "clockwork" is the level of "classical" natural science, especially physics and astronomy, and is probably the most completely developed level in the present state of knowledge, especially if we extend the concept to include the field theory and stochastic models of modern physics. Even here, however, there are important gaps, especially at the higher empirical levels. There is much yet to be known about the sheer mechanics of cells and nervous systems, of brains and of societies.

Beyond the second level, adequate theoretical models get scarcer. The last few years have seen great developments at the third and fourth levels. The theory of control mechanisms ("thermostats") has established itself as the new discipline or cybernetics, and the theory of self-maintaining systems or "open systems" likewise has made rapid strides. We could hardly maintain, however, that much more than a beginning had been made in these fields. We know very little about the cybernetics of genes and genetic systems, for instance, and still less about the control mechanisms involved in the mental and social world. Similarly the processes of self-maintenance remain essentially mysterious at many points, and although the theoretical possibility of constructing a self-maintaining machine which would be a true open system has been suggested, we seem to be a long way from the actual construction of such a mechanical similitude of life.

Beyond the fourth level it may be doubted whether we have as yet even the rudiments of theoretical systems. The intricate machinery of growth by which the genetic complex organizes the matter around it is almost a complete mystery. Up to now, whatever the future may hold, only God can make a tree. In the face of living systems we are almost helpless; we can occasionally cooperate with systems which we do not understand: we cannot even begin to reproduce them. The ambiguous status of medicine, hovering as it does uneasily between magic and science, is a testimony to the state of systematic knowledge in this area. As we move up the scale the absence of the appropriate theoretical systems becomes ever more noticeable. We can hardly conceive ourselves constructing a system which would be in any recognizable sense "aware," much less self conscious. Nevertheless as we move towards the human and societal level a curious thing happens: the fact that we have, as it were, an inside track, and that we ourselves *are* the systems which we are studying, enables us to utilize systems which we do not really understand. It is almost inconceivable that we should make a machine that would make a poem: nevertheless, poems *are* made by fools like us by processes which are largely hidden from us. The kind of knowledge and skill that we have at the symbolic level is very different from that which we have at lower levels—it is like, shall we say, the "knowhow" of the gene as compared with the knowhow of the biologist. Nevertheless it is a real kind of knowledge and it is the source of the creative achievements of man as artist, writer, architect, and composer.

Perhaps one of the most valuable uses of the above scheme is to prevent us from accepting as final a level of theoretical analysis which is below the level of the empirical world which we are investigating. Because, in a sense, each level incorporates all those below it, much valuable information and insights can be obtained by applying low-level systems to high-level subject matter. Thus most of the theoretical schemes of the social sciences are still at level (2), just rising now to (3), although the subject matter clearly involves level (8). Economics, for instance, is still largely a "mechanics of utility and self interest," in Jevons' masterly phrase. Its theoretical and mathematical base is drawn largely from the level of simple equilibrium theory and dynamic mechanisms. It has hardly begun to use concepts such as information which are appropriate at level (3), and makes no use of higher level systems. Furthermore, with this crude apparatus it has achieved a modicum of success, in the sense that anybody trying to manipulate an economic system is almost certain to be better off if he knows some economics than if he doesn't. Nevertheless at some point progress in economics is going to depend on its ability to break out of these low-level systems, useful as they are as first approximations, and utilize systems which are more directly appropriate to its universe—when, of course, these systems are discovered. Many other examples could be given—the wholly inappropriate use in psychoanalytic theory, for instance, of the concept of energy, and the long inability of psychology to break loose from a sterile stimulus-response model.

Finally, the above scheme might serve as a mild word of warning even to Management Science. This new discipline represents an important breakaway from overly simple mechanical models in the theory of organization and control. Its emphasis on communication systems and organizational structure, on principles of homeostasis and growth, on decision processes under uncertainty, is carrying us far beyond the simple models of maximizing behavior of even ten years ago. This advance in the level of theoretical analysis is bound to lead to more powerful and fruitful systems. Nevertheless we must never quite forget that even these advances do not carry us much beyond the third and fourth levels, and that in dealing with human personalities and organizations we are dealing with systems in the empirical world far beyond our ability to formulate. We should not be wholly surprised, therefore, if our simpler systems, for all their importance and validity, occasionally let us down.

I chose the subtitle of my paper with some eye to its possible overtones of meaning. General systems theory is the skeleton of science in the sense that it aims to provide a framework or structure of systems on which to hang the flesh and blood of particular disciplines and particular subject matters in an orderly and coherent corpus of knowledge. It is also, however, something of a skeleton in a cupboard—the cupboard in this case being the unwillingness of science to admit the very low level of its successes in systematization, and its tendency to shut the door on problems and subject matters which do not fit easily into simple mechanical schemes. Science, for all its successes, still has a very long way to go. General systems theory may at times be an embarrassment in pointing out how very far we still have to go, and in deflating excessive philosophical claims for overly simple systems. It also may be helpful, however, in pointing out to some extent *where* we have to go. The skeleton must come out of the cupboard before its dry bones can live.

3
Modern Systems Theory—An Outlook for Coping with Change

ANATOL RAPOPORT

It is not possible to give precise definitions for either "system" or "theory" because both of these words are understood in several different senses, all equally legitimate, being sanctified by wide usage. However, in the interest of clarity, it is advisable to spell out the different meanings of these words and to keep track as we pass from one to another.

Various Meanings of Theory

Let us examine some meanings of "theory" first. In one sense, the word is related to the word "theorem". A theorem is a proposition logically derived from other propositions, more specially a proposition established by the use of deductive techniques, such as those of mathematics. The "truth" of a theorem is established entirely by the validity of the deduction, that is, only with reference to the truth of the propositions from which the theorem was derived. The truth of these propositions is established by the same process until we arrive at certain "rock bottom" propositions, whose truth is simply assumed. These are called axioms or postulates. In short, a theorem is true if the axioms or postulates from which it was ultimately derived are true.

Until about 150 years ago the axioms and postulates of mathematics were regarded as self-evident propositions that could not be denied without violating common sense. Today they are regarded simply as propositions that for one reason or another we *agree* to regard as true. That some of the postulates of classical mathematics—of geometry, for example, are *not* self-evident has been demonstrated in modern mathematics where different mathematical theories have been constructed on different sets of postulates, all internally consistent and therefore all equally justified as theories (collections of theorems) in this purely deductive sense of the word.

The possibility of constructing equally justified but non-equivalent mathematical theories reveals mathematics as a "contentless" science. A mathematical theory, i.e., a collection of mathematical theorems, says nothing about the "real" world that we perceive by our senses. In fact, no mathematical theorem can be proved by an appeal to observations or experiments; that is to say, no mathematician will accept such a proof.

Take the familiar theorem of elementary geometry: the square of the hypotenuse of a right triangle equals the sum of the squares of the other two sides. In a practical sense we can verify the approximate truth of this theorem by measuring the three sides of several "right triangles." To the mathematician's way of thinking, however, this procedure is not a proof. To begin with, approximate verifications (as all measurements must be) are not good enough. The theorem says that the square of the hypotenuse must *exactly* equal the sum of the squares of the other two sides. It is impossible to establish "exact" lengths by physical measurements. Secondly, no matter how many triangles we examine, we cannot examine them all. Finally, there are no "right triangles" to get hold of, in the mathematical sense of "right triangle." All physical triangles are only crude approximations of the idealized triangles of geometry. In short, the assertions of mathematics are not about objects found in the world accessible to our senses but about things or events that have only a conceptual existence. Moreover, mathematical truth, being established only with reference to propositions assumed to be true, cannot be shown to be true in the sense of scientific truth, that is, observationally or experimentally verifiable truth. Bertrand Russell was not joking when he said that in mathematics we never know what we are talking about nor whether what we are saying is true.

Yet mathematics is an indispensable adjunct to all the mature sciences. This is because the mature sciences deal with situations described in terms of mathematical models. A right triangle may be taken as a model of the configuration formed by two roads at right angle to each other, both intersected by a diagonal road. In this configuration, mathematically derived properties of right angles are reflected with precision sufficient for most practical purposes. Similarly, physicists talk about perfectly elastic bodies, weightless rods, frictionless pulleys, etc., even though no such things exist. The mathematically derived properties of these idealized objects are approximately reproduced in real ones or else serve as a starting point of a theory, subsequently modified to fit better to the real world.

Practically the entire content of the physical sciences resides in mathematical models of portions of the real world. There are models of motions of heavenly bodies, of the propagation of electromagnetic waves, of chemical reactions, of transformations of energy from mechanical to electrical and vice versa, of phenomena involving heat, sound, light, etc. Thus, the theories of physical sciences, like those of mathematics, are essentially collections of theorems, that is, propositions mathematically deduced from basic propositions.

These basic propositions, analogues of postulates in mathematics, are called physical laws. There is, however, a fundamental difference between the physical sciences and mathematics. While in mathematics the truth of a theorem is established *only* with reference to the postulates, whose truth is simply assumed, in the physical sciences, the truth of an assertion must be established with reference to some observable event.

For example, the physicist may prove mathematically (as Archimedes did 2000 years ago) that a one pound weight can balance a two pound weight if it is twice as far from the fulcrum of a lever. But to establish the truth of this proposition he must demonstrate it with acutal weights and an actual lever. In 1846 two mathematicians deduced mathematically the existence of a hitherto unseen planet and its exact position in the sky. But the truth of the discovery was revealed only when Neptune appeared in the visual field of the telescope at the Berlin observatory. On the basis of Mendeleyev's periodic table, chemists deduced the existence of elements hitherto unknown. Their deductions were accepted as true only when the elements were actually found. In 1905 Einstein deduced purely theoretically that the energy contained in a gram of matter amounts to ninety trillion joules, but the truth of this proposition was demonstrated only forty years later when the first atomic bomb was exploded.

The connection between theoretically deduced propositions and observations endows the theories of physical science with predictive power. These theories call attention to what is possible and sometimes also to how the possible can be achieved. The burgeoning technology of Western civilization is a consequence of the realization and of the utilization of the predictive power of the physical sciences.

There are, however, two other by-products of physical science, not often appreciated by the layman but of extreme importance to man and of special relevance to our discussion. They are philosophical, specifically the epistemological by-products, related to conceptions of knowledge. In the light of the physical sciences, the world of matter is seen to be governed not by whims of gods or demons but by laws. The implication of this insight is that man's attempts to avoid misfortunes and to better his lot by bribing the gods or by trying to manipulate nature by incantations were misguided. The secret of power over the forces of nature lies in knowledge, not in acting out wishfulfilling fantasies.

The other epistemological by-product of physical theory pertains to the nature of knowledge itself. The source of knowledge, it turned out, was not someone's authority (which is the child's conception of knowledge), nor was it in the power of reason alone (as the idealistic philosophers conceive it), but direct contact with nature. To gain knowledge, we must learn to ask the right questions; and to get answers, we must act, not wait for answers to occur to us. The controlled experiment is an active (not passive) questioning of nature, a deliberate arrangement of conditions so as to elicit an answer to a question suggested by a theory.

Moreover, it turns out, all knowledge is tentative. The so-called laws of physics are only hypotheses, points of departure in the deduction of predictive propositions. The hypotheses are held onto only so long as the propositions deduced from them continue to be verified. If a deduced proposition is refuted by an experiment, the underlying hypotheses, even if they derive from long established physical laws, must be either modified or discarded. This is what happened to the classical laws of motion with the advent of relativity theory and to classical electrodynamics with the advent of quantum theory.

Combining these by-products of physical science, we discern the epistemological foundations of the philosophy of science. Knowledge of scientific truth is essentially the ability to predict events.

The predictive criterion of truth is a "hard" criterion. It emphasized the objective, public notion of scientific truth, its independence of what we, with our predilections, aspirations, and apprehensions, are often driven to believe. It is therefore in a way antithetical to the "soft," intuitive criterion of truth, where truth is identified with what "makes sense," with what makes impressions fit into an understandable pattern. Yet this "soft" component is also of paramount importance, even in science, in that it provides a motivation for the search for truth, other than the desire to predict and so control events.

The purely cognitive value of truth, the value of understanding in the intuitive sense of the word, leads to a third conception of theory—a conception based on explanatory appeal.

The explanatory appeal of a theory may be independent of its predictive power. For example, when the natural selection theory of biological evolution was first formulated, it had little or no predictive content. It was not possible on the basis of the theory to predict the future evolution of species, and even if it were, the scale of evolution would preclude the verification of the predictions. But the Darwin-Wallace theory of natural selection as the driving force of evolution had enormous explanatory appeal. Suddenly the idea of evolution, which philosophers had entertained since antiquity, made sense without recourse to anthropomorphic or mystical notions such as "will," "striving," "teleological causes," etc.

Similarly, the Marxist theory of history had great explanatory appeal especially for those who were already attuned to the idea of interpreting social history as a succession of struggles between oppressors and oppressed. In supposedly uncovering the economic "roots" of those struggles, Marx provided future Marxists with an outlook that made sense in the progressively more materialistic conception of the world.

Freudian theory "makes sense" to Freudians, and this feeling of having understood the sources of compulsion in the human psyche and in human conduct gives the theory its explanatory appeal, regardless of its predictive power, which is anything but impressive.

Prominent examples of theories that "hold up" in terms of their explanatory appeal are linguistic theories. The linguist singles out certain units in terms of which a language is described, such as phonemes (the fundamental sound units), morphemes (the smallest carriers of meaning), words, phrases, and sentences. Linguistic theory is a structural theory of language, that is, simply a description of how these units fit together in utterances. The theory makes no predictions to be verified by "controlled experiment." There are few logical deductions in it. But is makes possible a systematic description of languages. It operates with concepts that apply to all languages and so makes possible a systematic comparison of languages; it provides a conceptual scheme in terms of which language appears as a phenomenon that can be understood in its totality; it provides a *perspective* for studying language as a portion of reality.

In summary, three different aspects of theory are emphasized in different senses of the term. One is the logical or *deductive* component of a theory (as in mathematics). One is the *predictive* content of a theory (as in natural sciences). One is the *heuristic* aspect of a theory, its ability to provide intellectual points of leverage for investigations.

All three aspects are present in scientific theories. The heuristic aspect, however, is of special importance in areas where we are still groping for paths toward new knowledge, particularly new kinds of knowledge, areas where the deductive and predictive components of theories are still weak. The value of heuristic theories is in the opportunity they offer to look at things in a new way and so to gain a measure of "understanding," not yet justified by the hard criteria of a mature science but necessary for continuing the search. Actually all science began as dawning of an intuitive understanding of how "things hang together."

Systems theory can be viewed from all three of these perspectives, and we shall so describe it. First, however, let us examine the various meanings of the word "system."

"Hard" System Theory

Let us begin with the "hardest" definition. In this connection, I use the words "hard" and "soft" with reference to definitions. A hard definition is one that permits an unambiguous recognition of the thing defined. A soft definition provides only an intuitive understanding of the thing defined. A definition of a Frenchman as a person born in France is a hard definition to the extent that the borders of France are clearly specified. A definition of an intellectual as a person profoundly interested in ideas is a soft definition.

A hard definition of a system: it is a portion of the world which at a given time can be characterized by a given *state*, together with a set of rules that permit the deduction of the state from partial information. The state of a system (in its hard sense) is a set of values of certain variable quantities at the moment of time in question.

The definition can be best elucidated by examples. If a quantity of gas is confined in a container mechanically and thermally isolated from its environment, then eventually the temperature and pressure inside the container will become uniform. The gas will constitute a system in equilibrium, that is, a system persisting in a single state. The state of this system is completely described by three quantities: volume, pressure, and temperature. For a given gas, these three quantities are connected by a characteristic equation so that if two of the quantities are known, the third can be inferred. In this way the state of the system is inferred from partial information. The equation connecting the three state variables constitutes a static theory of that system. It is static because it says nothing about how the gas will behave if the equilibrium is disturbed. A *dynamic* theory permits the determination of the *succession* of states, once the initial state of the system is known.

The theory of the solar system is a good example of a dynamic system theory. The state of the solar system at a particular moment is completely described by the relative positions and velocities of the planets relative to the sun. The theory is the system of equations reflecting the rates of change of velocities of these bodies under the influence of their mutual gravitational attractions and all the assertions deduced from these equations. Given the positions and velocities of the planets at one moment of time, they can be deduced for all successive moments. Thus the sequence of states of the system can be deduced from the initial state, that is, from partial information.

A system isolated from its environment is called a closed system. One that receives inputs from the environment and/or acts on the environment through outputs is called an open system. Consider a system of chemical reactions where substances are fed into the system and removed from it at known rates. Such a system is an open system with known inputs and outputs. Knowledge of its laws of operation—for instance, of how the rates of change of the concentrations of the various substances depend on the momentary concentrations of the substances in the system—leads to a formulation of either a static or a dynamic theory of such systems: the theory is static if it predicts only the condition of the system in the steady state (when the concentrations remain constant); a dynamic theory predicts also the time courses of the concentrations.

It can be shown that many open systems of this sort exhibit so-called "equifinality." That is, the distributions of the concentrations in the steady state will be independent of the initial concentrations, as if the system "sought" to achieve that state and resisted external disturbances. Closed systems do not have this property. In them the distribution of concentrations in equilibrium do depend on initial concentrations. It was conjectured by some system theorists, notably by Ludwig von Bertalanffy, that "equifinality" (i.e., apparently purposeful behavior characterizing living systems) is a consequence of the fact that they are *open* systems. It is well known, of course, that a system cannot be living unless it constantly receives inputs from the environment in the form of food, information, etc. Here, then, is an example of a theoretical proposition arrived at through analysis of large classes of systems.

If both "system" and "theory" are to be understood in the hard sense, then a theory of a system is a mathematical model of it. The foundation of the model is a set of assumptions about how the several variables that define the state of the system are related to each other. If the theory is a dynamic one, the relations typically involve also the rates of change of the variables. The mathematical models are then systems of differential equations. Classical examples of such system theories are *deterministic*, for instance, theories of mechanical or electrodynamic systems or of systems of chemical reactions. That is to say, an initial state of an isolated system determines all of its subsequent states. Note that the determinism is not a matter of philosophical conviction (as is, for example, a denial of "free will" on metaphysical grounds) but rather a consequence of the mathematical model. Typically, the time courses of variables inter-related in a system of differential equations are determined, once the initial values of all the relevant variables are given. In this way the philosophical principle of determinism is derived logically rather than metaphysically. One need not accept this principle, of course. But rejecting it implies rejecting the classical models of physical processes. One then is faced with the theoretical problem of proposing other internally consistent models. This, in fact, was done in quantum mechancis. In that theory, the principle of indeterminism is also a consequence of clearly stated postulates rather than metaphysical conviction about "free will" or the like.

The modern system theorist (of the hard, mathematical persuasion) is concerned with the range of phenomena to which this sort of system theory can be applied. He already knows that it can be applied to a wide range of physical phenomena whenever the state of a system can be described with sufficient precision and whenever the laws of interaction among the variables describing the state of the system are known. The task of solving the equations that constitute the mathematical model may be a formidable one. As long, however, as the model is a reasonably good approximation of the actual structure and dynamics of the real system, the difficulties are only technical. With the advent of mathematical technology, the range of applicability of system theory can be continually expanded.

A case in point is meteorology. The state of the entire atmosphere at a given moment is describable in terms of the distributions of pressures, temperatures, concentrations of water vapor, velocities of air currents, etc. All of these variables are related by well known laws of thermodynamics, hydrodynamics, and aerodynamics. It is , however, out of the question to set up the equations governing these distributions and their rates of change, let alone to solve the equations. The meteorologist tries to single out the most important variables and to solve the equations approximately with reference to a limited region. With the advance of mathematical technology (e.g., high speed computers, accurate instrumentation, and instantaneous communication) the approximations can be improved and weather prediction can become quite accurate.

The greater accuracy of a theory is usually the result of taking into account more of the relevant variables and especially their complex interdependencies. That is, improvements of hard theories are consequences of an increasingly systemic conceptualization.

System engineering is the application of the same idea. The telephone system, the system of electric power distribution, a computer, an automated factory—all these are systems in the hard sense of the word. Knowledge of their laws of operation is essential if they are to be properly controlled and properly utilized. A dramatic instance of system failure occurred a few years ago in Northeastern United States and in the adjoining region of Canada when interruption of electric power supply affected the area. The failure was not foreseen because the operation of the entire system was not completely understood. Actually no system beyond a certain level of complexity can be completely known in all of its details. Therefore the system theorist is interested in singling out certain global properties of systems that characterize systems of a given type. Many aspects of systems can be understood in terms of these global properties even if a complete analysis is not possible.

As an example, an engine has a certain power, the rate of doing work. Knowledge of this quantity enables an engineer to tell in advance that the system will break down if a work load exceeding its power is imposed on it, even though he does not know the operation of the system in all its details. A work load that exceeds the power capacity of a system will *surely* cause a break down. But even smaller work loads may do it if certain subsystems of the total system become overloaded. Whether this happens depends on the internal organization of the system, in particular on the stability of its control mechanisms. Knowing the limits within which a system is stable enables the engineer to tell in advance the degree of control the system can exercise over its own operations. The above mentioned power failure of the Northeastern system was in all likelihood due not to an overload on the whole system but rather to the fact that limits of stability of the system were exceeded. The system was not able to adjust quickly enough to a local overload, and that failure in a part of the system spread throughout the whole system.

An important global property of modern communication systems is capacity for transmitting or processing information. Knowledge of this quantity enables the communication engineer to know the limits of the rate at which information can be transmitted or processed in a system without loss of accuracy. Information capacity is closely related to the degree of control in an automated system. The branch of system theory in which these global properties of systems are at the center of interest is called cybernetics. It comprises both theories related to the construction and use of high speed computers, and theories of servo-mechanisms—artificial systems capable of simulating "goal-directed" or "purposeful" behavior. The appearance of these devices that simulate logical thought and goal-oriented behavior has had a significant impact on the philosophical foundations of biology, psychology, and social science.

Systems Approaches to the Non-Physical World

This brings us to the interesting question posed in modern systems theory: to what extent can the hard system-theoretic approach be extended to other than physical systems?

The main difficulty is that, once we pass to systems other than the simple ones or the artificial ones studied in the physical sciences and engineering, we are not sure what variables best describe the state of such a system. In all likelihood they are not physical variables like masses, electric potentials, concentrations, etc. If we do single out certain variables which we think are important, we do not know the laws of interaction that govern their rates of change, since these variables do not as a rule obey the known, simple laws of physics. Nevertheless, certain portions of the non-physical world are being investigated from the mathematical system-theoretic point of view.

The clearest example is an economic system. Economics is the oldest of the "hardened" social sciences for the very good reason that economists have singled out certain easily quantifiable concepts. Therefore mathematical models of interaction among "economic variables" can be constructed as hypotheses. The variables of an economic system are prices, quantities of goods produced, man-hours of work required to produce them, capital investments, interest rates, tax rates, volumes of international trade, gold reserves, amount of money in circulation, etc. All of these variables are clearly inter-related in some way, but just how they are inter-related is not explicitly known. Nor is it easy to discover "the laws of inter-action," assuming they exist. This could conceivably be done if the variation of some of the variables in relation to others could be studied while all the other relevant variables were kept constant. But, unlike the physical variables studied in the laboratory (e.g., in a system of chemical reactions), the variables of an economic system cannot be subjected to rigorous control. Moreover, the fact that economists have singled out certain variables as relevant to economics does not mean that they are the only relevant ones. Economic events involve human behavior subject to variations stemming from political, cultural, historical, and psychological factors. This is not to say that human behavior is in principle unpredictable, as some insist in support of the argument that mathematical theories can never encompass human behavior. True, individual human behavior is often too erratic or too complex to be predictable in detail. Mass behavior, however, with which economics is typically concerned, may well be predictable (statistically speaking) if a sufficient number of relevant variables and their interactions could be taken into account.

Spotty as the successes of theoretical economics have been, the system point of view has undoubtedly helped it to mature. It may well follow in the footsteps of meterorology, increasing the scope of its accuracy as more and more relevant variables can be incorporated into models of large scale economic events. At any rate, concern with some global properties of economic systems is now commonplace—for example, concern with stability. A system becomes unstable when disturbances bring into play forces that aggravate the disturbances instead of counteracting them. Economic crises are now seen to be symptoms of system instability. Overproduction may result in large inventories, which may result in the closing of factories, which puts people out of work, which depresses their buying power, which aggravates the initial effects of overproduction. A runaway inflation also may be the result of a vicious cycle or, as the cyberneticians say, of the activation of positive feedback loops.

Understanding the properties of a system is a necessary condition for being able to control it. It is not a sufficient condition, of course, since historical, cultural, or political factors may well inhibit exercising control of a system, especially when questions arise about who is to exercise control, in what manner, and to what purpose. Still, understanding a system, even if it does not confer control over it, may reveal the reasons *why* control cannot be exercised, and this if often valuable knowledge in its own right. For instance, it may lead to changed attitudes toward a system that for certain revealed reasons cannot be subjected to control, even though it may be highly desirable or even imperative to control it.

Other important examples of systems beyond the scope of the physical sciences are ecological systems. A portion of the earth's surface, say a forest, or, better still, a body of water such as a lake, can be viewed as a living system in an environment: an ecological system. A state of an ecological system can be taken as the totality of concentrations of organisms of various kinds (including plants) in it, perhaps also their spatial distributions. These quantities change as organisms procreate and die, migrate or emigrate. The rates of change depend on the concentrations because some organisms feed upon others. One can well imagine cyclic fluctuations resulting from predator-prey interactions. As a very simple model, consider a population of foxes and rabbits. The former feed on the latter. As the rabbit population increases, foxes eat better and their population increases also. But as the foxes become more numerous, they catch more rabbits, reducing the rabbit population, which, in turn checks the fox population. It is conceivable that, if left alone, an ecological system may attain a steady state—the concentration of the various organisms being in equilibrium and the equilibrium being preserved by the mutual checks of the populations on each other.

It is now becoming evident that the advent of man has introduced a disturbing element into many ecological systems, and these disturbances have become increasingly severe as man's technology advances. For instance, the acquisition of firearms by the North American Indians led to the virtual extermination of the bison. The whaling industry has virtually exterminated many species of whale. Techniques of commercial fishing are depleting the fish population to the extent that the very improvements that initially made commercial fishing enormously productive are now propelling it toward ruin. The destruction of forests resulted in the formation of a dust bowl in Southwestern United States. The increase of desert area to almost 25% of the land surface is in part the result of the introduction of agriculture by man a few thousand years ago and of the attendant ecological disturbances.

It is commonplace to say that man's destructiveness (which in the long run becomes a danger to man himself) is a result of short-sightedness. But what is short-sightedness? It is failure to take into account the long run effects of one's actions—more specifically, failure to appreciate the *systemic* effects of one's actions, a result of being carried away by immediate or local effects. A system theory aims to reveal not only the immediate and local effects of some intervention but also the ultimate effects, perhaps on a system of whose very existence we may have been unaware. The systemic point of view practically forces itself on the medical profession, as powerful drugs become available in the treatment of specific conditions. It is now imperative to ask what *else* does a drug do? What is its effect on the entire physiological system?—not merely on the particular condition singled out for attention.

Again, insecticides when first introduced seemed a boon to agriculture, a break-through towards a solution of the global food problem. Only now are the deleterious systemic effects of insecticides to be appreciated, not the least of which is the appearance of insect strains resistant to insecticides.

Consider now the problem of war. The systemic point of view emphasizes the dynamics of the entire international system (conceived, perhaps, as nation states in interaction). In the systemic view, older notions that singled out rulers and their ambitions or specific international incidents as instigators of wars are de-emphasized. The international system is quite far removed from a physical system, presenting enormously difficult problems of conceptualization. How is the state of an international system to be defined? What are the variables to be singled out for attention? How are the relevant quantities to be measured? How do they interact? The task of constructing a "hard" theory of international relations seems insuperable. But so did once the task of describing the physical and the biological universes in all their complexity. One must begin somewhere if progress is to be made. Let us examine an instance of the system-theoretic approach to international relations.

A Model of an Arms Race

Lewis F. Richardson was a British meteorologist. He was also a Quaker pacifist. Both facts are important background information on his work. As a pacifist, Richardson was not interested in the political aspects of wars. To him the outbreak of war was simply a systemic failure, or a disaster like an epidemic or a flood. As a meterorologist, Richardson was well aware of the fact that some phenomena (like the weather) seem to be quite erratic and yet must be governed by physical laws. Determined to start somewhere in a system-theoretic exploration of inter-nation conflict, Richardson singled out two variables by means of which the state of the system could be described. One was the level of armaments of the nations, the other was the volume of trade among nations belonging to hostile blocs. Richardson knew very well, of course, that these variables cannot possibly be the only determinants of the state of an international system. But he followed in the footsteps of the early mathematical physicists: if you cannot solve the problem posed by the situation, pose a problem you can solve, then see whether you can do better. Accordingly, Richardson set up a mathematical model of an almost ludicrously simple international system consisting of two hostile nations or blocs. The fundamental assumptions of the model were the following:

1. The level of armanments of one bloc instigates proportionately to its magnitude the rate of increase in the armaments of the other.

2. Because increases of armaments levels cannot be boundless, the rate of increase of the armaments of each bloc must decrease as the level of armaments increases.

3. The degree of hostility between the blocs is measured by the difference between armament levels and inter-bloc trade (the latter being a measure of the degree of cooperation between them).

Translated into mathematical terms, these assumptions become embodied in a pair of differential equations with "degree of hostility" being the variable whose time course it to be determined.

Having solved the equations, Richardson showed that the solution fitted very well to the actual time course of intensifying hostility as reflected in the growing armament budgets of the Entente and of the Central Powers in the years preceding World War I. The fit of the solution to the data may well have been fortuitous, especially since the pre-World War I armament race lasted only a few years. However, Richardson's equations led to another conclusion, which may be of some importance in a systemic theory of international relations. Namely, the system described by his equations with the values of parameters estimated from available data, turned out to be inherently unstable. That is to say, a system of that sort could not persist in a state of equilibrium. Even if equilibrium were attained, the particular relations among the variables and their rates of change were such that the system was bound to move at an accelerated pace in either of two directions: either into a spiraling arms race (which Richardson interpreted as a drive toward war) or in the opposite direction toward disarmament. Which way the system would start moving turned out to depend on the initial values of the variables, namely the armament levels and inter-bloc trade. It happened that the state of the system at the start of the arms race in 1908 was just sufficient to propel it toward war rather than toward disarmament and possibly united Europe.

This result need not be taken seriously, but it is thought-provoking. In fact, today a great deal of attention is paid to the danger of a self-perpetuating arms race between the United States and the Soviet Union. Many feel that this race has an inherent dynamic of its own, that it is a systemic property—a result of the interactions in a polarized international system. Regardless of how the arms race is deplored, even by heads of states, the mechanisms of decision may be such that every technological advance in weaponry achieved by one side must be matched and, if possible, surpassed by the other. Each has staffs of professional men whose specific job is to watch and anticipate such advances and to make immediate provisions for "neutralizing" or surpassing them. Often it is useless to point out that the arms race is self-defeating and a mortal danger to humanity. Decisions on matters of national policy, especially when so called "security" is involved, are not governed by insights into the nature of systems but by the exigencies of the moment. This is called political realism.

The irony of the situation is that the problems with which the strategists are involved are also system-theoretic problems. Military planners are concerned these days not so much with particular weapons as with large, complex weapons systems. Because of the hypergrowth of military technology, the interdependence of the various parts of a military machine has become enormously complex. In Napoleon's time, logistics was a matter of having a sufficient number of wagons and horses to bring food and ammunition to an army marching on foot. Today logistics involves serving a huge complex of transportation and communication systems and providing armies of technicians to maintain them. Weapons systems depend for their effectiveness (so-called) on the precision of interaction of their parts at least as much as on their awesome destructive power. The design of these complexes requires sophisticated system thinking. Yet all of it must be confined to *that* system, which is only a subsystem in a large one, namely the *global* weapons system. If that global system should start operating "efficiently" it would destroy both itself and most of mankind. While this prospect is widely recognized at least in rhetoric, little serious thought has been devoted to what can be done about it. The reason is understandable: the existence of the global weapons system cannot be justified. Only the existence of its parts can be justified, and that by circular reasoning; it is said that each part must continue to exist because the other part exists.

I have departed considerably from our starting point, a discussion of "hard" system theory. This is because only a limited class of objects or phenomena can be described as systems in the rigorous sense of the term; moreover, we are looking for "philosophical spinoffs" of system theory. How has the awareness of systems changed ways of thinking, and what do these changes portend? To talk about these matters, we must turn to "soft" theories, those characterized by explanatory appeal rather than by predictive power.

"Soft" Systems Theory

According to a "soft" definition, a system is a portion of the world that is perceived as a unit and that is able to maintain its "identity" in spite of changes going on in it. While all the examples of systems given above in terms of the "hard" definition satisfy also the "soft" definition, once the demands of the "hard" definition are relaxed, a great many more interesting things can be viewed as systems.

First let us look at the systems already mentioned. The solar system undergoes changes all the time, since the positions of the planets keep changing. Yet the solar system "remains itself," as it were. The planets do not go wandering into space. The "unity" of the family is maintained.

Similarly, changes go on continually in a chemical system and in a social system. Yet the systems maintain their identities at least for a time, especially if they attain a steady state.

Many other "states of affairs" satisfy the "soft" definition of system. Consider a fountain. The identity of the drops of water in it keeps changing, yet the fountain maintains its shape. If a gust of wind disturbs it, it resumes its shape afterwards.

An example of system par excellence is a living organism. The material in it is constantly changing through metabolism, yet the organism maintains its identity throughout its life time.

Most interesting as systems are certain aggregates of organisms. Beehives and ant hills have many characteristics of living organisms. They can be so considered, namely as super-organisms composed of individual organisms in the same way as the latter are composed of living cells.

Similarly, human organizations and institutions fulfill the "soft" definition of system. A city, a nation, a business firm, a university, all of these are "organisms" of a sort. In fact, an entire civilization has many characteristics of a system.

Systems need not be material. A language, although it manifests itself in material things like books, documents, etc., and physical events like the sounds of speech, is not itself material. Yet a language, even while it changes, maintains its identity through long periods of history.

The systems just mentioned are too complex to be described in terms of succession of states or by mathematical models. Nevertheless they can be subjected to methodological investigation. Can we say anything general about all systems? That would depend of course on how we define a system. Our "soft" definition is a sort of generalization of a definition of an organism. Indeed, three fundamental properties of an organism appear in all organism-like systems.

Each has a *structure*. That is, it consists of inter-related parts.

If it is a material system, it maintains a short-term steady state. That is to say, it reacts to changes in the environment in whatever way is required to maintain its identity. It *functions*.

It undergoes slow, long term changes. *It grows, develops or evolves.* Or it degenerates, disintegrates, dies.

Organisms, ecological systems, nations, institutions, all have these three attributes: structure, function, and history; or, if you will, being, acting, and becoming. A non-material system like a language or a system of thought does not act. But it certainly has a structure (for example, a language, a grammatical one, a system of thought, a logical one) and an evolutionary history.

Is this general characterization of systems in any way enlightening? In a way it is, since it reveals a unified scheme among the various special sciences that are seen to treat one of or the other aspect of systems of various kinds. For instance, living systems can be organized into a hierarchy of types. A cell is a living system. An aggregate of cells may also be a system, such as an organ (heart, liver, lung) or an aggregate of organs, such as the circulatory system, the nervous system, the muscular system of an animal. The individual organism is a tightly organized system of organs and connecting parts. I already mentioned, some human aggregates as systems; some others are a family, a small group, a term, an organization, a bureaucracy, a military-industrial complex, a society, the international system, and humanity as a whole.

Imagine now a matrix or table with horizontal rows representing the levels of system and the vertical columns the three aspects mentioned: structure, function, and history. The "boxes" of the table are subject matters of various disciplines. Anatomy is concerned with the structure of individual organisms; cytology, with the structure of cells. Physiology is concerned with the functions (i.e., actions) of organs and organ systems; psychology and ethology, with the actions of the entire organism;

sociology, with the structure of a society. Embryology treats of the development of an individual from a fertilized egg; history, the evolution of a nation or a society or of humanity as a whole. Biological evolution is the history of species; synchronic comparative linguistics compares the structure of co-existing languages; diachronic comparative linguistics is concerned with the evolution of languages.

| | ASPECT | | |
LEVEL	STRUCTURE (BEING)	FUNCTION (ACTING)	EVOLUTION OR HISTORY (BECOMING)
Society	Sociology, Cultural Anthropology	Sociology, Economics, Cultural Anthropology	History
Institution	Theory of Organization	Political Science, Political Sociology, Theory of the Firm	Political Science, History, Cultural Anthropology
Small Group	Social Psychology	Social Psychology	
Individual	Anatomy	Psychology, Ethology	Developmental Psychology, Biography
Organ	Anatomy	Physiology	Embryology, Theory of evolution
Cell	Histology	Cell Physiology, Biochemistry	

Fig. 3-1 Schematic representation of "organismic" system theory (after R.W. Gerard).

In this way, the fractionation of science, an inevitable result of specialization, which is itself a result of the growing complexity of knowledge, can be to some extent counter-acted by this over-all systemic view of an entire field of knowledge.

The Use of Analogies

A methodological integration of the sciences can be furthered by drawing legitimate analogies between the methods of the different sciences. Therein lies, in my opinion, one of the most useful "philosophical spinoffs" of system theory. For a long time analogical thinking has been in disrepute. Indeed, naive analogies can be grossly misleading. In the Middle Ages, naive metaphorical analogies served to constrict rather than to emancipate thought. Thus social organization was sometimes compared to the human body in a way that reflected the ossified wisdom of the times. The king was the head of the body, the army its arms, the peasantry its back, the Church its heart, etc. Speculative metaphysics spun fantasies around analogies between the relations of heart to liver to spleen, and the relations of earth to moon to sun, etc., etc. Observations on animals were pervaded with anthropomorphic notions. Ants and bees were models of industry and foresight; foxes, of craftiness; lions, of courage. Alchemists attributed wills and aspirations to chemical substances, etc., etc.

Coupled with rigorous methods of observation, induction, and deduction, analogies can be extremely useful in the construction of theories both "hard" and "soft." This is especially true of mathematical analogies.

Let us return to "hard," i.e., mathematical system theory. At times two different physical systems can be described by the same or similar mathematical models. A famous example is the so-called harmonic oscillator. A weight suspended by a spring and undergoing oscillations in a resistant medium about its equilibrium position is an example of a damped harmonic oscillator. An alternating current with an inductance, a resistance, and a capacitance is another. Both systems can be described by exactly the same type of differential equation. The variables in the mechanical version are the position of the weight, its velocity, and its acceleration. In the electrical version, the variables are quantity of electric charge, the intensity of the current, and the electromotive force. Moreover, there are correspondences between pairs of constants that characterize both systems. The mass of the mechanical system is mathematically analogous to inductance; friction, to resistance; and the elasticity of the spring, to capacitance. Here, then, is an example of two systems with widely different "contents" but with exactly the same mathematical structure. All the theorems deduced for one system must be true of the other. Thanks to a mathematical analogy, two theories are merged into one. Again we see a countervailing force against fractionation of science—namely the unifying force of mathematical analysis.

The analogies of "soft" system theory are more difficult to defend. Yet they are at times compelling. Certain aspects of language evolution remind one so strongly of biological evolution that we cannot help suspecting the existence of certain principles governing both kinds of development. As an example, consider the anachronisms of spelling so common in English (the silent k's, p's, etc.) and the vestigial organs like the useless wings of non-flying birds, the gills in the embryos of mammals, the vermiform appendix, etc. We know also that certain "natural selection" principles are operating in the histories of such diverse things as languages and institutions. Certain real, not merely illusory parallels can be established between exchange of genetic material in sexual reproduction and cross-fertilization of cultures. Clearly, some of the parallels may be far-fetched or sterile. Some of them, however, almost certainly are manifestations of profound principles, which, once discovered, will surely stimulate rapid progress in the re-integration of the specialized sciences.

Of special interest in our day is the revival of the organismic conception of large human organizations. This is no longer a naive and literal analogy with a human body but rather a discernment of the operation of general organismic system principles. An organization has a structure. It maintains itself, often has specialized "organs" for maintaining and protecting its continued existence. It grows, sometimes metastasizes, matures, eventually becomes "senile," and dies. It often transmits information within itself through specialized channels. It often processes information in specialized centers. Some of its parts may have specialized decision functions. It interacts with other organizations. It is commonplace in business circles to speak of the "health" of a business firm. This is not a far-fetched metaphor. Distinct parallels can be drawn between the health of a business firm and the health of an organism in terms of its adaptability, vigor, immunity to harmful disturbances, survival potential, etc.

Of paramount importance in our lives is the super-organism known as the nation state and the society embodied in it. It seems natural to talk about the "health" of a society. Yet we would be hard put to define it unambiguously, that is, in terms that would enable most people to agree whether a given society is healthy or sick. Yet it is imperative to find acceptable criteria of social health, because political decisions, at least in a democracy, are supposed to be guided by goals directed at improving and maintaining the health of a society.

When as individuals we get sick, we usually know we are sick. How can a social consciousness be developed so that a society knows it is sick when it gets sick? Some diseases escape our awareness until it is too late, cancer being a notorious example. Do societies succumb to analogues of cancers, that is, growths within a society that eventually become autonomous organisms indifferent to the needs of the society and rob the society of its "nourishment," impair its adaptability to change, and finally kill it? Is the monstrous hypergrowth of military establishments in the two greatest powers of our time a structural and functional (not merely a metaphorical) analogue of a cancer? Do societies like individuals succumb to psychoses? Was the Nazi nightmare an example of one? Was Stalinist terror another?

These are the sorts of questions that spring from the "philosophical spinoffs" of "soft" systems theory.

Summary

In summary, the influence of systems theory on modern thought is along three distinct lines. "Hard" systems theory is an outgrowth of the development and maturation of the exact sciences, into which mathematical methods inevitably become incorporated. As more and more complex systems become objects of investigation by rigorous methods (e.g., atmosphere, complex communication and control technology, complex economies), mathematical methods must keep pace. In this way hard system theory grows and matures.

Another direction of influence is toward a reintegration of the sciences around the concept of a structured entity, maintaining its identity, and evolving. This conception provides a link between the biological and the social sciences. It emphasizes the structural, homeostatic, and historical (in the broad sense) aspects of certain especially interesting portions of the world that can be perceived as organized wholes.

The third direction, an outgrowth of the neo-organismic view of human organizations, has a strong ethical component. If human organizations as well as human beings are "organisms," what are their "rights," if any? Do so-called "primitive cultures" that sicken and die in contact with "civilization" have the right to autonomous existence, a right to identity of which they are deprived? Powerful nation states pursue their "national interests," that is, organismic needs of these systems as perceived by their leaders. In the course of satisfying these needs, powerful states often injure and even destroy other social organisms or prevent the "birth" or growth of new ones (as in containment of revolutions). Ought this be a matter of moral concern? If so, to whom?

What are the ethical implications of juxtaposing certain formally recognized rights of individuals to the needs, real or imagined, of societies of which individuals are component parts? Can we distinguish between real and imagined needs of organizations or societies? Do societies have "psyches"? What happens to the psyche of the individual who has identified himself with a larger organization, in particular with the nation state and its interests as defined by its leaders? Is social strife a symptom of a disturbance to be eliminated by the restoration of "systemic equilibrium" or, on the contrary, a symptom of the development of a society toward a form of organization more responsive to the needs of the people in it? Is a revolution an instance of social pathology or of social therapy?

Questions of this sort reflect "soft" rather than "hard" thinking. They are not well-formulated questions, the sort that pose concrete problems of interest to practical men. We must keep in mind, however, that practical men are practical precisely because they pose only those problems that can be solved within existing conceptual frameworks. But it may very well be the case that the existing conceptual frameworks are entirely inadequate to deal with the problems with which humanity is now confronted. Modern system theory should be viewed not only as a set of techniques for solving problems arising in conventional frameworks of thought, such as problems of increasingly complex technology, but also as a harbinger of a new outlook, one that is better equipped to cope with the accelerating rate of historical change.

4
Definition of System

A.D. HALL AND R.E. FAGEN

The plan of the present chapter is to discuss properties of systems more or less abstractly; that is to define *system* and to describe the properties that are common to many systems and which serve to characterize them.

Definition of "System"

Unfortunately, the word "system" has many colloquial meanings, some of which have no place in a scientific discussion. In order to exclude such meanings, and at the same time provide a starting point for exposition we state the following definition:

A system is a set of objects together with relationships between the objects and between their attributes.

Our definition does imply of course that a system has properties, functions or purposes distinct from its constituent objects, relationships and attributes.

The "definition" above is certainly terse and vague enough to merit further comments, the first of which should, in all fairness, be a note of caution. The "definition" is in no sense intended or pretended to be a definition in the mathematical or philosophical sense. Definitions of the mathematical or philosophical type are precise and self contained, and settle completely and unambiguously the question of the meaning of a given term.

To reduce the vagueness inherent in our definition, we now elaborate on the terms *objects, relationships,* and *attributes.*

Objects

Objects are simply the parts or components of a system, and these parts are unlimited in variety. Most systems in which we will be interested consist of physical parts: atoms, stars, switches, masses, springs, wires, bones, neurons, genes, muscles, gases, etc. We also admit as objects abstract objects such as mathematical variables, equations, rules and laws, processes, etc.

Attributes

Attributes are properties of objects. For example, in the preceding cases, the objects listed have, among others, the following attributes:

atoms—the number of planetary electrons, the energy states of the atoms, the number of atomic particles in the nucleus, the atomic weight.

stars—temperature, distances from other stars, relative velocity.

switches—speed of operation, state.

masses—displacement, moments of inertia, momentum, velocity, kinetic energy, mass.

springs—spring tension, displacement.

wires—tensile strength, electrical resistance, diameter, length.

Relationships

The *relationships* to which we refer are those that "tie the system together." It is, in fact, these relationships that make the notion of "system" useful.

For any given set of objects it is impossible to say that no inter-relationships exist since, for example, one could always consider as relationships the distances between pairs of the objects. It would take us too far afield to try to be precise and exclude certain "trivial" relationships or to introduce a philosophical notion such as causality as a criterion. Instead we will take the attitude that the relationships to be considered in the context of a given set of objects depend on the problem at hand, important or interesting relationships being included, trivial or unessential relationships excluded. The decision as to which relationships are important and which trivial is always determined by the person dealing with the problem; i.e. the question of triviality turns out to be relative to one's interest. To make the idea explicit, let us consider a few simple examples.

Examples of Physical Systems

First, suppose the parts are a spring, a mass, and a solid ceiling. Without the obvious connections, these components are unrelated (except for some logical relationships that might be thought of, such as being in the same room, etc.). But hang the spring from the ceiling and attach the mass to it and the relationships (of physical connectedness) thus introduced give rise to a more interesting system. In particular, new relationships are introduced between certain attributes of the parts as well. The length of the spring, the distance of the mass from the ceiling, the spring tension and the size of the mass are all related. The system so determined is *static*, that is, the attributes do not change with time. Given an initial displacement from its rest position, however, the mass will have a certain velocity depending on the size of the mass and the spring tension; its position changes with time, and in this case the system is *dynamic*.

A more complex example is given by a high-fidelity sound system. The parts of this system are more numerous, but for simplicity we could consider only the turntable and arm of the record player, the amplifier, the speaker, and the cabinet. Again, without connections, these parts in themselves would not behave as a sound reproducing system. With connections, in this case electrical coupling of input to output, these parts and their attributes are related in that the performance in each stage is dependent on performance in the other stages; mechanical vibrations in the speaker are related to currents and voltages in the amplifier, etc.

Examples of Abstract or Conceptual Systems

An example of a nonphysical nature is given by a set of real variables. The most obvious property of a real variable is its numerical size; in other words in this example *object* and *attribute* are closely related (in fact, in any example an object is ultimately specified by its attributes). Familiar relationships between variables take the form of equations. For concreteness, consider two variables x_1 and x_2 satisfying the two linear equations.

(1)
$$a_1 x_1 + a_2 x_2 = c_1$$
$$b_1 x_1 + b_2 x_2 = c_2$$

The equations provide constraints on the variables; together the two equations constitute a system of linear equations; the parts of the system are the variables x_1 and x_2, the relationships being determined by the constants and the simultaneous restrictions on the given quantities. The system of equations (1) might be termed *static*, by way of analogy with the static spring and mass system. The analogy is determined by the fact that the numbers which satisfy the equations are fixed, just as the length of the spring is fixed in the mechanical analogue.

On the other hand, introduction of a time parameter t gives rise, for example, to equations of the form

(2)
$$\frac{dx}{dt} = a_1 x_1 + a_2 x_2$$
$$\frac{dx}{dt} = b_1 x_1 + b_2 x_2$$

The system (2) might, by further analogy with the spring and mass example, be termed *dynamic*. Here the solutions are functions of time just as the length of the spring in the dynamic system is a function of time.

The terms "static" and "dynamic" are always in reference to the system of which the equations are an abstract model. Abstract mathematical and/or logical relationships are themselves always timeless.

Abstract Systems as Models

The two examples of the preceding section provide more than incidental illustrations of the idea of system; they suggest one of the most fruitful ways of analyzing physical systems, a way that will be immediately recognized as a fundamental method of science: the method of abstraction.

A return to the simple example of the coupled mass and spring provides a direct illustration of the idea. In the static case, the attributes of interest are the spring constant K, displacement x, and weight W. These are related (within elastic limits by Hook's law) by the linear equation

$$Kx = W$$

which is of the form (1) for one variable. This further suggests the intimate relationship between an abstract system such as (1) and its *physical realization*. To study the physical system, we substitute for it an abstract system with analogous relationships and the problem becomes a mathematical one. In the dynamic case as well, it is not hard to show that the same sort of analogy obtains, the system being replaced in this case by a differential equation instead of a linear algebraic equation.

This practice is certainly a familiar one to physicists, chemists, and engineers; usually it is spoken of as the creation of a mathematical *model*. The extent to which a model agrees with the actual behavior of a system is a measure of the applicability of the particular model to the situation in question. On the other hand, the ease with which a given system can be represented accurately by a mathematical model is a measure of the ease of analyzing the given system.

In order to be completely amenable to mathematical analysis, a system must possess rather special properties. First, the relationships must be known explicitly; secondly, the attributes of importance must be quantifiable and not so numerous as to defy listing, and finally the mode of behavior (as would be given by a physical law such as Hooke's law), under the given set of relationships must be known. Unfortunately, it is a rare system indeed that has all these properties; more exactly, systems possess these qualities in degrees, the more interesting systems such as living organisms exhibiting less of a conformance than simpler systems such as mechanical systems of which the spring and mass is a special case.

Definition of Environment

At this point it seems worthwhile to introduce the notion of *environment* of systems. Environment for our purposes can best be defined in a manner quite similar to that used to define system, as follows:

**For a given system, the environment is the set of all
objects a change in whose attributes affect the system
and also those objects whose attributes are changed
by the behavior of the system.**

The statement above invites the natural question of when an object belongs to a system and when it belongs to the environment; for if an object reacts with a system in the way described above should it not be considered a part of the system? The answer is by no means definite. In a sense, a system together with its environment makes up the universe of all things of interest in a given context. Subdivision of this universe into two sets, system and environment, can be done in many ways which are in fact quite arbitrary. Ultimately it depends on the intentions of the one who is studying the particular universe as to which of the possible configurations of objects is to be taken as the system. A few examples may serve to illustrate this idea.

Systems and their Environments

First, let us return to one of our original examples, the high fidelity sound system. Suppose the whole system is situated in a living room, and that a record is being played over the system. The environment of the system could consist of the record being played, the room in which it is situated, and the listener. It is easily seen that each of these objects bears some relationship to the behavior of the system; the record determines the succession of electrical impulses and mechanical vibrations in the various stages of the system. The output of the system, in turn, affects the pattern of sound waves in the room as well as the mental state of the listener (which might range from sheer ecstasy to nervous apprehension depending on the excellence of the output). Any or all of these environmental objects could be considered to be part of the system instead of the environment. For certain purposes this might be an artificial designation. Each time a different record is played, one would be considering a different system in this case, whereas actually the system of interest to a sound engineer would not include any specific record, and so would not change in nature from record to record. On the other hand, if one is interested in a system to reproduce one specific announcement, it would make more sense to consider the record as part of the system.

The example above is cited only to make clear what is meant by system and environment and why the dichotomy of sets of related objects into system and environment depends essentially on the point of view at hand. However, the general problem of specifying the environment of a given system is far from trivial. To specify completely an environment one needs to know all the factors that affect or are affected by a system; this problem is in general as difficult as the complete specification of the system itself. As in any scientific activity, one includes in the universe of system and environment all those objects which he feels are the most important, describes the inter-relationships as thoroughly as possible and pays closest attention to those attributes of most interest, neglecting those attributes which do not play essential roles. One "gets away" with this method of idealization rather well in physics and chemistry; massless strings, frictionless air, perfect gases, etc. are commonplace assumptions and simplify greatly the description and analysis of mechanical and thermodynamical universes. Biologists, sociologists, economists, psychologists, and other scientists interested in animate systems and their behavior are not so fortunate. In these fields it is no simple task to pick out the essential variables from the nonessential; that is, specification of the universe and subsequent dichotomization into system and environment is in itself, apart from analysis of the inter-relationships, a problem of fundamental complexity.

Subsystems

It is clear from the definition of system and environment that any given system can be further subdivided into subsystems. Objects belonging to one subsystem may well be considered as part of the environment of another subsystem. Consideration of a subsystem, of course, entails a new set of relationships in general. The behavior of the subsystem might not be completely analogous with that of the original system. Some authors refer to the property *hierarchical order* of systems; this is simply the idea expressed above regarding the partition of systems into subsystems.[1] Alternatively, we may say that the elements of a system may themselves be systems of lower order.

In passing it may be worthwhile to note that this idea of examining subsystems and their behavior has a rather widespread significance in mathematics, particularly in set theory and modern algebra. Just to mention an example, the study of groups (collections of mathematical objects having certain algebraic properties) includes considerations of the properties of sub-groups; moreover, subgroups do not necessarily "behave" (behavior here is in the algebraic sense) the same as their parent groups in all respects.

Returning to our example of the high-fidelity system, we see that the idea of division into subsystem is clearly illustrated. The amplifier itself is a system of considerable complexity; the pick-up arm and speaker, themselves systems of a different character, can be quite naturally considered as parts of the environment of amplifier. In turn, the amplifier could be further divided into its stages, and each circuit considered as a separate subsystem.

Macroscopic vs. Microscopic Views of Systematic Behavior

One technique for studying systems which are exceedingly complex is to consider in detail the behavior of certain of its subsystems. Another method is to neglect the minute structure and observe only the macroscopic behavior of the system as a whole. Both of the methods above are common and familiar in many fields, and are of fundamental importance. Before discussing these ideas further, we cite a familiar example.

The difference between these two approaches can be seen by considering the roles of the physiologist and psychologist in the study of the human system. The physiologist is interested in the internal properties and characteristics of the body; he isolates and studies separately the functions of the various internal organs in relationship to bodily activity. When studying the heart, for example, the blood stream, lungs, kidneys, etc. might well be considered as parts of the environment. On the other hand, the psychologist, while not completely neglecting visceral conditions, is primarily concerned with patterns of behavior of the system under various external conditions. It may well be that the psychologist could theoretically improve his knowledge by a complete physiological approach. From the practical standpoint this may be virtually impossible. The variables and their relationships are still beyond description and comprehension; the psychologist is left with the realization that his investigation of behavior is more fruitful from a macroscopic point of view.

Some Macroscopic Properties of Systems

So far we have been talking in detail about systems as though by implication there were in the background some sort of unified theory of systems. Actually, there is as yet no such theory, although attempts have been made at one. It is always a good idea when considering such general theories to be sure the types of system under discussion are clearly understood and, where generalizations to systems of other types are claimed, to see if all the analogies and correspondences used are valid.

Nevertheless, there are some properties that belong to certain classes of systems, and are worth mentioning briefly. Also, there are some valid and useful analogies concerning the behavior and properties of certain types of systems that often aid in analysis, at least conceptually, of particular systems. As a notable example, the concept of entropy, useful in thermodynamic systems, has an interesting and valuable analogue in the concept of entropy as defined for message sources in information theory.

Properties that are frequently mentioned by various authors in discussing systems include *wholeness and independence, progressive segregation, progressive systematization and centralization.*[2]

Wholeness and Independence

In our definition of system we noted that all systems have relationships between objects and between their attributes. If every part of the system is so related to every other part that a change in a particular part causes a change in all the other parts and in the total system, the system is said to behave as a *whole* or *coherently*. At the other extreme is a set of parts that are completely unrelated: that is, a change in each part depends only on that part alone. The variation in the set is the physical sum of the variations of the parts. Such behavior is called *independence* or *physical summativity*.

Wholeness or coherence and independence or summativity are evidently not two properties, but extremes of the same property. We may speak of 100% wholeness being at the same end of a scale with 0% independence, but such use of these terms would be merely a matter of verbal convenience. While wholeness and independence may be matters of degree, no sensible method of measuring them yet exists. Nevertheless, the property provides a useful qualitative notion. In fact, since all systems have some degree of wholeness, this property is used by some writers to define "system."

Since all systems have wholeness in some degree, we have no difficulty illustrating the property. Near the 100% end of the scale we have such systems as passive electrical networks and their mechanical analogues. At the other end of the scale we have difficulty finding examples. In fact, most of the literature uses the term "heap" or "complex" to describe a set of parts which are mutually independent and the term "system" is used only when some degree of wholeness exists. We prefer to call sets of parts with complete independence "degenerate systems" because, as we noted before, it is impossible to deny systematic relationships in a heap of sand or odds and ends.

Progressive Segregation

The concepts of wholeness and summativity can be used to define another qualitative property often observed in physical systems. Most non-abstract systems change with time. If these changes lead to a gradual transition from wholeness to summativity, the system is said to undergo *progressive segregation*.

We can distinguish two kinds of progressive segregation. The first, and simplest kind, corresponds to decay. It is as though, through much handling, the parts of a jigsaw puzzle become so rounded that a given piece no longer fits the other pieces better than another. Or suppose an open-wire carrier telephone system were suddenly deprived of maintenance. Vacuum tubes would wear out, poles would rot, and so on, and eventually there would be a group of parts that no longer behaved as a system.

The second kind of progressive segregation corresponds to growth. The system changes in the direction of increasing division into subsystems and sub-systems or differentiation of functions. This kind of segregation seems to appear in systems involving some creative process or in evolutionary and developmental process. An example is embryonic development, in which the germ passes from wholeness to a state where it behaves like a sum of regions which develop independently into specialized organs. Another example, often observed in the creation and development of a new communication system, occurs when an idea appears, or a need is defined, and the original conception of a system segregates through planning effort into subsystems whose design and development eventually proceed almost independently.

Progressive Systematization

This is simply the opposite of progressive segregation, a process in which there is change toward wholeness. It may consist of strengthening of pre-existing relations among the parts, the development of relations among parts previously unrelated, the gradual addition of parts and relations to a system, or some combination of these changes. As an example, consider the development of the long distance telephone network. First, local telephone exchanges sprang up about the country. Then exchanges were joined with trunk lines. As transmission techniques improved, more exchanges were added at greater distances. Later, toll dialing was added, placing the network at the command of operators and eventually at the command of customers. The record has been one of increasing unification of the whole system.

It is possible for progressive segregation and systematization to occur in the same system. These two processes can occur simultaneously, and go on indefinitely so that the system can exist in some kind of steady state as with the processes of anabolism and catabolism in the human body. These processes can also occur sequentially. Consider the early history of America during which groups of people colonized various parts of the country. These groups became more and more independent of their parent countries. Gradually, the new country became more coherent as more interchanges occurred between the groups, a new government was formed, etc.

Centralization

A *centralized* system is one in which one element or subsystem plays a major or dominant role in the operation of the system. We may call this the *leading part* or say that the system is *centered* around this part. A small change in the leading part will then be reflected throughout the system, causing considerable change. It is like a trigger with a small change being amplified in the total system. An example from politics might be a totalitarian regime, decisons of an autocrat affecting behavior of the entire system.

Either progressive segregation or progressive systematization may be accompanied by *progressive centralization*; as the system evolves one part emerges as a central and controlling agency. In the case of embryonic development previously noted, segregation does not proceed to the limit for several reasons, the most important perhaps is that the brain emerges as the controlling and unifying part.

Natural and Man-Made Systems

To enhance the meaning of "system" we distinguish natural systems and man-made systems. Engineers are directly interested in man-made systems; however, in the environment of these man-made systems are natural systems which also require investigation since their properties interact with the system under study. Furthermore, there are certain properties that both types of systems have in common; man-made systems are often copies of natural systems or at least are constructed to perform analogous functions.

Natural Systems

The description of these is the task of the astronomer, physicist, chemist, biologist, physiologist, etc., and again the amount one can say about a given natural system depends on the number of essential variables involved.

Open and Closed Systems

Most organic systems are *open,* meaning they exchange materials, energies, or information with their environments. A system is *closed* if there is no import or export of energies in any of its forms such as information, heat, physical materials, etc., and therefore no change of components, an example being a chemical reaction taking place in a sealed insulated container. An open system becomes closed if ingress or egress of energies is cut off.

Whether a given system is open or closed depends on how much of the universe is included in the system and how much in the environment. By adjoining to the system that part of the environment with which an exchange takes place, the system becomes closed. For instance, in thermodynamics, the second law is universally applicable to closed systems; it seems to be violated for organic processes. For the organic system and its environment, however, the second law still holds.[3]

Adaptive Systems

Many natural systems, especially living ones, show a quality usually called *adaptation*. That is, they possess the ability to react to their environments in a way that is favorable, in some sense, to the continued operation of the system. It is as though systems of this type have some pre-arranged "end" and the behavior of the system is such that it is led to this end despite unfavorable environmental conditions. The "end" might be mere survival; evolutionary theory is based heavily on the notion of adaptation to environment.

There are many examples of adaptive behavior in the body. Many of these are mechanisms that tend to keep within certain physiological limits various bodily conditions such as body temperature, physical balance, etc. Mechanisms of this sort are sometimes called "homeostatic mechanisms." One example is the inborn reaction to cold by shivering, tending to resist a drop in body temperature by a compensating movement producing warmth. Closely related to the concept of adaptation, learning, and evolution is the notion of *stability*.

Stable Systems

A system is stable with respect to certain of its variables if these variables tend to remain within defined limits. The man-made thermostat is an example of a device to insure stability in the temperature of a heating system; the notion of stability is familiar also in mechanics and especially in the communications field. Note that a system may be stable in some respects and unstable in others. An adaptive system maintains stability for all those variables which must, for favorable operation, remain with limits. In physiology, "motor co-ordination" is intimately connected with stability; clumsiness, tremor, and ataxia are examples of deficient or impraried motor co-ordination and instability.

Systems with Feedback

Certain systems have the property that a portion of their outputs or behavior is fed back to the input to affect succeeding outputs. Such systems are familiar enough to the communications engineer; servo-mechanisms in general are man-made systems utilizing the principle of feedback. Systems with feed-back occur quite frequently in nature as well; posture control in the human body is an example. It is a well known fact that the nature, polarity, and degree of feedback in a system have a decisive effect on the stability or instability of the system.

Man-Made Systems

Man-made systems exhibit many of the properties possessed by natural systems; simple notions such as wholeness, segregation, and summativity have meaning for both types of system. On the other hand, it has not been until recently that man-made machines have shown what might be termed adaptive behavior even on a modest scale. Other kinds of man-made systems, such as language and systems of social organization, have always shown adaptive behavior.

Adaptation for man-made systems is not strictly analogous to that for natural system; in fact, what might be considered mystical behavior on the part of a natural system is perfectly explainable for the man-made system. Any seemingly purposeful or intelligent behavior on the part of a machine has been built into it by its designer. Also, adaptive behavior on the part of a machine is not to ensure the survival of the machine necessarily, but instead to insure a specified performance in some respect.

Compatibility (or Harmony)

Often the problem arises of constructing a system to match a given environment, or what amounts to virtually the same thing, of adding new parts to already existing systems, or of connecting two systems to operate in tandem. There is no guarantee that a system constructed for a given purpose will function properly if its environment is changed (not all fountain pens write under water). Similarly, two systems independently might be quite satisfactory in certain respects, but in tandem could have completely different and not necessarily favorable characteristics.

Systems might be compatible in some respects and incompatible in others; it depends on the purpose for which the systems are introduced as well as the environmental factors. Also, systems may be compared as to the degree of compatibility with a given system. In terms of the high fidelity system, we might consider as an example the problem of matching a speaker to the rest of the outfit. Different speakers would function with varying degrees of success; some of the environmental factors might be the size of the room, the amount of money available to spend on the speakers, etc. A speaker with perfectly matched impedance and excellent mechanical construction might produce beautiful results in the given setting, but if it cost a few thousand dollars it could easily be called incompatible with respect to at least one environmental factor.

Optimization

Compatibility considerations lead naturally to the problem of optimization. As the term implies, it means adapting the system to its environment to secure the best possible performance in some respects. Optimum performance in one respect does not necessarily mean optimum performance in another; again it is a question of intent on the part of the system planner. Often, the factor of interest in an optimization problem is economic: how much bandwidth to allocate to a telephone channel, how many interoffice trunks to provide, etc. Note that the optimum bandwidth for transmitting all the subtle voice characteristics is not the same as the optimum from an economic standpoint.

Systems With Randomness

In either natural or man-made systems it is sometimes necessary to take into account random behavior. What randomness means and when to introduce it in analysis of a system are questions that can be hotly debated by philosophers. In practice it is usually introduced as a factor when the variables that may affect a given attribute are so great in number or so inaccessible that there is no choice but to consider behavior as subject to chance. One example is the noise in a vacuum tube due to random emission of electrons from the cathode.

Random variables enter in at both the microscopic and macroscopic levels. Statistical mechanics and modern physics are both dependent on assumptions of microscopic randomness. Economic conditions, numbers of potential customers, and so on are macroscopic factors also subject to chance fluctuation.

The operation of some systems with randomness can best be described in terms of stochastic processes (also called random processes or time series). Familiar examples in the field of communications are random message sources and disturbing noise in information theory, and the theory of waiting lines in telephone traffic.

Isomorphism

As has been suggested before, there are instances in many sciences where the techniques and general structure bears an intimate resemblance to similar techniques and structures in other fields. A one-to-one correspondence between objects which preserves the relationships between the objects is called an *isomorphism*. For instance in the electrical-mechanical duality, an R-L-C circuit is isomorphic to its mechanical dual since each circuit element has its corresponding mechanical interpretation and the relationships are formally the same.

Isomorphisms of this type are rather numerous; in fact, their prevalence has led to several attempts at unifying various fields of science using the idea of "system" as a fundamental concept, but these attempts are as yet incomplete. There are, however, several disciplines with more modest aims that have achieved notable success. To quote a well-known mathematician[4]:

> "As for practical usefulness, it should be borne in mind that for a mathematical theory to be applicable it is by no means necessary that it be able to provide accurate models of observed phenomena. Very often in applications the constructive role of mathematical theories is less important than the economy of thought and experimentation resulting from the ease with which qualitatively reasonable working hypotheses can be eliminated by mathematical arguments. For example, in geology we are confronted with random processes which have been going on for millions of years, some of them covering the surface of the earth. We observe that certain species go through a period of prosperity and steady increase, only

to die out suddenly and without apparent reason. Is it really necessary to assume cataclysms working one-sidedly against certain species, or to find other explanations? The Volterra-Lotka theory of struggle for existence teaches us that even under constant conditions situations are bound to arise which would appear to the naive observer exactly like many of the cataclysms of geology. Similarly, although it is impossible to give an accurate mathematical theory of evolution, even the simplest mathematical model of a stochastic process, together with observations of age, geographical distribution, and sizes of various genera and species, makes it possible to deduce valuable information concerning the influence on evolution of various factors such as selection, mutation and the like. In this way undecisive qualitative arguments are supplemented by a more convincing quantitative analysis.''

In addition to the Volterra-Lotka theory mentioned in the quotation above, there are other theories of the same nature unifying several subdomains of science. Mathematical biology, for instance, has had considerable success in this direction. There have been attempts at proposing a mathematical theory of history, cybernetics is widely quoted as unifying the communication field with the study of the behavior of living organisms, demography is a study of the growth and spread of populations, etc., but these attempts, while offering hope that certain areas will be unified eventually, are yet incomplete.

That there are isomorphisms, either total or partial, is neither accidental nor mystical. It just amounts to the fact that many systems are structurally similar when considered in the abstract. For example telephone calls, radioactive disintegrations and impacts of particles, all considered as random events in time, have the same abstract nature and can be studied by exactly the same mathematical model. It is not surprising then that properties shown by systems of gases with diffusion are useful in analyzing waiting lines of telephone calls and vice versa.

References and Notes

1. Bertalanffy, Ludwig von, "An Outline of General Systems Theory," *The British Journal of the Philosophy of Science.* Vol. 1, No. 2, 1950.
2. Stebbing, L. S., *A Modern Introduction to Logic,* New York: t. Y. Crowell Co., 1930.
3. Bertalanffy, Ludwig von, "The Theory of Open Systems in Physics and Biology," *Science,* Vol. 111, 1950.
4. Feller, W., "On the Theory of Stochastic Processes with Particular Reference to Applications," *Proc. Berkeley Symp. on Math. Stat. and Probability,* University of California Press, 1949.

5
Basic Constructs of Systems Philosophy

ERVIN LASZLO

Systems philosophy is predicated on the assumption that thinking about man and the world in terms of systems is not to force the facts of experience into the Procrustean bed of a preconceived abstract scheme, but rather is warranted by the applicability of systems concepts to many spheres of inquiry. We perceive and understand in systems terms because phenomena are perceivable and constructable as systems.

In this chapter, I should like to concentrate on the pure or theoretical aspect of systems philosophy, and suggest some constructs which are basic in the formulation of a general theory of systems. These constructs can then be used as the premises of a general philosophical theory having the required properties of synthesis and empirical relevance.

All theory construction presupposes that the world beyond human knowledge and experience is in some respects rationally ordered. There can be no theory of a chaotic universe. Inasmuch as we do have theories of the universe we hold them on the expectation that the universe is not—or not entirely—chaotic. Once this assumption is made, we confront the dilemma of special methods and special constructs to deal with particular phenomena with optimum fidelity, or using some general conceptual tools and frameworks to attempt to understand the interconnection of diverse phenomena.

The specialist is motivated by a desire to achieve optimum adequacy to the phenomena in his constructs, and builds models and proposes theories with an eye solely on the accuracy of the match with nature. The generalist believes, on the other hand, that one does not adequately understand any phenomenon unless one knows its interconnections with other phenomena. He seeks to produce those general concepts and frameworks which could prove to be adequate for the understanding not only of isolated events, but of general patterns of relationships.

The methodological position of the specialist would be superior to that of the ''generalist'' if phenomena would indeed lend themselves to accurate mapping only through specific laws and concepts. But phenomena do not impose their own categories with finality, and a number of different theories can be confirmed in regard to any set of phenomena. The selection between theories depends in the last analysis on the preferences of the investigators. These preferences are not "merely" psychological quirks, however, but underlie all rational modes of thoughts. They are the values of thinking with empirical accuracy and yet with heuristic power conferred by economy, internal consistency, and wide range of applicability.

Theories which combine empirical ideals of accuracy with the rational ideals of economy, consistency, and generality have the edge over theories that sacrifice one component for the sake of others. It is my belief that systems philosophy reflects an optimal combination of both the empirical and rationale ideals.

The foundation of systems philosophy is the recurrent applicability of empirically precise systems concepts in diverse fields of investigation. Cybernetics, general systems theory, information and game theories, and an entire constellation of mathematical and empirical disciplines emerged with striking rapidity since the 1950s. They are not unprecedented in contemporary or even classical thought, of course. "Organistic" thinking was characteristic already of Greek cosmologies and reappeared in the modern age in the works of Lloyd Morgan, Henri Bergson, Alfred North Whitehead, Samuel Alexander, and John Dewey—to mention only the key proponents. But the empirical accuracy which this mode of thought could now achieve is unparalleled by earlier attempts. The insights of past generations of thinkers may have been as great as or greater than those of systems thinkers at present, but they lacked the empirical base which is now applied by the natural and social sciences. These sciences give us not only mere sophisticated theories, but qualitatively different ones: they are, on the whole, no longer atomistic, mechanistic and reductionist, but tend toward the appreciation of wider contexts, general theories, and irreducibilities.

Systems philosophy is envisaged as a general philosophy of man and nature, using the invariant constructs which recur in the various systems-oriented sciences. The scientific theories are used as anchor points for constructing an embracing philosophy which is general in scope.

Empirical sciences map phenomena from a particular disciplinary perspective. For example, man, perhaps the most complex of all phenomena, is mapped from the perspectives of biology, psychology, the social sciences, and diverse philosophies, e.g. existentialism, idealism, spiritualism, etc. Each strand of order elucidated by inquiries from these different perspectives tells us something about man. But none does him justice, for man is a biological, as well as a psychosocial entity. In an integrated systems philosophy he can be recognized as such, by taking the isomorphies appearing in different perspectives as a starting point, and finding the invariance underlying them, which is man himself.

If systems concepts do indeed apply to a wide realm of empirical phenomena, the invariances which they code become adequate for wide-ranging application. For example, although the concept of negative feedback control is a simplification and organization of a wide variety of data, it permits one to comprehend the principle of operation in phenomena as diverse as the ordinary room thermostat, the sonar-guided underwater torpedo, the instrument landing system of modern airplanes, and the homeostasis of the human body. There is no mechanistic—or even essentialistic or spiritualistic—explanation which would have comparable integrative power without loss of empirical accuracy.

I shall now suggest four basic constructs of systems philosophy. I have found them to be extremely useful for constructing a general model of systems, which is applicable in empirical fields as diverse as physics, biology, psychology, and the social sciences. The four constructs jointly define the general system's attributes. The set of general systems we are dealing with are those called "natural systems," i.e. systems which arise independently of conscious human planning and execution. (Since almost all social and cultural systems arise in this way, they, too, are included in this defintion. The primary set of excluded systems are the artificial systems.)

Ordered Wholeness

An ordered whole is a non-summative system in which a number of constant constraints are imposed by fixed forces, yielding conditions with enduring mathematically calculable parameters. A system of this kind always contains an element of order; complete randomness is excluded from it.

Wholeness defines the character of the system as such, in contrast to the character of its parts in isolation. A whole possesses characteristics not possessed by its parts singly. Insofar as this is the case the whole is other than the simple sum of its parts. For example, an atom is other than the sum of the component particles taken individually and added together; a nation is other than the sum of individual beings composing it, etc. However, no mysticism is implied or involved in this assertion. Traditionally, wholes were often considered to be qualitative and intrinsically unmeasurable entities because they were seen as "more than the sum of their parts." This conception is spurious. Wholes can be mathematically shown to be other than the simple sum of the properties and functions of their parts.

Consider merely the following basic ideas. Complexes of parts can be calculated in three distinct ways:

(1) By counting the *number* of parts
(2) By taking into account the *species* to which the parts belong, and
(3) By considering the *relations* between the parts.[1]

In (1) and (2) the complex may be understood as the sum of the parts considered in isolation. In these cases the complex has *cumulative* characteristics: it is sufficient to sum the properties of the parts to obtain the properties of the whole. Such wholes are better known as "heaps" or "aggregates," since the fact that the parts are joined in them makes no difference to their functions—i.e. the interrelations of the parts do not qualify their joint behavior. A heap of bricks is an example of this. But consider an atom, an organism, or a society: the particular relations of the parts bring forth properties which are not present (or are meaningless in reference to), the parts. Examples of this range from the Pauli exclusion principle (which does not say anything about individual electrons), through homeostatic self-regulation (which is meaningless in reference to individual cells or organs), all the way to distributive justice (likewise meaningless in regard to individual members of a society). Each of these complexes is not a mere heap, but a whole which is *other* than the sum of its parts.[2]

The mathematics of non-summative complexes apply to systems of the widest variety—physical, biological, social, and psychological. These systems form ordered wholes in which the law-bound regularities exhibited by interdependent elements determine the functional behavior of the totality. The fallacy of reducing a whole atom to the sum of the properties of its parts is well known to atomic physicists; the analogous fallacy of reducing the whole organism to biochemical reactions and physical properties manifested by particular components is becoming increasingly recognized too.[3] Social scientists, as well as individual psychologists daily accumulate evidence concerning the unfeasibility of explaining social or psychological events by reference to the qualities of the individual components, e.g. the motivations, wishes and habits of individuals, and the properties of particular cognitive or emotive factors.

Self-Stabilization

A whole is an entity that forms a dynamic balance between internal, fixed constraints, which impose its enduring structure, and external, unrestrained forces, which mold the structure and evolve the entity. The presence of fixed forces brings about a steady, or stationary state when all flows induced by unrestrained forces vanish. When unrestrained forces are introduced into a dynamically balanced system disposing over fixed constraints, the system will tend to buffer out forces which perturb its stable configuration. As Katchalsky and Curran[4] have shown, any fluctuation in such a system gives rise to forces which tend to bring it back to its stable configuration due to the fact that the flow caused by the perturbation has the same sign as the perturbation itself. Hence the flow will reduce the perturbation and the system will eventually return to its steady state. If the perturbations vanish, the system is characterized by the parameters of its fixed constraints. If both the fixed and the unrestrained forces vanish, the system reaches a state of thermo-unrestrained dynamic equilibrium, that is, it becomes a heap rather than a dynamically ordered whole.[5]

In the stationary state the systems are the most economical from the energetic viewpoint since they lose the minimum amount of free energy. (A still more economical state is the state of thermodynamic equilibrium; in that state, however, the systems are no longer ordered wholes.) Minimum entropy production characterizes the complex systems we term "living," which slow down the process of thermodynamic decay during their lifetime and remain in stationary states characterized by the typical constraints making up the species-specific organization of the individual. As Katchalsky and Curran point out, living systems are endowed with a series of regulating mechanisms that preserve the steady state and bring the organism back to its unperturbed condition in a way which resembles the action of a restoring force coming into play in any fluctuation from a stationary state in a physical system.[6] Inasmuch as both physical and biological systems maintain themselves in stationary states, characterized by the parameters of the fixed forces within the systems, life as cybernetic process is analogous to any physical system describable, by our definition, as an ordered whole. But we must recognize that in a biological system the stationary states are not fully time-independent: they are *quasi*-stationary.

The general system property discussed here abstracts from many varieties of regulatory mechanisms and generalizes the concept of adaptation to the environment through the self-maintenance of systems forming ordered wholes. The generalized conclusion may be stated thus: within a limited range of perturbation, an ordered whole will tend to return to the stationary states characterized by the parameters of its constant constraints. Inasmuch as the systems reorganize their flows to buffer out or eliminate the externally introduced perturbations, they *adapt* to their environments. This is adaptation in a limited sense—a more striking form of it, involving the reorganization of the fixed forces themselves, will be discussed next.

Self-Organization

We have shown that ordered wholes, i.e. systems with calculable fixed forces, tend to return to stationary states following perturbations introduced from their surroundings. It is likewise possible to show that such systems *reorganize* their fixed forces and acquire new parameters in their stationary states when subjected to *constant* perturbation in their environment.

This conclusion follows if we consider Ashby's principle of self-organization with some modifications. According to Ashby, natural systems in general go to ordered stationary states. Now most of a natural system's states are non-stationary. So in going from any state to one of the stationary ones, the system is going from a larger number of states to a smaller. In this way it is performing a selection, in the purely objective sense that it rejects some states, by leaving them, and retains some other state by sticking to it. Thus, as every determinate natural system goes to its stationary state so does it select.[7]

The selection described by Ashby involves not merely the re-establishment of the parameters defining a previous stationary state of the system after perturbation, but the progressive development of new stationary states which are *more resistant* to the perturbation than the former ones.

Ashby suggests the following example. Suppose the stores of a computer are filled with the digits 0 - 9. Suppose its dynamic law is that the digits are continuously being multiplied in pairs and the right-hand digit of the product is going to replace the first digit taken. Since even × even gives even, odd × odd gives odd and even × odd gives even, the system will "selectively evolve" toward the evens. But since among the evens the zeros are uniquely resistant to change, the system will approach an all-zero state as a function of the number of operations performed.

Ashby concludes that this is an example of self-organization of the utmost generality. There is a well-defined operator (the multiplication and replacement law) which drives the system toward a specific stationary state—"equilibrium state." It selectively evolves the system to maximum resistance to change. Consequently all that is necessary for producing self-organization is that the "machine with input" (the computer-dynamic-law system) should be isolated. Adaptive self-organization inevitably leads toward the known biological and psychological systems. *"In any isolated system, life and intelligence inevitably develop"* (italics in original).[8] Or, to quote his more general conclusion, *"every isolated determinate system obeying unchanging laws will develop organisms that are adapted to their 'environments'"* (italics likewise in original).[9]

The above argument applies to the present thesis with the suggested two modifications: (a) it is restricted to natural (as opposed to artificial) systems, and (b) the operator drives not toward a state of equilibrium in the system, but toward stationary or quasi-stationary *non-equilibrium* states. The reasons are potent for discarding the concept of the equilibrium state in favor of that of a non-equilibrium stationary state in *natural* systems: (1) equilibrium states do not dispose over usable energy whereas natural systems of the widest variety do; (2) equilibrium states are "memoryless," whereas natural systems behave in large part in function of their past histories. In short, an equilibrium system is a dead system —more "dead" even than atoms and molecules. Thus, although a machine may go to equilibrium as its preferred state, natural systems go to increasingly organized *non*-equilibrium states.[10]

The modified Ashby principle shows that in àny sufficiently isolated system-environment context, the system organizes itself in function of maximal resistance to change in the environment. Its new level of organization is measurable both as negative entropy, and as the number of "bits" necessary to build the system from its components.

Every system produces entropy relative to time. The positive, negative or zero entropy change is governed by the relative values of the terms in the Prigogine equation: $dS = dS_e + dS_i$, where dS_i denotes entropy change through the input and dS_e entropy change due to irreversible processes within the system. Whereas dS_e is always positive, dS_i may be positive as well as negative. If the latter, the system "imports negentropy" (Schrodinger) and can not only offset disorganization by work performed within its boundaries, but can actually use the excess free energy to organize itself. Thus there is nothing mysterious or *sui generis* about self-organization to states of higher negative entropy: it is a physical property of systems, regardless of their materials or origin.

Self-organization conduces systems toward more negentropic states; self-stabilization maintains them in their pre-existing state of organization. In an environment in which constant forces are operative, and the perturbations they occasion are within the range of correction by self-stabilization, systems not only survive, but evolve. The development of systems in such environments can be conceptualized as a sequence of parallel, or irregularly alternating, stabilization around the parameters of existing fixed forces and re-organization of the fixed forces in function of increasing resistance to the constant forces in the environment.

Hierarchization

Self-stabilizing, self-organizing and ordered wholes which share a common environment impose systemic order on that environment. Sets of mutually interacting systems form supra-systems and organize themselves as parts within the emerging whole. The system thus formed can interact with other systems on its own level, and form still higher level suprasystems. Each of these systems exhibits the properties of irreducibility, temporal and spatial order, homeostatic self-stabilization, and evolutionary self-organization. The coexistence of systems on multiple levels results in a highest-level system which is hierarchially organized. That structure is the totality of all systems, welded into systematic unity by means of their mutual self-stabilizations and self-organizations.

The concept of a multilevel hierarchy can account for the manifest diversity of phenomenal properties as well as the multiplicity of structures and functions consistently with the invariant framework of a general systems theory. Fresh qualities and properties can emerge in the form of new transformations of invariant systems attributes. The diversity of structures and functions can be shown to be the consequence of the manifestation of some recurrent basic function in particular variations, corresponding to the hierarchic level of the system. This is explained by the fact that systems at each level contain systems at all lower levels plus their combination within the whole formed at that level. Hence the possibilities for diversity of structure and function increase with the levels, and one need not reduce the typical characteristics of higher-level entities to those of lower levels, but can apply criteria appropriate to their particular hierarchical position.

The higher we raise our sights on the hierarchy, the more diversity of functions and properties we are likely to find, manifested by a smaller number of actualized systems. Thus atoms exist in greater numbers than molecules but have fewer properties and variations of structure; organisms exist in smaller numbers than molecules but have an enormously wide repertory of functions and properties and are capable of existing in untold variety of structural forms. And the number of ecologies and societies is smaller than that of organisms but manifests within their small populations greater diversity and flexibility than biological phenomena.

It is evident that both the numerical and the functional differences are due to the hierarchical position of the systems on the various levels. Many systems on one level constitute one system on a higher level and consequently higher level systems are less abundant and have a wider repertory of functional properties than systems on lower levels. Thus to claim that all systems exhibit invariant properties and types of relationships does not entail reductionism: the invariances express themselves in specific non-reducible transformations corresponding to the degrees of freedom proper to each level of the hierarchy.

Now, the concept of "hierarchy" while much used in the contemporary literature of natural science and philosophy, is seldom defined rigorously, and when it is so defined, it is often inapplicable.[11] A rigorous definition implies a governing-governed or "bossing" relation between levels, so that a diagram of a hierarchy becomes a finite tree branching out of a single point, without loops. Such hierarchies apply at best to military or quasi-military organizations with established non-reciprocal chains of command.

But hierarchies have found their most fruitful application in nature, where rigorously unidirectional action is hardly ever the case. Hence in the present use the concept of "hierarchy" will not be given its rigorous meaning but will denote a "level-structure" or a "set of super-imposed modules[1], so constituted that the components of modules at one level are modules belonging to some lower level. Using the term "system" for "module" we can speak of a hierarchy as a level-structure in which the systems functioning as wholes on one level function as parts on the higher levels, and where the parts of a system on any level (with the exception of the lowest or "basic" level) are themselves wholes on lower levels.

Systems belonging to a level below that of any chosen level are called "subsystems" in relation to the system of the chosen level, and the system belonging to the next higher level is a "suprasystem" in relation to it. The relativity of these terms is evident: a given system a may be a subsystem in relation to b and a suprasystem in relation to c. Merely that $(c<a) < b$ is required, where $<$ is a symbol of relative inclusion. Then b is a suprasystem in relation to a, and c a subsystem in relation to b. We can readily see how a theoretically infinite hierarchy may be constructed in this way. But if our postulates take account of the empirical world as their sphere of applicability, our hierarchy will be finite: although there may be a large number of levels of systems in the observable universe, there is no serious warrant for believing that the series is infinite. Thus a more realistic task is to propose a finite-level hierarchy and identify each of its rungs with one predominant type of observable.

Attempts of this kind have been often made and, until relatively recently, came under the heading of an ontological category scheme. One of the latest major systems of this kind was that of N. Hartmann. More recently, this type of endeavor has been taken over by general systems theorists. Thus Boulding supplied key notions of a "hierarchy of systems" which Bertalanffy formalized into a table of system levels, theories and models, and empirical descriptions.[12] It includes both natural and artificial systems.

The hierarchy we are concerned with here is less inclusive than this, dealing only with *natural* systems, and more rigorous in one basic regard: its levels follow the hierarchical scheme of relative inclusion without gaps or redundancies. Thus we seek to order natural phenomena into a "vertical" order wherein any given system, with the exception of those on the lowest or *basic* level and that on the highest or *ultimate* level, is both a suprasystem in regard to its hierarchical parts and a subsystem with respect to the system(s) which it forms together with other systems in its environment. Hence, from the viewpoint of a system of level n there is an *internal hierarchy* of its structural-functional constitution, made up of the hierarchically ordered series $[(a<b)<c]<n$ as well as an *external hierarchy* consisting of the structural-functional wholes constituted by its environmental coordinations with other systems, $[(n<x)<y]<z$. Since n is situated at the intersection of the internal and the external hierarachies, the number of levels in each defines n's specific position within the objective level structure in nature, ranging from atoms to ecologies and beyond.

A hypothetical identification of the principal levels and interrelation of the micro- and macro-heirarchies is given in figure 5.1. Note that the emergence of each higher level out of systemic structurations of units from lower levels is contingent upon local conditions and results in the uneven build-up and distribution of modules of intermediate levels (-H7 through - H1, including - h6—h) within the space-time manifold.[13]

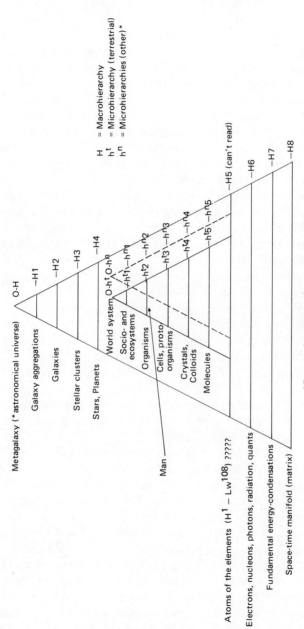

Fig. 5-1

Metagalaxy (* astronomical universe) O-H

Galaxy aggregations —H1

Galaxies —H2

Stellar clusters —H3

Stars, Planets —H4

World system O-h^{t}O-h^n

Socio- and ecosystems —h^{t}1—h^{n}1

Organisms —h^{t}2—h^{n}2

Cells, proto organisms —h^{t}3—h^{n}3

Crystals, Colloids —h^{t}4—h^{n}4

Molecules —h^{t}5—h^{n}5

Man

Atoms of the elements (H^1 – Lw^{108}) ????? —H5 (can't read)

Electrons, nucleons, photons, radiation, quants —H6

Fundamental energy-condensations —H7

Space-time manifold (matrix) —H8

H   = Macrohierarchy
h^t = Microhierarchy (terrestrial)
h^n = Microhierarchies (other) *

* Form and evolution of upper levels undetermined.

If a hierarchy of this kind could be confirmed by empirical data, a basic ideal of science would be realized: the many entities investigated by the diverse empirical sciences would be plotted on a map of hierarchical organization and the theories applicable to them could thereby be interrelated. Such confirmation encounters serious difficulties at this stage of scientific development, as the uncertainties concerning relationships of wholes to parts emerge in all disciplines (e.g. is the "particle" itself a system of more primitive units such as quarks; is a tissue a level below the organ, or above, or equal to it; is a community of people on the same multiorganic level as a beehive or above it, etc.). But empirical difficulties of identification do not adduce evidence for the inapplicability or falsity of the concept of a hierarchy of natural systems, only for the methodological and observational problems of confirming any given hypothesis about it.

Atoms and organism, molecules, cells and societies—units of investigation which appear ordered in their own special way when approached within the framework of the special empirical sciences, reappear as units of the same general species in a generally ordered realm of nature when the special theories are integrated within the framework of systems philosophy. We may never know whether the "real" world—that ultimate reality which surely underlies all our observations and constitutes our very existence—is truly ordered, and if so, whether it is divided into distinct types of special orders or manifests one overarching type of systematic order. What we do know is that the human mind seeks order and that the more general and simple the order it discriminates the more meaning it confers on experience. As long as no direct metaphysical insights into the nature of reality are available, we must reconstruct reality through rational theories with empirical applications. In systems philosophy such understanding is elicited by the integration of the findings of the empirical systems sciences by means of the invariances exhibited by their respective systems models.

The basic constructs of systems philosophy described here provide the conceptual reference points for the discovery of such invariances and the consequent integration of empirical scientific findings. Every set of enduring entities that comes about in the natural world must exhibit the basic properties of ordered wholeness, self-stabilization and self-organization, and hierarchization. These are the very conditions of systematic endurance in a dynamic universe. If we take them as our conceptual gestalt, invariant orders are revealed to us across a wide range of transformations. Atoms, organisms, and societies share these invariant orders, and man finds himself in a world which is no longer a stranger to him. The implications of this new way of organizing experience and integrating scientific knowledge are tremendous. A broad and rich field of philosophic-scientific investigation opens up. Its exploration is among the most exciting challenges available to us today.

References and Notes

1. Bertalanffy, Ludwig von, *General System Theory*, New York: George Braziller, 1968, Chapter 3.
2. Wholes may be more than the sum of their parts, e.g. in information content, qualitative diversity, function, sensitivity, etc.; and they may be less than their parts, e.g. in measure of entropy, thermodynamical equilibrium, range of variation, etc. The terms "more than" and "less than" are relative to the scale by which the whole is compared to its parts.
3. Selye, Hans, *In Vivo: The Case for Supramolecular Biology*, New York: Liveright, 1967.
4. Katchalsky, A., and P. F. Curran, *Nonequilibrium Thermodynamics in Biophysics*, Cambridge, Mass.: Harvard University Press, 1965, Chapter 16.
5. *Ibid.*
6. *Ibid.*
7. Ashby, Ross W., "Principles of the Self-Organizing System," *Principles of Self-Organization*, Foerster, Zopf, eds. London and New York: Pergamon, 1962.
8. *Ibid.* p. 272.
9. *Ibid.* p. 270.
10. Ashby himself seems to be aware of the difficulty in regard to living systems. He suggests that intelligence, as well as such phenomena as conditioning, association, learning, etc., may be the result of a process where the input comes to a system with many equilibria. But such a system would be cogently defined, it would seem, not as an equilibrium system, but as one with a number of fixed internal constraints.
11. A case in point is Bunge's formal definition, *Hierarchical Structures*, Whyte, Wilson, and Wilson, eds., New York: Elsevier, 1969.
12. Bertalanffy, Ludwig von, *General System Theory*, New York: George Braziller, 1968, pp. 28-29.
13. Laszlo, Ervin, *Introduction to Systems Philosophy: Toward a New Paradigm of Contemporary Thought*, New York and London: Gordon and Breach, 1972.

SECTION II
Communication and
Levels of Human Organization

In "General System Theory—The Skeleton of Science," Boulding suggests two complimentary methods of systemic definition.

> . . . the first approach is to look over the empirical universe and to pick out certain general phenomena which are found in many different disciplines, and to seek to build up general theoretical models relevant to these phenomena. The second approach is to arrange the empirical fields in a hierarchy of complexity of organization of their basic individual or unit of behavior, and to try to develop a level of abstraction appropriate to each.[1]

For human communication study, we believe a particularly useful combination of the two methods which Boulding suggests is possible as exemplified by the contributions in this section of the volume. We have included works which serve well as primary building blocks in an integrated taxonomy of thought about communication systems. Each piece reflects a view of human communication which has internal order, crossdisciplinary validity and applicability, and stresses the interdependent-relationship between human systems and their environments.

Chester Lawson focuses on language and communication and their role in biological organization. He explores the view that communication processes are a useful means of comprehending the complexities of embryonic development and evolution. Drawing on the works of David Berlo, Kenneth Pike, and an earlier book entitled, *Language, Thought and the Human Mind,* Lawson provides a description of human organisms as homeostatic systems maintaining themselves as an *organization* only through communication in and with their environments.

Harold M. Schroder, Michael J. Driver, and Siegfried Streufert have been significant contributors in the area of cognitive psychology and human information processing. In their work included here, they focus attention on what they consider to be an overemphasis on the importance of *what* information people learn, and considerably too little attention to *how* people learn to combine and use information for adaptive purposes. They suggest four different intrapersonal information organizing structures based on different rules for thinking, deciding, and interrelating information. In all this, the function of human communication relative to informational transactions between individual and informational milieu is central.

Using intrasystem organization as a point of focus and departure, Alfred Kuhn offers a characterization of system functions in which he lists detector, selector, and effector components. In moving to a discussion of intersystem organization and social processes he enumerates what he terms the communication, transaction, and organization functions which he views as parallel to those at the intrasystem level. Kuhn also offers an insightful discussion of the question of what is a *system,* and provides a highly useful taxonomy in which his view of social systems and social control take shape. The notions of social processes and organization build on those of Lawson and Schroder, Driver, and Streufert, and on the basic concept of communication as one of two critical life processes, in and through which human organizations at all levels are established, maintained and altered.

In what serves as an excellent summary piece for the section, Lawrence Frank presents a similar view of communication as it relates to social processes of cultural organization. Utilizing the concept of transaction, Frank provides an articulate discussion of the nature of the communicative interchange between an individual and his socio-cultural milieu from which both take their existence. He notes the sense in which individuals are subject to the pressures and sanctions of their social environment to which they must adapt, and stresses the role of communication as the critical link in the process. He emphasizes also the notion that personality development is not passive adjustment by an individual to his environment, but rather an active interchange through communication between the individual and environmental forces.

Common to each of these pieces is a view of communication as a continuous, transactional process with no clear beginning or end, serving a variety of functions all of which are essential to human existence at particular levels of organization.

References and Notes

1. Boulding, Kenneth, "General System Theory—The Skeleton of Science," *General Systems,* Vol. 1, 1956, and Chapter 2, of this volume.

6
Biological Organization

CHESTER A. LAWSON

Language, Communication, and Biological Organization

During the last few years geneticists have been speaking of the genes of organisms as code systems that function in guiding development. A code is a language of some kind and language is used in communication. Thus, because both embryonic development and evolution are dependent on gene action, it is possible that a theory based on the communication process might serve to integrate the various data related to these areas. However, before discussing communication and code systems, it is necessary to discuss the nature of the physical environment and the relation of organisms to this environment.

The Relation of the Organism to the Physical Environment

The physical environment of organisms consists of a narrow zone where earth and atmosphere meet. From the earth and the atmosphere organisms obtain the ingredients necessary to maintain life. Minerals come from the earth; essential gases and water come from the atmosphere; light and heat, of course, are obtained from the sun through the atmosphere.

The amounts of gases, water, minerals, light and heat vary from place to place on the earth and also they vary in any one place from time to time. In general this variation is cyclical. For example light and dark alternate daily. Temperatures range from a high to low daily and also from another high to another low over the period of one year. Water falls on the earth as rain and is drawn into the atmosphere again to form clouds and thus the earth roughly alternates from wet to dry.

Over long periods of time, such as geological time, the physical environment may change drastically but for shorter periods the changes are in general cyclical and within fairly constant limits.

Thus it is within a cyclically changing environment with fairly fixed limits of change that organisms live. However, organisms do not merely "live in" the physical environment in the sense that humans live in a certain climate and endure it or enjoy it depending on its nature. This sense of "living in" connotes an independence of the organism from the environment. It implies that the organism could move out of its environment if it wished, just as I could move out of my present location to some more favorable climate if I wished.

The relation of an organism to its environment is much more intimate and dependent. The stuff that makes up the organism comes directly from the environment and the organism can not be separated from it. The conditions under which the organism lives are the conditions found within its surroundings. In a very real sense the organism is an organized concentration of the matter and energy of the environment that exists only by virtue of its organization.

Organisms have been described as dynamic, homeostatic systems. As such, life is a process that continues so long as matter and energy are obtained from the environment and so long as the temperature remains within a certain range. Life is a system of activities intimately coordinated with the physical environment. Thus life must change as the environment changes or it must perish.

Because of this constant interaction of the organism with its environment and the dependence of the organism on the environment the organism must be sensitive to changes that occur. For example, the organism must sense food sources, changes in temperature, changes in light and in humidity. This means that it must be in communication with various elements of its environment. It must receive messages, decode them, and react appropriately. Since organisms depend on communication, it is possible that the ideas, developed as a result of the study of human communication, may be useful in interpreting the behavior and organization of non-human organisms.

Human Communication

Three studies related to human communication were used as a guide in developing a communication theory of biological organization. The first was *The Process of Communication* by Berlo.[1] The second was *Language in Relation to a Unified Theory of the Structure of Human Behavior* by Pike.[2] The third was *Language, Thought, and the Human Mind* by Lawson.[3]

Berlo utilized a model of the communication process in humans that included the following elements (1) source of message (2) message (3) encoder (4) channel (5) receiver (6) decoder.

In this model the source is defined as "some person or group of persons with a purpose or reason for engaging in communication." A message is defined as a code or systematic set of symbols. In order for the source to generate a message it has to translate the ideas, purposes, etc., into muscular movement of some kind producing sound, writing or various gestures of hands, arms, or face. This translation of ideas into a message is accomplished by the encoder.

The channel is "a medium, a carrier of messages," while the receiver is the person who receives the message. In order for communication to occur the receiver has to decode or retranslate the message and put it in a form that the receiver can use.

Berlo used his communication model to interpret the learning process in humans. For this purpose he equated the message of the communication model with the stimulus involved in perception and learning, the decoding process with the act of perception, and the encoding process with the overt response.

I have used Berlo's communication model including its relation to the learning process but have modified it somewhat to produce a model that might explain the interaction of individual organisms with their environments. This model is described as follows.

Individual Organisms and Communication

In terms of a model of communication the environment can be described as the source of messages. However, this source differs from Berlo's in that the environment has no need or purpose. The message is any stimulus that the organism is sensitive to. The sense receptors of organisms are the receivers but they may also be decoders and encoders, because any stimulus received by the receptors must be transmitted by way of internal conductors to some effector if the organism is to respond appropriately to the stimulus.

Thus our communication model for reflexive organisms includes (1) source (2) external message or stimulus (3) external channel (4) receptor (5) decoder (6) encoder (7) internal message (8) conductor (internal channel) (9) effector (10) response.

The communication system of reflexive organisms is conceived as being built into the organisms. The receptors, conductors, and effectors are structures synthesized by the developmental process and once built they are fixed in their functional relationships so that no change is possible after their synthesis. This, of course, is not entirely true because there is evidence that some very primitive organisms can learn. However, in terms of survival, such learning is too slow and limited to be sufficient. Other learning processes to be described later are required.

Returning to the concept of an organism as a dynamic, homeostatic, metabolic system with a built-in communication system it is possible to conceive of an organism-environment relationship in which there would be no death. For this we would need an environment that changed cyclically but that was stable in that it lacked novelty. We would also need an organism so equipped that it could receive, decode, and react appropriately to every necessary message within the stable environment.

Theoretically such an organism-environment relationship could last forever. There would be no death.

Probably it is safe to say that no such stable organism-environment relationship ever existed or ever will exist. The actual environment changes and organisms must also change or perish.

Any dynamic system such as our hypothetical organism that operates within a cyclically changing physical environment is capable of some change. As the environment changes the organism changes accordingly. Such capabilities of change are due to the operating receptor-conductor-effector systems. But such built-in ranges of behavior have limits. If the change in the environment exceeds these limits the organism can no longer adjust. What is needed is a wider range of responses or an entirely new set of responses.

To achieve this the receptor-conductor-effector systems must change. Presumably this could be accomplished by switching the connections between receptors and effectors so that stimuli already accepted by the receptors would activate different effectors or the same effectors in different ways. Berlo states that learning occurs if the individual (1) continues to make the same responses, but to a different stimulus, (2) makes a different response to the same stimulus. Reorganization or modification of the conducting pathways between receptors and effectors could produce this kind of learning.

In addition it is possible that the receptors and effectors could change. The old receptors could become sensitive to new stimuli or new receptors could be built. Similarly the effectors could become capable of making completely new responses, or new and different effectors could appear.

Normally individual organisms cannot reconstruct their physical systems. Once the body structure is developed it remains. Thus, in those organisms where little or no individual learning occurs, changes in receptor-conductor-effector systems cannot be made at the level of the individual. Another level of interaction of organisms with the environment is required. This new level is the population of organisms.

Populations and Communication

A population as defined by Pearl is a group of living individuals set in a frame that is linked and defined in respect of both time and space.[4] The individuals that make up a population are related to one another not only in terms of space and time but also by reproduction. Individuals of a population breed together and have a continuity through time from one generation to another.

A population operates as a unit and has properties or attributes characteristic of the group that are unique to the group and not possessed by any individual of the population. Such group attributes are essentially statistical. They are birth rates, death rates, dispersion, or numerical distribution in space and in time, density, changes in size through time, etc.

A population is a group of interbreeding or asexual organisms living within a physical environment. Our initial description of the organism-environment relation pictured the individual organism as the living, dynamic, homeostatic unit operating within and interacting with the physical environment. Now our focus shifts to the population or group of organisms operating within, and interacting as a unit, with the physical environment.

Populations as units represent a new level of interaction of organisms with the environment and just as the interaction of the individual with the environment required a communication process so does the population interaction. However, the communication process at the population level is different than and complimentary to the individual communication process.

One essential behavior of a population as a unit is reproduction. The population survives if it can reproduce enough organisms to replace those that die. Birth rate must equal or exceed the death rate. If we assume that the death rate is due to factors in the physical environment effecting individual organisms, a population would have an advantage if it could produce individuals with receptor-conductor-effector systems that permitted the individuals to live at least long enough to reproduce. In a nonchanging environment established populations presumably would have no problem. In an environment that changed sufficiently so that the receptor conductor-effector systems of the individuals were outmoded and no longer able to cope with the new conditions the death rate might rapidly exceed the birth rate with the consequent destruction of the population.

Berlo's communication model did not quite fit the population level. For this we need different concepts. One point to be stressed is that while the population is an organized unit that is responsive to its environment it, nevertheless, "perceives" its environment only through the individual organisms. It is the individuals that come in direct contact with the environment by means of their receptor-conductor-effector systems. It is through reproduction of individuals that the population as a unit waxes or wanes. Thus, a population consisting of individuals having receptor-conductor-effector systems efficient enough to maintain the organisms until it reproduces will survive. The population lacking such individuals will not survive. In a changing environment a population able to produce individuals with new and more adequate receptor-conductor-effector systems will be able to adjust to the changed environment and survive.

The key to such change is the gene pool or the total system of genes contained in the population. This gene pool is to be conceived as a code or language. Each organism within the population contains within its germ cells a portion of this code, which it passes on to the next generation. The function of the code is to give directions for the construction or synthesis of the new organism. If the code system for any population were completely uniform then each new generation would be like the last and no change would be possible. However, gene pools or code systems probably are never completely uniform. Gene mutation produces small changes in the code, while in sexual forms fertilization produces recombination of genes at each generation. The new gene combinations control the synthesis of modified individuals which may or may not be better adapted to the changed environment.

This process of gene mutation, sexual recombination, and natural selection is, of course, the current theory of evolutionary change. However, viewed in terms of a communication process it takes on a new meaning.

Human Language and the Genetic Code

Two studies of human language in relation to human behavior were used as a guide in interpreting the function of gene systems as a code. One was *Lanugage in Relation to a Unified Theory of the Structure of Human Behavior* by Pike and the other was *Language, Thought and the Human Mind* by Lawson.[5]

Pike developed a detailed and involved theory of human behavior which included the use of communication as a part of that behavior. I have borrowed only a part of Pike's theory, principally his concept of the behavioreme or behavior cycle.

According to Pike, human behavior, in which language or communication between two or more people is involved, has a structure or pattern with a beginning, a duration, and an end. The behavior consists of a succession of actions on the parts of the persons involved, with the action of each being stimulated by a message from another person. One example Pike used to illustrate a behavior cycle was a church service. In this service the participants were the minister, the members of the choir, and the members of the congregation. The entire service was a succession of behaviors by the participants which depend on (1) each participant having a general knowledge of the entire pattern of behavior, (2) each participant having a specific knowledge of his own role in the pattern, and (3) intercommunication among the individuals.

Communication among the behaving elements in a behavior cycle is essential for the continuation of the integrated activity, but also it is essential that each individual have sufficient knowledge to react to the proper cues to play his role in the pattern. This knowledge constitutes a code or a set of specifications that can be transmitted from one generation of church-goers to another either by imitation or by written language.

Such a code or set of specifications would include statements naming the kinds of elements or participants in the behavior cycle. In the church service these would be the minister, the choir, the congregation, and any other. It would include descriptions of the behaviors required of each participant and the sequence of behaviors from the beginning to the end.

Lawson was unaware of Pike's work when he wrote *Language, Thought and the Human Mind,* but therein was developed the concept that all human behavior was guided by systems of ideas that had a structure similar to that of deductive systems. The postulates of the deductive systems were statements that named and described (1) the elements or participants in the behavior, (2) the kinds of behavior of each different element, and (3) the succession of behavior that made up the whole sequence. The idea of the deductive system was essentially the same as Pike's behavior cycle.

Language as a Substitute Stimulus

In addition to Pike's behavior cycle and deductive systems another concept relative to codes or language is essential. Organisms were described above as being homeostatic systems with receptors, conductors and effectors by means of which the organism could receive and respond to messages from the environment. Such messages could be of any form, the only requisite being that they originate from some aspect of the environment to which the organism must react, and that the organism decode them properly in order that the appropriate reaction could follow.

Messages in this form are transient changes in the environment of the organism. They could be changes in light, heat, moisture, chemicals of various kinds, etc. These changes have no permanence; they proceed directly from the source, and they elicit a direct response, after which as functional entities they disappear.

A code of language can be conceived as a variation of this kind of stimulus when such language is used by humans for giving commands or for any purpose where a behavioral response is expected. On the other hand a code or language can be thought of as a substitute for the "real" stimulus. For example, if in a crowded theater the audience suddenly sees flame and smoke coming from a part of the building the response is apt to be a stampeding for the exists. The fire and smoke in this case would be a direct, that is a "real," stimulus. The same response could occur if someone yelled "FIRE" under the same circumstances. The sound "FIRE" would be a substitute stimulus.

A further characteristic of a code or language is that as a substitute stimulus it can consist of arbitrary things or events. Marks on a paper, having no resemblance to what they represent, can nevertheless stimulate appropriate behavior; to be preserved and used over and over again. They can be transmitted from person to person, from generation to generation, and so long as there are organisms to receive and decode the message they can function as a stimulus and as a guide to behavior.

Page 15.

Behavior cycles or deductive systems can be translated into a code or permanent message or stimulus and used as a guide for the development and operation of the behavior cycle. Among humans, language descriptions of behavior cycles, such as the church service mentioned above, would serve such a guiding function. Among organisms gene systems or chemical codes could serve the same function.

Application of the Pike-Lawson Model to Organisms

Returning now to non-human organisms, an attempt will be made to fit the concept of the behavior cycle and of codes to systems of organisms living in a physical environment. We have described individual organisms and populations of organisms. We must now introduce the concept of the community of organisms.

Allee, *et al*, defines a community as follows:

> . . . . the major community may be defined as a natural assemblage of organisms which, together with its habitat, has reached a survival level such that it is relatively independent of adjacent assemblages of equal rank: to this extent, given radiant energy, it is self-sustaining.[6]

In a community the various kinds of populations have special functions integrated so that each population is dependent on other populations for living requirements, and the community as a whole is dependent on the proper function of the respective populations. For example, food is a requirement of all organisms. Green plants produce their own through photosynthesis. Some animals eat plants and other animals eat animals. Saprophytes get their food from dead organisms or from excreta of living organisms.

The concept of the community is illustrated by the following quote from Allee, *et al*.

> Many years ago Möbius recognized that a natural assemblage of organisms constitutes a community, and stated: "Every oyster bed is . . . a community of living things, a collection of species, and a massing of individuals, which find everything necessary for their growth and continuance . . . ." Obviously Möbius did not mean that the oysters alone formed the community, but that the collection of species, which were mutually interdependent, and hence self-sustaining, formed the community. Thus, the important copper ion concentration necessary for the setting of the oyster spat . . . , and the location of the oyster bed in marine littoral areas where this ion could be available from river systems, the plankton upon which oysters feed, the oyster sponges (*Clionidae*) and oyster drill (*Urosalpinx*) and starfish (*Asterias*), which prey upon the oyster, the collective ectoparasites and entoparasites—all these and many other elements combine to form the oyster community. . . .[7]

The oyster community described above can be conceived as a behavior cycle—the elements of participants of which are the various interacting organisms in a particular physical setting. The community is a process depending for its continuance on the respective behaviors of the various members. Each different member plays a specific role in the community and this role-playing requires communication among the members. Also each member must be able to respond to the appropriate cues to produce the sequence of behaviors that constitute community process or behavior cycle.

However, because a part of the role-playing in a community includes dying and being consumed in one way or another by other participants, the continuity of the community process requires some method of replacing the individual members that die. Reproduction of participants supplies the replacements.

Thus the community as a behavior cycle includes two levels of communication. One level is that of the individual with its receptor-conductor-effector systems which permit it to behave appropriately to other individuals or to the physical elements of the environment. The other is the communication from generation to generation through reproduction and development that supplies the continuity of participants over time.

In the church service the knowledge required for correct behavior was transmitted from generation to generation by language. In the oyster community this knowledge is transmitted from generation to generation by another kind of language—the gene system or genetic code.

For the integrated behavior represented by the community it is not necessary to invoke some centralized controlling factor. All that is needed is a set of directions (the genes) for each kind of organism, that guides the development of individuals to produce receptor-conductor-effector systems appropriate for the system.

Changes in the physical environment in which the community lives might require changes in the behavior of the organisms of the community. Changes in behavior of organisms would require changes in the receptor-conductor-effector systems of the individual organisms. Some such changes might be accomplished through the learning of individuals, but where this was not possible changes in the code system by mutation and sexual recombination would permit the production of new behaviors, some of which might be more appropriate behaviors.

Communication and Progressive Evolution

The evidence from historical evolution studies have suggested to some that evolutionary changes have been guided by some inner force; that evolution is progressive and moving to some pre-determined goal. Others have assumed that the change has simply been a matter of blind chance. The present attempt to interpret the evolutionary process in terms of communication has nothing to offer relative to this debate, but there is one type of apparently progressive evolution to which communication theory is relevant. This is the evolution from simple to complex, from lower levels of integration to higher levels as exemplified by the presumed progression from single-celled forms to the many-celled organisms and from the simple social organizations to the more highly integrated societies such as those of bees, ants, and termites.

It is possible to explain such evolution in terms of a communication theory if we first make the assumption that any individual organism has a limited capacity for utilizing energy. That is, we can assume that each individual is endowed with the capacity for taking in and using in its lifetime only a certain amount of energy and no more. To use a metaphor, each individual has a bank account containing a fixed sum which it can withdraw and use. When the bank account is depleted the organism dies.

The organism could use this energy in two major ways. One would be for metabolic processes that maintain the organism and the other would be for reproduction. If all the energy were used for metabolism there would be none left for the reproductive process. However, as both processes must operate if life is to continue some balance in the use of energy resources would be necessary. Enough energy would have to be expended for metabolism to maintain the individual and enough for reproduction to maintain the population.

Let us also assume that an increase in metabolic efficiency would permit the expenditure of more energy on reproduction with the result that the population would gain an advantage in the race for survival.

There are two general ways in which greater efficiency might be achieved. One would be to take in energy in a more concentrated form and thus eliminate the necessity of performing the initial steps in the synthesis of food. The other would be to join with other organisms and parcel out the various functions—some performing one function such as digestion, while others excrete, etc.

To illustrate the consequences of the first method of increasing the efficiency of energy use, let us imagine a population of single-celled organisms living isolated in the physical environment. Let us assume this to be near the beginning of life on earth so there is only this one population made up of one kind of organism. Each cell has the ability to take in energy from the sun, to synthesize food, and to perform all the other metabolic functions necessary for life. Also each cell reproduces.

Because light and certain inorganic molecules in the physical environment are essential for life maintenance the receptor-conductor-effector systems are designed to permit sensitivity and response to these stimuli. The genetic code operates to direct the synthesis and maintenance of these receptor-conductor-effector systems.

Now let us assume that through a change in the code system of one or more individual organisms a new kind of receptor-conductor-effector system is created. The new system would permit the organism to be sensitive to, and to respond to, new stimuli in a different way. The new stimuli could come from the excreta of other organisms, the dead bodies of other organisms or the living forms. The new response is to digest and absorb the organic molecules from these other organisms.

Such a change in method of intake of energy would presumably release energy for reproduction because it would permit the elimination of the initial stages of food synthesis and thus give these new forms an advantage in survival. However, it would also make them dependent on the food synthesizing forms. They would have to live with them and integrate their activities so that the food source would never be completely consumed. But this is essentially what a community of organisms is—an integrated collection of populations of organisms each dependent on others and with at least one kind capable of synthesizing food from an inorganic energy source.

The second method of increasing efficiency of energy utilization mentioned above involved a division of labor among individual cells such that some cells became specialists in one or the other of the metabolic functions while they delegated to other cells the other functions.

To illustrate the second method of increasing efficiency in energy utilization let us begin with the hypothetical population of single-celled forms. Again a change in the genetic code would cause the synthesis of new receptor-conductor-effector systems with the result that the cells would lose one or another of the living functions. This loss of activity presumably would increase the efficiency of the cells, but at the same time it would make them dependent on others for the functions they no longer perform. Such cells must live very close together and integrate their activities if they are to survive. The result, however, would be a many-celled unit—a new form of life. The first step toward the evolution of a new level of complexity would have been made. This scheme is similar to the hypothesis of Beadle and Coonradt concerning the evolution of sexuality.[8]

There are at least two ways in which such metazoa might have originated: (1) Similar, but initially independent, cells might have united and gradually specialized their functions. The slime molds have a life cycle that actually reflects this process; (2) single cells reproducing by asexual cell division might not become physically separated. Various colonial protista represent this possibility. Either one or both processes may have occurred historically to produce modern metazoan forms.

The first method of increasing the efficiency of energy utilization that presumably would lead to the creation of communities made up of different populations of organisms would offer no problem relative to reproduction. Each organism would retain its reproductive function. However, the second method that presumably could have lead to the creation of many-celled forms would create a problem for reproduction.

How would the newly created many-celled form produce another one like it? There are at least two possibilities. One is that each cell would retain its ability to divide, that the cells would separate long enough to accomplish this division and then join again into two integrated units.

The other possibility is that the individual cells not separate, but that some cells become specialized to produce the next generation. These specialized cells, the reproductive cells, could separate from the others and by cell division and development produce another edition of the integrated organism.

Again historically both methods may have been used but for the majority of metazoa the specialization of some cells for reproduction became the selected process.

Embryonic Development and Code Systems

The production of a new integrated many-celled organism from a single-celled organism would require some method of directing the orderly change from the beginning single cell to the adult organism. The general pattern for such orderly change is for the single cell to divide to produce two cells which divide again. This process of division continues until in some organisms thousands, millions, or billions of cells are produced. These cells are joined physically or at least are not separated by great distances and as development proceeds they form into layers and masses that fold and migrate and interact until the various integrated and specialized tissues, organs, and systems that characterize the adult are produced.

The whole process can be conceived as a behavior cycle with the cells as participants. The built-in receptor-conductor-effector systems of the cells would determine the cell's behavior and such systems would be sensitive to messages from other cells. The gene systems contained by each cell would control the synthesis of the necessary receptor-conductor-effector system for that cell. Thus the genetic code would be the ultimate controlling device for the developmental process.

A code system present in all cells could direct and control such development if the operations of such a code could be integrated with that of other cells. According to modern theory, genes control the synthesis of enzymes which in turn direct the synthesis of the various protoplasmic components of cells. A single genetic code system in the nucleus thus can be conceived as being sensitive to conditions in the cytoplasm and could, by directing the synthesis of enzymes, direct the metabolic and synthetic processes that create the receptor-conductor-effector systems of that cell. Such receptor-conductor-effector systems could be sensitive to messages from other cells and thus coordinate their various behaviors. However, in development it is not individual cells that persist and interact to produce the adult organisms, but populations of cells. During development, cell division goes on producing more and more individual cells. At the same time at different stages in the developmental process cells behave differently depending on the stage of development and the relation of the particular groups of cells to other groups. Thus embryonic development involves progressive or successive changes in individual cells and in populations of cells integrated with changes in behavior of other populations of cells.

Embroyonic development can be compared with a behavior cycle involving "wheels within wheels." The following quotation from Pike concerning a church service illustrates this aspect of a behavior cycle.

Although the preceding paragraphs were not specifically designed to show that behavior structure is built like "wheels within wheels," very little can be said about the details of any complex behavior pattern without this fact being implicit in the description. The church service includes the singing of a hymn, the hymn a stanza, the stanza a line (a phrase), the line a word, the word a sound, and the sound is sung by a composite of articulatory movements; or the song leader attends the service, he leads the singing throughout, stands, gestures and sings for a particular note, his small motions are part of a larger series of motions which is a part of a segment in a larger series.[9]

In embryonic development the total behavior cycle or pattern begins with the fertilized egg and ends with the establishment of all the tissues, organs, and systems that comprise the basic form of the organism. This total behavior cycle contains many smaller behavior cycles some of which are in series and some parallel. One such behavior cycle is repeated cell division that divides zygote to produce the thousands or millions of cells that make up the adult.

There are patterns of movement of cells or groups of cells. These may be migrations from place to place or they may be infoldings or outfoldings of layers of cells. There are changes in form or structure of individual cells. All of these divisions, movements, and changes are integrated and controlled so that the whole behavior cycle is completed and an integrated organism results.

The smallest pattern or unit of behavior in this total pattern of development probably is the metabolic activity within each cell. At the same level, perhaps, is mitotic cell division. The metabolic activity results in the synthesis of the cytoplasmic receptor-conductor-effector system of each cell and the mitotic cell division produces populations of cells. A higher level unit of behavior might be the migrations and foldings of groups of cells and the changes in the structures of cells as they gradually differentiate into the various forms that represent muscle, bone, nerve, etc.

The integration of the various subpatterns to achieve the total pattern requires intercommunication among the elements or participants and each element or participant must know his role in the whole pattern. In the church service illustration of a behavior cycle each member of the congregation knew the role he played in the total pattern. Each participant reacted to the appropriate cues and behaved according to his role with the result that the total behavior cycle, the church service, was enacted. A single code or description of the service detailing the behavior of the various members was all that was necessary to serve as a guide for the enactment of the service. Each member of the congregation knew this code and also, of significance, is the fact that each congregation member persisted as an entity during the whole of the service.

A different situation exists in embryonic development. The cells, that contain the genetic code that presumably guides and directs the developmental process, do not persist as single entities during the whole developmental process. Individual cells, containing a code of the entire pattern plus their own role in it, cannot be compared directly with the individual members of the congregation. The cells divide producing successive generations during the developmental process. The congregation members do not.

To overcome this difficulty it is necessary to assume more than one code. One code, which we will call a subcode, presumably directs the behaviors of single cells. It controls the behavior of a cell from its beginning as the result of a cell division to its end when it also divides. A second code, the supercode, presumably controls and directs the subcode. The span of behavior controlled by the subcode is one-cell generation. The span of behavior controlled by the supercode is the entire developmental pattern. The supercode contains information concerning the successive changes that must occur in the subcode in order to effect and control the successive changes in the cytoplasm of cells that produce the total integrated pattern of development.

The Emergence of Higher Level Communication Systems

It was mentioned above that with the appearance of many-celled forms a new living unit was created. This new unit was presumed to be more efficient in energy utilization because of the division of labor among the various cells or groups of cells. However, the new unit also has significance in terms of the communication process.

In single-celled forms the receptor-conductor-effector system with its decoding, encoding, and transmission functions is built of molecular units. In the metazoa, however, with the development of the nervous system, special receptors such as eyes and ears and special effectors such as muscles and glands, plus the integrating communication system is built of cellular units. The same functions are performed, but in the metazoa they are performed at a new level, with new units.

This process of emergence of new levels of integration apparently did not stop with the metazoan individual organism, for these also became units in still higher forms of integration. This level is represented by the associations of multi-celled forms into aggregations, herds, flocks, families and finally the closely integrated societies of insects and man.

The social insects such as wasps, bees, ants, and termites are populations that achieved a division of labor and integration to produce colonies that act as units in relation to their environment. In relation to this division of labor and integration Allee, *et al.* states:

> Division of labor and integration are associated principles. Integration has no function unless there are differentiated parts that must act in relation to the whole. Specialization of function cannot occur unless the specialized parts are coordinated. Efficient homeostasis follows an increase in the special functions of the integrated parts. These principles apply to every organismic level from the cell to the ecosystem, but are particularly well exhibited by the population of a colony of social insects.[10]

Social insect colonies vary somewhat in the kinds of insects that make up the colony but they all contain at least a reproductive caste and a worker caste. Some have soldiers that serve a protective function. The structure of all forms in any one kind of colony is basically the same. That is, they are all recognizably ants, wasps, or termites, but they also differ in morphology, and these differences are associated with their function within the colony.

The production of the different castes within a colony apparently is not directly controlled by differences in the genetic system. Allee, *et al.* states, "With the exception of sex differentiation the different castes of most social insects seem to develop from genetically similar eggs."

The control of the development of specific types is related to the presence or absence of that type in the colony.

In termites the presence of mature males, females, or soldiers, respectively, inhibits the development of the same caste from undifferentiated nymphs. According to Allee, *et al.*, "the most adequate theory to account for the facts is that castes gives off an exudate or "exohormone that passes to the developing individuals, or possibly to the unlaid eggs in the Hymenoptera, by licking or feeding or nutritive physiology, thus inhibiting the development of either reproductives or soldiers. . . ."

The point to be made is that just as embryonic development of metazoa required communication among cells the development of insect societies requires communication among insects. The two processes are analogous with communication operating in both instances. Also in both cases the messages transmitted are presumably chemical.

A complete development of this thesis in relation to human society is impossible in the present essay. However, it is generally agreed that genetic systems control human embryonic development and also determine certain simple behaviors in infants. Nervous and hormonal communication systems operate to coordinate the functions of the individual bodies, but in addition there has appeared an entirely new code or language system that functions in the social development and social integration of individuals. Human society seems to be a culmination of an evolutionary process that has produced successive levels of integration, by the creation of new levels of intercommunication. With human society there has appeared a new evolutionary unit, the tribe, state, or nation integrated by means of a new code or language system. It is interesting to speculate on what the next step in evolution might be, whether still higher levels of integration will produce still higher levels of units.

References and Notes

1. Berlo, David K., *The Process of Communication*, New York: Holt, Rinehart and Winston, 1960.
2. Pike, Kenneth, *Language in Relation to a Unified Theory of the Structure of Human Behavior*, Glendale, California: Summer Institute of Linguistics, 1954.
3. Lawson, C. A., *Language, Thought, and the Human Mind*, East Lansing: Michigan State University Press, 1958.
4. Pearl, Raymond, "On Biological Principles Affecting Populations Human and Other," *American Naturalist*, 1937.
5. Pike, Kenneth, *Language in Relation to a Unified Theory of the Structure of Human Behavior*, Glendale, California: Summer Institute of Linguistics, 1954 and Lawson, C. A., *Language, Thought, and the Human Mind*, East Lansing: Michigan State University Press, 1958.
6. Allee, W. C., Alfred E. Emerson, Orlando Park, Thomas Park, and Karl P. Schmidt, *Principles of Animal Ecology*, Philadelphia: W. B. Saunders Company, 1949.
7. *Ibid.*
8. Beadle, G. W., and Verna L. Coonradt, "Heterocaryosis in Neurospora Crassa," *Genetics*, Vol. 29, 1944, p. 291-308.
9. Pike, Kenneth, *Language in Relation to a Unified Theory of the Structure of Human Behavior*, Glendale, California: Summer Institute of Linguistics, 1954.
10. Allee, W. C., Alfred E. Emerson, Orlando Park, Thomas Park, and Karl P. Schmidt, *Principles of Animal Ecology*, Philadelphia: W. B. Saunders Company, 1949.

7
Intrapersonal Organization

HAROLD M. SCHRODER
MICHAEL J. DRIVER
SIEGFRIED STREUFERT

Implications of Information Processing Variables

In the rapidly expanding technology of our society, development and training have almost become synonymous with the acquisition of knowledge and skills. In overemphasizing the importance of the information a person learns, we pay considerably too little attention to the ways people learn to combine or use information for adaptive purposes. Given the same amount of information, different people use different conceptual rules in thinking, deciding, and interrelating. A sharp distinction is made between *what* a person thinks and *how* he thinks.[1] This chapter introduces and summarizes the main points taken up in depth.

Relationship between Information-Processing Structures and Information Content

One of the most common observations made about the behavior of organisms, at all points along the evolutionary ladder, is their consistency under similar conditions. Organisms either inherit or develop characteristic modes of thinking, adapting, or responding. Such modes or adaptive orientations not only differ among species but are observed as individual differences within species, and change in the same organism as a result of change in environmental conditions.

According to their theoretical preference or problem orientation, psychologists refer to these adaptive strategies as response patterns, attitudes, needs, defense mechanisms, norms, and so on. Much of psychology is directly concerned with the conditions surrounding the development, generalization, and persistence of such orientations. However, two distinct classes of information are relevant to the understanding of adaptation.

"Content variables" provide information about the acquisition, direction, and magnitude of responses, attitudes, norms, needs, and so on. From this standpoint, we are interested in what and how much a person learns, how long it is remembered, what attitudes or needs he holds, and how intense they are. Here the criterion or metric for describing adaptive orientations is the behavioral outcome measured in terms of the components involved, their magnitude (how much), and their direction (which stimuli are evaluated negatively or positively).

"Structural variables" provide a metric for measuring the way a person *combines* information perceived from the outside world, as well as internally generated information, for adaptive purposes. In this book, it is maintained that an adaptive orientation acts, first, like a set of filters—selecting certain kinds of information from the environment—and, second, like a program or set of rules which combines these items of information in specific ways. The first aspect is the component or content variable, and the second aspect is the structural or information-processing variable.

We will postulate various conceptual rules that persons could use to process information. These rules, or information-processing systems, will be ordered in terms of their complexity.

We emphasize the contribution of structural variables to the understanding of development, personality, attitudes, intelligence, performance, and interpersonal and intergroup relations. The emphasis will be upon *how* a person thinks or uses an attitude as a structure for processing new information, as opposed to an emphasis upon content, upon *what* a person thinks, what his attitudes are, and so forth.

Instead of treating differences in information processing as error, we hope to show that if the same informational components are processed in different ways—regardless of the content of the outcome—different adaptive consequences follow. For example, two persons may reach the same conclusion in a situation or hold the same attitude, but if the conclusion or judgment was reached by a different thought process or if the same attitude is used in a different way for processing information, then very different adaptive consequences would be expected to follow.

Human Thought and Information Processing

Compared to that of lower animals, human "thought" is characterized by the generation of more alternatives. More meanings can be attributed to objects, and a greater number of connections (relations) between these meanings arise. In this way, human thought is less stimulus-bound; action can be delayed; a given stimulus gives rise to a greater number of outcomes, creating more uncertainty and ambiguity. Taking an extreme case, the moth has no alternative when faced with a "light" and immediately flies toward it, whereas a human engaging in complex thought processes can perceive stimuli in many ways and can consider many ways of interrelating these perceptions for his adaptive purposes. In this sense, human thought has more degrees of freedom.

The difference between man and the higher-order animals lies not so much in the ability to learn or to utilize the meanings of a large number of stimuli, but rather in the ability to learn and to utilize alternate meanings of the same stimulus and to build up and use different patterns of interrelationships within the same set of meanings. This change, from lower to higher levels of thought, is a matter of degree, paralleling the evolutionary scale across species and developing with age (to an upper neurological limit under optimal environmental conditions) within species.

In developing a metric for measuring the level of information processing, a sharp distinction has been made between the degree to which rules are fixed or emergent. Static structures with fixed rules are exemplified by instincts in insects, by lower centers of the central nervous system, by most present-day computers, and by rigid, concrete thought structures representing an inability to take more than one perspective. Within this class, these structures differ in terms of the amount of informaion processed and the speed with which it is processed, but they are similar in that the rules of information processing are minimally modifiable within the system.

Emergent rule structures, on the other hand, are exemplified by exploratory and creative behavior in animals at the upper end of the evolutionary scale, as well as by other forms of integratively complex thought in which many perspectives and ways of interrelating these perspectives occur, and in which *new* rules can be generated for decision-making purposes. Within this class also, systems differ in terms of the amount and speed of information processed, but they are similar in that new information-processing rules emerge within the system itself.

Levels of Human Information Processing

In this model, two interdependent properties of information-processing structures are postulated: the parts of dimensions; and the integrating rules. Dimensions are the units of conceptual functioning and represent the elements or "content" of thought. Judgments, attitudes, decisions, or perceptions concerning a range of stimuli can be based on few—or many—dimensional units of information. For example, in making judgments about different kinds of light, the human being appears to be able to differentiate at least three different aspects or dimensions: brightness, saturation, and hue. On the other hand, a simple (much less differentiated) organism, such as the amoeba, may only have one dimension for "reading" differences between light stimuli; namely, degrees of brightness. This difference between the person and the amoeba in reference to a range of light stimuli illustrates the property of differentiation.

The same property could be used to describe the differences between two people, one of whom is capable of using more dimensions of information than the other in preceiving an art object, a person, a problem, or any other part of the environment. The same objective stimulus may be mediated by more or less differentiated conceptual structures. Each structure will be composed of dimensions representing an independent attribute along which the stimuli can be scaled such as length, weight, or power.

The number of dimensions is not necessarily related to the integrative complexity of the conceptual structures, but the greater the number of dimensions, the more likely is the development of integratively complex connections or rules. Low integration index is roughly synonymous with a hierarchical form of integration, in which rules or programs are fixed. Schemata for organizing alternate sets of rules are not present. Consequently, a hierarchical structure can have a small or a large number of parts (rules and procedures), but the relationships between the parts are relatively static and may be expressed as a single circle, as in Figure 7.1.

High integration index structures have more connections between rules; that is, they have more schemata for forming new hierarchies, which are generated as alternate perceptions or further rules for comparing outcomes. High integration structures contain more degrees of freedom, and are more subject to change as complex changes occur in the environment.

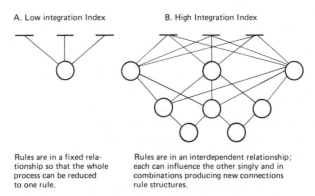

A. Low integration Index   B. High Integration Index

Rules are in a fixed relationship so that the whole process can be reduced to one rule.

Rules are in an interdependent relationship; each can influence the other singly and in combinations producing new connections rule structures.

Fig. 7-1 Variation in Level of Conceptual Structure

Many gradations or structural levels could be described along the conceptual-complexity dimension; however, in the pages to follow, we will describe only four: low, moderately low, moderately high, and high integration indices. We would like to emphasize that these are merely points on a somewhat continuous dimension which have been selected solely for purposes of communication. For an identification of these four conceptual levels see Figures 7.2, 7.3, 7.4 and 7.5.

Low Level Organization

Simple (concrete) intervening structures are characterized by compartmentalization and by a hierarchical integration of parts (rules). Regardless of the number of dimensions or the number of rules and procedures involved, the integrating structure is absolute. It lacks sets of alternate interacting parts. When the structure is hierarchical, the dimensional "readings" of a range of stimuli are organized in a fixed way.

A number of implications concerning the functioning of concrete structure (low degrees of freedom) can be derived from these characteristics: (a) At any given time, stimuli are "read" or interpreted unidimensionally. Such a system identifies and organizes stimuli in a fixed

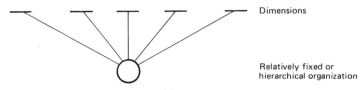

Dimensions

Relatively fixed or hierarchical organization

Fig. 7-2   Low Integration Index

way, and the rules derived from existing schemata are explicit in defining this one way. (b) Comparatively few degrees of freedom exist. The more undifferentiated the schemata, the lower the potential for generating conflict or ambiguity or for resolving ambiguity by means other than exclusion. (c) Dimensions are dichotomous with respect to the distribution of stimuli. A single hierarchy of rules for stimulus placement in a given category, which is compartmentalized so as to be independent of other subrules, has little potential for developing scaled dimensions. Stimuli are matched against yes-no categories, which they either do or do not fit.

In information processing, a concrete structure has comparative certainty and determinate character. Stimuli are evaluated more or less unidimensionally, and, from the subject's point of view, the problems of choice or error arise less frequently. Rules can be explicated more definitely, and there is a minimum of ambiguity. The structure can generate many hierarchically related categories about a given stimulus or stimulus range, as well as unrelated or compartmentalized categories about dissimilar stimuli.

The central feature is the development of rules for categorizing stimuli, for articulating structure and order. When the major work of an information-processing structure is the explication of rules for placing stimuli on discrete dimensions, three characteristics are present: (a) Once categorized in a particular way, a stimulus tends to remain in that category. It is minimally affected by placements of the same stimulus on other dimensions. This is associated with comparative absence of conflict within the system. (b) New stimuli are either distorted to fit existing dimensions or excluded. (c) Environmental conditions may change the way in which a stimulus is categorized but can affect the structure of the integrative schemata only minimally.

What are some of the familiar behavioral patterns generated by low integration index properties, regardless of the particular population of stimuli or content area?

These general characteristics of behavior include:

1. Categorical, black-white thinking. The discrimination of stimuli along dimensions is minimally graduated; for example, if a person holds an extremely concrete attitude toward Negroes, and "Negroes" are categorized in a single way, it follows that all Negroes will tend to be lumped into one category (for example, "bad") and contrasted with others. A structure that depends upon a single fixed rule of integration reduces the individual's ability to think in terms of relativeness, of "grays," and "degrees."

2. Minimizing of conflict. Stimuli either fit into a category or are excluded from consideration. There is no conceptual apparatus that can generate alternatives; the result is fast "closure" in choice or conflict situations. When conflict is introduced (as with the presentation of attitudinal refutation or dissonance), it quickly is minimized and resolved. Theories which argue that cognitive dissonance is followed by strategies aimed at reducing the conflict have validity particularly in describing the behavior of persons with concrete structure in a particular attitude area.

3. Anchoring of behavior in external conditions. If a stimulus is categorized in an absolute way, there is a corresponding restriction of internal integrative processes, and alternate resolutions or interpretations fail to arise. In structures with a low integration index, behavior is maximally controlled by external stimulus conditions. With increasing conceptual level, alternative perspectives and interrelationships can be generated from the same dimensional values of information. This represents an increase in the concept of "self" as an agent, a going beyond any single or externally given interpretation and an increase in the conception of internal causation.

4. The more absolute the rules of integration, the greater the generalization of functioning within a certain range, and the more abrupt or compartmentalized the change when it occurs. For example, if a stimulus person is categorized as holding the same attitude as the self, this perception (of agreement) will persist unchanged as the degree or nature of agreement becomes less or more complex. Conflicting attitudes tend to be misperceived or "warded off" because of the absoluteness of the stimulus categorization and the lack of alternate schemata for "sensing" shades of difference. In this sense, the perception of the other person is overgeneralized. When a person continues to perceive the world completely in terms of his own schemata, ignoring subtle situational changes and the alternate interpretations of others around him, he is "projecting." Thus, projection may be considered to be a defense mechanism commonly used by individuals low in integrative complexity. If the changes in the situation exceed a certain limit (which is defined in terms of the conditional rules for categorizing stimuli), the categorization of the stimulus person will change rather abruptly, and he will be perceived in a drastically different way. Another compartmentalized hierarchical set of rules negatively related to the first takes over.[2]

Moderately Low Organization

Many transitional systems could be described as the level of structure increases. Generally, the most significant aspect of change is the extent to which the system becomes less determinate. Increasing abstractness implies an increasing number of degrees of freedom. The system must itself generate conflict and ambiguity if it is to evolve beyond an adaptation characterized by fixed rules; for example, although a digital computer program may generate complex solutions, the rules are explicated, fixed, and externally determined. The program cannot change itself in the face of a changing environment. It is thus incapable of the behavior that most strikingly characterizes higher organisms.

One of the major requirements for the evolvement of abstract properties is the potential to generate alternate interpretations of a stimulus on any one dimension at a particular time (see Figure 7.3). It is one thing to categorize a stimulus on one dimension under one set of conditions, but it is a different matter to interpret the same stimulus at two places on the same dimension by using alternate rules at the same time. In more abstract structures, more information is generated and evaluations are less fixed. Decisions can be—and are—made on the basis of more information, yet there is less certainty owing to the presence of conflict.

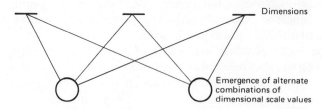

Fig. 7-3   Moderately Low Integration Index

The major characteristics of this second structural level are:

1. The presence of a conceptual apparatus that is able to generate alternate organizations of dimensions. That is, if there are three dimensions, such a structure would provide at least two possible rules for combining these dimensions. A given stimulus could be placed at two different points on any or all of the dimensions. For example, a mother helping a child to dress could be coded as "plus" or "minus" on a given dimension (such as control) depending on which of the alternate sets of rules the judgment was anchored.

2. At this level, there is, however, a lack of conceptual apparatus for relating or organizing differentiated rules. In these structures, schemata are related in the most primitive way. The integrating rules loosely specify conditionality; for example, in situation X, weight rule A higher than rule B. This does not involve the simultaneous use of schemata by superordinate rules other than conditional principles. In this sense, once a rule is engaged, moderately low integration index structure functions much like low integration index structure except that other schemata are available.

This moderately low level of organization is characterized by the delineation of several alternative ways of structuring the world. Although such conceptual properties are not effective for relating or organizing differentiated sets of rules for decision-making processes, they do usher in the problem of choice and probability. The generation of alternatives or of uncertainty is an important step in increasing abstractness, but at this level the system is characterized by ambivalence. Unlike low-level structure, for which the problem of choice is minimal, moderately low structure generates alternate interpretations without a fixed basis for choice or organization. For example, there is no fixed rule for what is right or wrong. Here conditions affect the choice not only of dimensions, as is the case in structures with a low integration index, but also of schemata.

One of the most general implications of moderately low structure is that the discrimination of stimuli on dimensions remains relatively constant. That is, since each alternate organization is minimally modified by or related to the other, stimuli are still being "read" primarily via a single schema. However, the dimensional structure is more complex in the sense that stimuli can be differentiated within a single dimension (that is, can be evaluated at more than one point). It is differentiation of stimulus placement within a single dimension that opens up the developmental possibility of relating the differentiated organizations and furthers the evolvement of higher-level structural properties.

Some of the consequences of moderately low structural properties include:

1. A movement away from absolutism. Because of the availability of alternate schemata, "right" and "wrong" are not fixed as they were in structures with low integration index.

2. The emergence of primitive internal causation. A fixed system, based on a rigid set of absolutes, requires and expresses no internal processes. There is no freedom of choice. When alternates are available, the individual must make choices; internal processes, however minimal, begin to emerge. At the second level, the internal processes are mainly conditional, and in this sense they are primitive compared to the internal processes of more abstract structures.

3. *Instability and noncommitment.* In the absence of both absolute ways of evaluating environments and complex rules for integrating alternate schemata, there is ambivalence and lack of consistency in decision making and judgment. From the observer's point of view, conditional rules may appear inconsistent, and their application may indicate lack of commitment. In psychoanalytic terms, the person might be described as having a weak superego.

4. *A form of rigidity still present, as in the first level.* Rigidity there was used in the sense that external stimuli are perceived in a minimally differentiated and complex way; thus, the richness and range of experience is small. At this second structural level, the rigidity is due to the fact that, after the selection of a given schemata when one perceptual organization has been accepted, alternate schemata are almost completely ineffective. Information that could have entered the system via the rejected schemata is not available. There is, consequently, a failure to consider certain environmental pressures under some conditions.

5. *A "pushing against" or negativistic orientation.* When alternate schemata can be selected by a set of conditional rules, the person is able to generate and understand two or more ways of perceiving a given situation. But since the two evaluations are used in a compartmentalized manner, failure to utilize one schema can be interpreted by an outside viewer as "negativism." Further, the process of generating alternate schemata itself implies a "pushing against" present or alternate schemata and can again be viewed as an expression of negativism.[3]

In our discussion of moderately low structural levels, we refer to a wide range of transitional systems that go from vague doubts concerning a single schema, through the use of simple conditional rules, to the development of a structure that is more complex than is shown in the diagram (Figure 7.2), for selecting alternate organizations. Research may show that certain of the possible structures in this range are frequently found, or are of great predictive value, in certain situations. These moderately low organizations would then be particularly interesting and worth describing in greater detail.

Moderately High Organization

Increasing levels of information processing involves the emergence of more complex and interrelated schemata. In turn, more dimensions are generated, and discrimination between stimuli becomes more linear. If the adaptive significance of moderately low structure is the delineation of alternate rules, the significance of moderately high structure may be described as the initial emergence of rules for identifying more complex relations than alternation (see Figure 7.4).

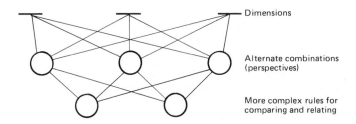

Dimensions

Alternate combinations (perspectives)

More complex rules for comparing and relating

Fig. 7-4 Moderately High Integration Index

At this level, the person is able to combine schemata. In moderately low structure, the rules could not be effectively combined. The arrangement of stimuli generated by each alternate set of rules was relatively fixed. However, the delineation of alternate schemata increased the level of uncertainty and decreased the fixity of outcomes. This shift from absoluteness to the generation of alternatives increases the amount of functional information available at a given time. Uncertainty increases with the presence of more abstract properties, not in the sense that the world is more chaotic, but rather in the sense that alternatives exist. Much more information is sought before resolutions are made; when they have been made, these resolutions are less fixed, and the system remains open to the perception and effects of alternatives.

At the minimum, moderately high levels of structure require rules for matching, comparing, and relating pairs of schemata. Each of these three processes utilized *both* "readings" for arriving at decisions or resolutions. In low-level structure, the rules determine conditions that govern the choice of stimulus categories; in moderately low-level structure, additional rules specify conditions under which alternate schemata are used; and at the third level, additional rules specify various ways in which schemata are compared. The process is one of "comparing" or "matching" in such a way that alternate schemata become organized more or less independently of other organizations.

A number of important behavioral implications are associated with moderately abstract properties:

1. The system is less deterministic. Combining and using two alternate systems of interpretation greatly increase the number of alternative resolutions that can be generated. Even when the individual closes on a particular decision, he is still open to a number of alternative pressures. At this level, abstractness (that is, lack of fixity) becomes a formal rule of the system.

2. When system properties begin to permit the simultaneous utilization of two schemata, the environment can be tracked in many more ways. While moderately low integration index structure permits different ways of tracking or interpreting an environment at different times, moderately high integration index structure can vary combinations of alternate schemata. A person who is functioning at this level may view a social situation in terms of two points of view, see one in relationship to the other, perceive the effects of one upon the other. He is able to generate strategic adjustment processes, in which the effects of behavior from one standpoint are seen as influencing the situation viewed from another vantage point. This implies, for example, that a person can observe the effects of his own behavior from several points of view; he can simultaneously weigh the effects of taking different views. The adaptive utilization of alternate schemata here is much less compartmentalized than at moderately low levels.

3. The presence of choice makes possible the use of internal processes. Such processes emerge in a rudimentary way in moderately low-level structure. However, the "comparing" or "relating" function, which is entirely an internal process, is characteristic of more integratively complex levels than the second. At the third level, sttructure is potentially self-reflective. The awareness of "self" (and the "self" as a causative agent) is greatly enhanced, although it does not reach its climax until the development of high-level structure. In moderately high levels of integrative complexity, rules are minimally fixed. They are no longer completely anchored in the past. When relationships are not thus anchored, the process of relating alternate schemata to each other is a highly internal one. It is internal in the sense that it is not anchored in established rules, in the sense that it represents a projection into the future, and in the sense that many different interactions can be generated in the same external situation. Functioning is decreasingly dependent upon immediate external stimulus conditions, and behavior is decreasingly predictable from a knowledge of the individual's past. In order to predict behavior, it becomes increasingly important to understand the internal processes of the structure.

High Level Organization

While moderately high structure generates rules for comparing and combining the effects of specific pairs (or small groups) of schemata at a time, high level structure includes additional and more complex potentialities for organizing additional schemata in alternate ways. At the fourth level, comparison rules can be further integrated. Alternate complex combinations provide the potential for relating and comparing different systems of interacting variables. As with other system differences, the difference between the moderately high and the high levels is one of degree. In the latter, the potential to organize different structures of interacting schemata opens up the possibility of highly abstract functions (see Figure 7.5).

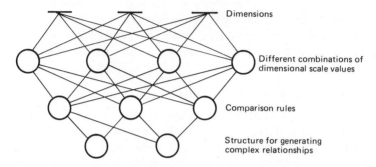

Fig. 7-5 High Integration Index

In a very loose sense, and by analogy, the difference between moderately high and high levels may be described as the difference between an empirical and a theoretical outlook. At the moderately high level, a number of classes of empirical relationships are possible; in high-level functioning, it is possible to generate or apply general laws that systematize a large and differentiated body of information generated by simpler schemata in various related ways. Unlike the low level, which consists of a hierarchical set of established rules and procedures, high-level functioning (which again reaches a form of unity in the system) is characterized by the ability to generate the rules of the theory, the complex relations and alternate schemata, as well as the relationships between the various structures. It has the potential to generate alternate patterns of complex interactions.

As with other levels, an increase in the number and complexity of the parts of the mediating structure is accompanied by (a) an increase in the degree of diversity the system can generate and handle, in the number of schemata and dimensions, and in the complexity of their organization; (b) greater discrimination between stimuli within dimensions; and (c) an increased potential for the structure to generate alternate patterns of interaction and new schemata without the imposition of new external conditions. Internal processes can produce alternate organizations of rules for viewing the world. These schemata can then be tested by exploration.

This very abstract orientation should be highly effective in adapting to a complex, changing situation. It is certainly much more effective than a structure that is dependent upon external conditions for building rules and upon past experiences for predicting events. The effectiveness of high level properties would be maximized if the criteria of performance were based upon (a) the utilization of many alternate interactive processes, and (b) the ability to cope with situational change over time. Highly abstract structure permits the delineation of many systematically related alternatives, and decisions should be most effective for adapting to a future event. At this level, the ability to discover and utilize information about a range of stimuli at any given time is maximized. High-level structure requires a rich set of empirical relations (evolved at lower levels), which can then be ordered in various ways through the emergence of superordinate rules.

Attitudes, Personality, and Information Processing

Level of conceptual structure refers to the way an individual receives, stores, processes, and transmits information. Thus, beliefs, hypotheses, attitudes, needs, concepts, and so forth, may be viewed as structures for organizing or processing information. Although personality often is described in terms of a profile of the directionality and magnitude of needs and attitudes, there is evidence to argue for the inclusion of information based on structural variables.[4]

It is well known, for example, that two persons may express the same attitude but use it differently in thinking, arguing, and decision making. The same is true for expressions of conformity, assertiveness, and so on. In many situations, particularly where complex decision making and intergroup and interpersonal relations are involved, it would seem appropriate to weight the *way* a person thinks about a given problem more highly than *what* he thinks.

Structural variables measure the nature of the relationship between a person and the objects in his world. Consequently, in any area—political, religious, interpersonal—of the life space we can measure the level, or the integrative complexity, of the conceptual rules for processing information. In higher-level structures with more rules and interconnecting linkages, the individual has more ways to relate to persons and objects and to generate new aspects of relating.

In this manner, conceptual level enters as an important determiner of self-definition. In a particular area of stimulation, we define that aspect of the self as both the directionality (what a person believes, desires, and so on) and the nature (conceptual level) of these subject-object ties.

The more integratively complex the information-processing structure, the more the "self" enters as a causal agent in generating new perspectives and new ways of relating to objects. In simple attitudes, the ways of relating are fixed and absolute and the potential for generating alternate perspectives is low. Conceptual level defines the level of awareness of self as agent and provides an objective measure of self-development. Higher levels of conceptual structure are associated with more flexible, adaptive orientations to stress and greater resistance to its various forms.[5]

Flexibility—rigidity in various forms has been recognized as an important personality variable from the earliest periods in psychology. However, the present conceptualization differs from traditional descriptions in three ways. First, it is not viewed as an additional aspect of personality; for example, as a "trait." Rather, it is viewed at a different level of analysis—the information-processing level—*which has no necessary relationship to content variables. Second, it is not conceptualized as a trait or a cognitive style that is independent of a particular content area.* We contend that conceptual level is dependent upon developmental conditions, and therefore can vary across different areas if developmental conditions also vary across these areas; for example, in dealing with interpersonal and with religious stimuli.[6] According to this view, most persons are integratively simple in a number of content areas and complex in others. Third, the level of information processing in a given area is not held to be necessarily static over time. A number of experiments demonstrate the temporary effect of conditions on the level of information processing in a given area.[7] In this approach, there is relatively great emphasis on the interaction between person and situational variables.

Perhaps the most important distinction between information-processing or structural variables and traditional conceptions of rigidity-flexibility is in their relationship to motivation. In agreement with Hunt,[8] we regard motivation as being triggered or initiated on the content side by the perception of a stimulus incongruent with a given adaptation level; for example, the perception of a discrepant communication. However, the nature and processes involved in ensuring goal-directed activity will differ as a function of the conceptual level in that area. The nature of goals, their number and interconnection, vary as a function of conceptual level, and the pattern of goal-oriented behavior would be expected to differ in different information-processing systems. The empirical relationships between content variables, such as needs and traits, and behavioral measures thus are expected to differ in different information-processing systems.

Intelligence, Creativity, and Information Processing

Low-and high-level information-processing systems can be equally intelligent. If intelligence is measured by the amount of information known or by the degree to which learned rules can be invoked by certain cues, no matter how complex the rules, then the level of intelligence in higher and lower systems is not necessarily different. High-and low-level structures can have an equal number of parts, or a low-level system can have more parts (dimensions and rules), as in the case of a computer. But if intelligence is measured by the amount of new information that can be generated by new rule combinations, higher-level information-processing structures would be more intelligent.

From the point of view of performance, lower-level structures can function effectively if there are sufficient parts and if the appropriate performance is known and remains constant. Higher-level structures can function more effectively in situations that are undergoing change and in which new perspectives and solutions are required. In this sense, the degree of creativity is synonomous with the conceptual level in any given area. Here, then, creativity has no necessary relationship to "success," if success is defined by a performance criterion. Success often is achieved by following a fixed theory or set of rules and persisting to limits to which others do not aspire. Although such activity is necessary and useful, it is not always creative.[9]

While the traditional concepts of creativity and level of information processing are similar if they are interpreted in the framework we have suggested, two additional distinctions may be made. It is assumed that the level of information processing can vary across content areas, so that a person can be creative in one field and conceptually very simple in another. Further, the level of information processing in a given area can vary as a function of different forms of environmental stress. That is, creativity is not viewed as a fixed, generalized ability but as the potential to engage a complex, interrelated set of conceptual rules in information processing in a given area. Creativity and intelligence are thus anchored in a sociopersonality theoretical framework.

Group Development and Information Processing

The integrative complexity of the way persons process attitudinal and interpersonal information is expected to have a considerable influence on interpersonal interaction and the evolvement of group organization. The higher the conceptual level of group members: (a) the greater the diversity of information and alternative perspectives opened up, producing new and more creative adaptive orientations; (b) the less members define themselves by the content or directionality of their own judgments, attitudes, or beliefs, adopting each other's perspectives as new organizations leads to better interpersonal relations—particularly with disagreement— and the evolvement of a higher-level information processing structure; (c) the less salient the power orientation and the lower the probability of aggression under conditions of intragroup or intergroup conflict.

Much of our research in this area is directed toward the investigation of the hypothesis that the level of the information processing of group members sets limits to the level to which group organization can evolve.[10] Many face-to-face groups composed of persons, matched on all major variables including intelligence but differing in conceptual level, have been observed in long term, complex, decision-making situations, such as inter-nation simulation, stock market simulation, and tactical war games, as well as management games.

Norms, rules, roles, and so forth, are viewed as structures for processing information that emerge through face-to-face interaction in groups. Groups composed of members with lower-level conceptual structures are expected to generate less diversity, fewer alternative perspectives, rigidly constricted norms, and fixed role relationships. The implication is that such groups, in complex experimental situations, evolve an organization that closely resemble autocracy, whereas groups composed of members with more complex information-processing structures can develop more complex organizations given favorable developmental conditions.

The relationship between group structure (or the level of conceptual structure of members composing a group) and performance depends upon the criterion of performance. If the goals, member roles, relevant stimuli, and processing rules are known and the situation remains static, the performance of simple structure groups can equal or perhaps surpass that of more complex group organizations. However, to the extent that the criterion of performance involves: (a) the perception of subtle environmental change, (b) the evolvement of new interconnected ways to solve problems, and (c) the consideration of many alternatives and of diverse information in decision making, and to the extent that the experimental situation is sufficiently interesting and complex to engage high-level information processing, more integratively complex groups should perform better.

According to this view, the structure or the decision-making or political organization of groups basically depends upon an interaction between the conceptual level of group members in face-to-face situations and the specific environmental conditions. This is not meant to imply that the group does not have an effect on the conceptual level of its members; obviously, there is an interaction here also. It implies that decision-making or administrative organizations cannot be imposed on groups—small or large—and that the structural characteristics of groups are developmental. In groups, as in persons, structural evolvement begins at the simpler level and progresses to higher levels only if the conceptual level of individual members permits and if the developmental conditions are favorable.

Training and Information Processing

The content-structure distinction is highly relevant to training and development. Training can refer to the development of two independent aspects: (a) response patterns, attitudes, roles, and rule application; and (b) information-processing structures. From the structural point of view, the question is not what a child is taught—what habits, attitudes, and so on—but what adaptive orientation he develops while he is learning these responses in a given training environment. That is, the training agent sets up a particular kind of training environment, and the subject, in addition to learning a specific response or rule, also begins to learn to cope with this class of stimuli in a given way.

In training a child to adopt certain responses, some sequences may teach him to look externally for rules to avoid uncertainty and alternatives. Such an environment would be expected to develop simple structural properties. Other sequences, while aiming to "train in" the same subject matter, may teach a person to search for diversity, develop alternatives and uncertainty, and practice rule generation. This environment would be expected to lead to a more integratively complex structure in the particular stimulus area.

In Chapter 1V of *Human Information Processing* various training environments and their hypothesized structural outcomes are presented. It is there suggested that which training method is superior again depends upon the criterion applied. Mass society with its emphasis on the learning of rules and how to use them, and mass education with its emphasis on the acquisition of more and more information in more and more fields, increasingly use the content criterion. Good performance often is measured by how much a person learns in a given period of time. Further, a vast array of technology, including many types of teaching machines, textbooks, and so on, has been developed against a content criterion. The approach described here emphasizes the significance and implications of the structural criterion in many situations.

The more a task can be successfully performed by a fixed, predetermined set of procedures (and providing the task and interpersonal roles remain static or can be prescribed), the less the significance of structural variables. But in changing task environments in which the environment and the adapting persons interact, and in which exploration and alternate goals, means, strategies, and decisions are required, information-processing variables should be weighted more heavily.

Successful performance in most complex reactive task environments requires (a) sufficient performance skills and knowledge, (b) a near optimal level of interest or motivation, (c) adequate competence in interpersonal relations (since most complex task environments require group activity for decision making purposes), and (d) the capacity to engage in complex information processing.

References and Notes

1. This chapter introduces and summarizes the main points taken up in Schroder, Harold M., Michael J. Driver, and Siegfried Streufert, *Human Information Processing*, New York: Holt, Rinehart, Winston, 1967.
2. The nature of this black-white change or the black-white effect of anchors on stimulus placement (J. Bieri, ''Cognitive-simplicity and Predictive Behavior,'' *Journal of Abnormal Social Psychology*, Vol. 51, No. 2, 1955, pp. 263-268), is discussed in detail in Chapter 5 of *Human Information Processing*, Schroder, et al.
3. Negativism also occurs in low integration index structures. In that case, it implies a rejection of any possible alternate and represents absolutistic thinking.
4. See, *Human Information Processing*, Schroder, et al., Chapters 2-10 for supporting material.
5. *Ibid.*
6. *Ibid.*
7. Hunt, J. McV., ''Motivation Inherent in Information Processing and Action,'' *Motivation and Social Interaction, Cognitive Determinants*, O.J. Harvey, ed. New York: Ronald, 1963, pp. 35-94.
8. See, *Human Information Processing*, Schroder, et al., Parts II and III.
9. *Ibid.*

8
Social Organization

ALFRED KUHN

Types of Social Systems and System Controls

Every science classifies and categorizes the phenomena within it. The goal of a classification system is a condition in which the act of identifying some phenomenon as belonging to a certain category will tell you something about it—if you already know something about that category. Such knowledge is possible under certain conditions. First, all items within the category must be similar in certain respects, those similarities being the things one can know from the act of categorizing. Second, different categories must be reasonably discrete. Biological categories, for example, are kept nicely discrete by the fact that cross fertilization occurs across only a very narrow species spectrum. Were this not so, we would long ago have arrived at the point where every individual would, in effect, be its own species—as, for example, if we could cross fleas with elephants and then cross breed their progeny with the offspring of dogs and salmon.

If you tell me something is a mammal or a lever, I immediately know something about it. But if you tell me something is a system, I am not sure there is anything I can know from your statement that I did not know before, however well versed I might be in systems analysis. While this situation may have been inevitable in the early days of a science, it seems about time we try to do something about it. In that spirit, the purpose of this chapter is to suggest some sub-categories of the genus "system" so that to identify something as a particular kind of system will provide information. There are undoubtedly loopholes in this proposal, some of which reflect my orientation in the social sciences. We have nevertheless got to start somewhere, and this is a tentative trial.

The Classification Scheme

Since a classification scheme is clearest in outline form, an outline of this one is appended. I have included in it examples of each type of system, but with sharp reservations, knowing that examples, like analogies, are apt to be more controversial than the generalizations they

114

illustrate. The difficulty is that no real system is a precise counterpart of the pure analytical construct.

Before dealing with the divisions shown in the outline, I would like to distinguish even more broadly between systems and non-systems, to counter the current tendency to refer to practically anything as a system. An automobile crankshaft, for example, is not a system when viewed solely as a component of the engine. No two parts or characteristics of it change relative to one another. The crankshaft, of course, changes position relative to the engine block and the pistons. Hence, the crankshaft plus those other components do constitute a system. But the crankshaft alone is a non-system. The term "mountain system" is also common. While I will not try to change the layman's usage, my point is simply that various parts of a mountain "system" do not interact in any sense relevant to the typical user of the term. For most purposes we could level the whole of the Appalachians north of the Mason-Dixon and precisely nothing would happen to the part south of the line. However, if a geologist is dealing with some developments in which the parts *do* interact, he may legitimately refer to the mountain chain as a system. In this vein I would like to require every systems analyst to make a long list of things that are *not* systems and paste it over his desk.

Acting vs. Nonacting (or pattern) Systems

The first division is between (1) action systems and (2) pattern, or nonaction systems. Action systems *do* something. By contrast, pattern systems have things *done* to them, but do not themselves do anything. I see this as a fundamental distinction, and feel sure that no significant analysis that applies to one will also apply to the other.

To deal first with pattern systems I would sub-classify these into real pattern systems and analytical or conceptual ones. The distinction is the reasonably familiar one between information level and matter-energy level. In this connection I would note Peter Caws' 1968 presidential address to the Society for General Systems Research.[1] He observed that theories about systems are themselves also systems. This he considered a serious ambiguity. I would strengthen his point by saying that only chaos can result if we do not sharply distinguish real systems from the pattern systems which are their analytical counterparts. There is an important sense, of course, in which statements about an analytical model are also true of its real counterpart, as we shall see below. But there is also a fundamental difference, as you would quickly discover if you thought you had been put in charge of General Motors and were then told you were only in charge of its analytical model. A map of North America is not North America, and the schematic of your TV set will not bring you Walter Cronkite.

There are many real pattern systems. For example, the skeletal shape of a skyscraper and the structural characteristics of steel beams are related in a systematic way. Yet the shape does not *do* anything to the characteristics of steel beams, which are the same whether or not they are put into the skyscraper, and whether or not skyscrapers are ever built. Conversely, the characteristics of steel beams do not themselves *do* anything to the shapes of buildings. The only *doing* that occurs is done by the human being. Once he has learned the constraints placed upon him by the traits of steel he then shapes his building according to his own criteria of safety, appearance, cubic capacity, land values, and the like. Although there is a "systematic" relationship between steel strength and building shape, neither *acts* on the other. Only the human being acts in this case.

Similarly, the parts of language are interrelated in highly systematic fashion, and a sentence holds together only if its parts follow the system. But if by accident or ignorance one half of a sentence is utterly inconsistent with the other, neither half *does* anything to rectify the discrepancy. Only if some human intervenes will change be made. Again, the human acts; the language does not. The same general logic also applies to the pattern system which is mathematics.

As of the moment I am extremely skeptical that systems analysis, as such, has, or ever will have, anything to contribute to understanding pattern systems. If anything we learn from studying language systems is applicable to our understanding of steel-skyscraper systems, this result, I think, will be purely fortuitous. I certainly have no objection if someone can find some common traits among all kinds of pattern systems, but I think it unlikely. A Gregorian chant is a pattern system and so is the theoretical structure of neoclassical economics. Again, I doubt if any generalizations about one will be applicable to the other. If linguistic and mathematical analysis have some things in common I suspect the reason is that mathematics is in an important respect also a language.

If an analytical system is created as a model of an acting system, then the logic of the acting system may also be said to be valid for this corresponding pattern system. This is only so because the analytical system *is* a model of an acting system, and the logic is that of the acting system. For example, if I use a mathematical formula to compute the traits of a particular transitor the result is determined by the laws of electrons, not of mathematics. Only to the extent the analytical and mathematical model happens to fit the electronic reality can the former be used for the purpose at all. By the same token if several models (pattern systems) of different acting systems show similarities, the similarities are those of the acting systems they represent, not of any logic of pattern systems themselves.

By contrast, my strong suspicion is that any systems science that can be developed will apply solely to acting systems. Here I think we can already say that as soon as something is identified as an acting system we *know* something about it. The things we know are those already widely discussed by systems analysts, and include:

1. Under certain conditions the system can reach and maintain equilibrium. The best known condition is negative feedback, in which a deviation from some point sets in motion an opposite action which pushes the system back toward that point. Less widely discussed is positive feedback when one or more variables reach a limit. A fire, for example, is subject to positive feedback in that the hotter it gets the faster it burns and the faster it burns the hotter it gets. The system may nevertheless reach an equilibrium if fuel or oxygen is supplied at only a limited rate, or if a temperature is reached at which heat is dissipated as fast as it is generated. Social analysis has many such positive feedback equilibria. For example, the more accurately people communicate the more similar their ideas become and the more similar their ideas the more accurately they communicate. Here we have an equilibrium at the asymptotic limit of identity.

2. A system will be subject to explosion or shrinkage under positive feedback without any limit to its variables.

These two points give us some information. As to the first, unless a particular system is subject to some equilibrium it is not likely to last long enough to be worth investigating as a system. Hence merely to identify something as a continuing system implies that within it can be found either some negative feedback relation, or positive feedback with at least one variable limited. Hence the basic understanding of any continuing system lies in identifying its negative feedback elements or the asymptotically limited positive ones. I cannot recall where I saw a generalization to the effect that the first law of system is that they tend to maintain themselves. This is an interesting and basically correct statement, but to my mind it reverses the logic of things. The proper statement, it seems to me, is that only those things that tend to maintain themselves are worth classifying and studying as systems. The other version has a mildly anthropomorphic quality, and seems to overlook something important about the basic nature of science.

3. If the system is closed it will be subject to entropy, which in its broadest sense may be construed as loss of differentiation. By contrast, if the system is open and in some way subject to positive feedback, it may undergo evolutionary change into greater differentiation. Stated in reverse, if the system *does* evolve, then we know it is open and subject to positive feedback.[2]

4. The final state of a closed system, or any intermediate state, is determined by those forces and processes already within it at the moment of closure.

5. The final state of an open system, or any intermediate state, is determined by both the forces within the system at the moment it became open and the forces of the environment.

I do not know how many extant generalizations are applicable to all *action* systems, or how many more may eventually be developed. So far as I can see, however, none of these applies to pattern systems, as I have defined them.

Controlled (cybernetic) vs. Uncontrolled (noncybernetic) Systems

Action systems can again be subdivided into controlled or cybernetic systems and uncontrolled or non-cybernetic. The former has some kind of goal and behavior as a unit, and maintains at least one variable within some specified limits. Whenever the variable moves beyond those limits, the system reacts to bring it back. The household thermostat is the classic example.

By contrast, an uncontrolled system will presumably reach some equilibrium since if it does not it is probably not worth analyzing—as indicated above. But it has no "preference" for any *particular* level of equilibrium. A river system, for example, at any given moment will reach a level which equilibrates such factors as amount of rainfall, area of watershed and width, depth, and slope of river channel. But if rainfall increases or the channel becomes clogged and the river, therefore, rises, the new equilibrium is "accepted" just as readily as the old one. The river system does nothing to restore its previous level. Similarly in microeconomic theory the equilibrium price of a commodity is that which clears the market. If supply increases, as through lower cost of production, a new equilibrium will prevail. The new equilibrium is just as "right" as the old one. The system will not respond to restore the previous equilibrium, which would now be "wrong" under the increased supply.

Note that the word "controlled" here refers only to internal system controls, not external. For example, the path of a purely ballistic missile can be externally controlled when one sets its angle of fire and propulsion energy. But no internal mechanisms rectify its course if it goes astray, in marked contrast to the controlled guided missile, which detects and corrects such deviations.

The obvious reason for distinguishing controlled and uncontrolled systems is the difference in applicable analysis. Although both are subject to the five generalizations stated above, and possibly others, that particular sub-species of system analysis called 'cybernetics' is applicable solely to controlled systems. This distinction between controlled and uncontrolled systems will be elaborated below in connection with human organizations. Pattern systems obviously cannot be subdivided into controlled and uncontrolled. The distinction is relevant only to systems that act, and pattern systems do not.

Organizations (of humans) vs. Non-organizations

Both controlled and uncontrolled systems must, I think, be subdivided between those whose elements consist of multiple interacting human beings and those which do not, to reflect fundamental differences in the nature of system interactions. To give them a name, we will call all systems consisting of multiple humans,"organizations." Although system analysts widely use "organization" and "system" interchangeably, much other usage is already in accord with the present one.

The distinguishing differences between organizations and non-human systems are indicated in the outline. First, communications between humans and their organizations are mainly linguistic or semiotic. They are based on (pattern) systems of signs and referents in semantic communications. Now there is plenty of communication going on inside an amoeba or the genes of human beings, and much of it is amenable to rigorous information and communications analysis. But it is not amenable to linguistic analysis. By contrast, in the linguistic communication so typically human, communication theory may tell us something about the quantity of information as measured by numbers of signs. But it can tell us nothing about the quantity of information which constitutes the referent of any particular sign in the head of any individual.

The second distinction is the transactional. Systems other than humans engage in many transfers (inputs and outputs) of matter and energy. These exchanges are based on certain technical characteristics of the systems, and can be described in terms of principles of biology, chemistry, or physics. By contrast, the transactional exchanges between humans are based on the *values* of the things exchanged. Except in some primitive, analogic sense the kinds of transactions dealt with in bargaining power theory and supply and demand analysis, for example, occur only among humans. No other systems similarly engage in negotiations and establish terms of trade based on utility functions of the interacting systems. Human systems are therefore distinguished because the interactions between them are subject to utterly different analysis than are those between nonhuman systems.

Formal vs. Informal Organization

Since this chapter is directed primarily at social systems I will deal in further detail only with systems of humans. Here I suggest calling controlled systems "formal organization" and uncontrolled ones "informal organization." The main distinctions are:

1. The formal organization has some kind of preference as a unit; the informal does not.

2. The formal organization makes and executes some kinds of decisions as a whole unit—possibly of a sort that will optimize something—while the informal does not.

3. The formal organization to some degree determines its own internal structure; the informal does not. By this we mean that it specifies its own subsystems and the role each is to play in the whole system. How well the controls operate will depend on some of the control mechanisms to be indicated below.

4. The analysis of formal organization (like that of any controlled system) can be focused on its detector, selector, and effector functions—of which more later. By contrast the uncontrolled system cannot be said to have any detector, selector, or effector functions as a unit.

The biological eco-system can be viewed as a lower prototype of informal organization. All its significant subsystems are themselves controlled systems, of which each seeks its own goals in its own ways. The subsystems also interact in numerous ways, but only in pursuit of their own separate goals. The total set of components and interactions constitute a system in a very full and clear sense. But the system engages in no behavior as a unit, and has no goal beyond those of its separate subsystems. So far as the whole system is concerned, any equilibrium it reaches is as good as any other and it will institute no behavior as a unit to move toward a different one. If and when controls are instituted, as in the Tennessee River system and the American economy during the 1930's, by definition the system then moves into the controlled category.

I mentioned earlier that my examples may be arguable and I will try to clarify several. For example, I have listed a laissez-faire economy as one particular kind of social system at the level of the whole society. One might argue, for example, "But the American economy is a laissez-faire system, and yet it has lots of controls!" This is the typical problem of classifying complicated real phenomena into pure analytic categories. By a laissez-faire economy I mean a laissez-faire economy—that is, one with no controls. If an economy that is primarily laissez-faire nevertheless has some controls, then to that extent it must be categorized as a controlled system, not uncontrolled. We must then apply the analysis of formal organization to the controlled part and of informal organization to the uncontrolled part. The fact that much of reality is very messy does not mean that our analytical system must also be. Elementary physics tells us nice things about perfectly hard, perfectly spherical objects rolling down perfectly hard, perfectly plane surfaces. But most phenomena of the real world do not fit the neat categories of the physicist—like the rubber headed mallet bouncing down your cellar steps. Although physics is enviable in that many pieces of its reality are, or can be made, very similar to analytical models, for most other sciences (and many physical phenomena) we can make precise statements only about the analytical models, not about reality. We can all regret this, but there is not much we can do about it.

Similarly I classify a cocktail party as informal on the assumption its sole aim is amusement of its individual members. But if its members are brought together with some collective intent, such as to found a new chapter of Alcholics Anonymous, then that cocktail party is to that extent a formal organization. To understand its behavior may then require both kinds of analysis.

In the outline I have classified the social system as informal. More strictly it probably justifies an intermediate category, which elsewhere I call the semi-formal. It is informal insofar as it has no central controlling mechanism and no single goal. But it does contain some formal elements in that many behaviors of many individuals are directed toward their views of the total good, not solely their own. The social organization of tribal societies lies closer to the formal end of the spectrum. They are small enough so that any reasonably perceptive person has some sense of his own effect on the total society. If additional controls are exerted by individuals on their peers, even without controls by a chief, these provide some degree of formality in being directed toward a preferred state of the whole society. Again, however, the validity of the overall classification scheme does not depend on how precisely we can categorize particular real entities.

Interactions with Organizations (and between humans)

The next question is why the above references to interactions among human beings and organizations have been described as communications and transactions. This formulation arises from work I have been doing elsewhere in connection with "unified social science", and is related to system analysis as follows. Human beings are controlled systems behaving in an environment. Any such adaptive behavior seems to involve a logically irreducible list of three ingredients: (1) The environment, (2) the system, and (3) the adaptive response.

Now a system does not respond to its total environment, but only to those aspects which impinge upon it, or are "known" to it in some sense. It is only to the extent that the system has itself been modified by its environment that it can respond to it, and in the strict sense the system responds only to these modifications, not to the environment as such. When the system has been thus modified, we will say that it "contains information" about the environment. The process by which a system acquires such information can be referred to as its *detector* process.

But all systems do not respond alike to a given environmental situation. Due to differences in their internal logic or goal structure they "select" different responses. These differences may characterize a whole species of systems, or they may differ from individual to individual within a species, depending upon their built-in and learned differences. The tendency of a system to respond in a certain way will be construed as its goal or value structure. This is the sense in which a system selects behavior, and the function of doing so will be referred to as its *selector* function.

Having selected a response a system then effectuates it, and the processes or structures of doing so will be referred to as its *effector* function. Couched in this language we then say that, given its structure, the behavior of any controlled system can be diagnosed by examining the state of its detector, selector, and effector processes. For systems such as human beings we can say that these three things represent respectively the concept-perception function which processes information about the environment, the goal or value function of the individual, and the ability of the individual through muscular strength and coordination or other mechanism actually to carry out the selected behavior. The effector process normally involves a transformation of the environment or of the individual's relation to it. For the present chapter we need not be concerned whether that environment consists of nature or other human beings. The same three functions—detector, selector, and effector—very closely correspond respectively to the Stimulus → Organism → Response relationship of behaviorist psychology. They also correspond to the three functions of watching, comparing, and responding or adjusting as used by Philip Chase in his discussion of armaments races and the correspondence is not coincidental.[3] The same trio is widely found elsewhere including the head, the heart, and the hands of the Campfire Girls. Further, the detector and selector functions correspond to the distinction between factual or scientific judgments and value or preference judgments which date from at least the Fifth Century B.C.

For purposes of unified social science I have been suggesting a parallel trio in the relations between humans or organizations. Parallel to the detector, which processes information, is the *communication* which transfers it from one person to another. Parallel to the selector, which deals with values or preferences, is the *transaction* which transfers valued things from one person to another. More strictly, communications and transactions are transfers analyzed with respect to their information and value contents, respectively. The third intrasystem function is the effector, and the corresponding intersystem behavior is *organization,* which is the joint effectuation of some behavioral response or transformation of environment.

For reasons which need not be spelled out here, but which are probably intuitively obvious, organization necessarily fulfills the definition of a higher level system, whose components are the two or more individuals comprising it. To the extent the behavior of the organization is analyzed as a unit we turn back to the tools of intrasystem analysis—namely detector, selector, and effector. This then leaves the communication and transaction as the only distinctively intersystem types of behavior, and they can occur between either persons or organizations.

In this connection we should refer to the earlier distinction between acting systems and pattern systems, and the related suggestion that only chaos will result unless we sharply distinguish the two, and apply systems analysis solely to the former. In a similar spirit we must equally sharply distinguish between system action and systems. Again only chaos will result if we attempt to deal with actions of systems as if they are themselves systems. It is perfectly true that various actions of a given system are interrelated, and those who yearn to use the term may refer to these relationships as a system. But if so, it should be noted that this is a pattern system, to which, I think, systems analysis does not apply.

In this same vein I also have some reservations about calling a particular collection of things a system on the basis of a particular kind of interaction among them. I cannot state this as clearly as I would like, but will try to illustrate. General Motors is a system. It consists of many subsystems, which communicate in certain ways. It is common to list or diagram these parts and the information flows among them and to refer to the whole as a "communication system." Certainly this is not a subsystem of General Motors in the same sense that a vice president, the Buick division, or a research department is a subsystem. The latter three *act* in a sense that the "communications system" does not, since communication is itself already an action of a system. If one insists on calling it a system, I would view it as a pattern system. Given free choice I would probably avoid the problem entirely and call it simply a communication net or pattern. I would similarly talk of the *pattern* of power within organization, formal or informal, but not of the *system* of power. Here as elsewhere, if we want to develop a body of tight generalizations about systems we may have to be a bit more discriminating about the kinds of things we will call systems.

System Controls

I have not dealt directly with "systems controls." Differences in types of control, however, are implicit in the classification system itself, and are, in fact, part of the definition of some types of systems. For example, the formal organization is one which specifies—i.e., controls—its own subsystems. In present language this means that it specifies the detector, selector, and effector functions of each subsystem, and the kinds of communications and transactions they engage in, either within the main system or across its boundaries. The internal controls of the formal organization are themselves assumed to take place by communications and transactions. For example, a system does not respond to its environment as such, but only to its information about it. To the extent such information depends on the communications received, an organization's control over the information flowing to its subsystems controls their behavior. In addition, with a formal organization the control exercised by transactions is essentially that of authority, which I have defined transactionally as the ability to grant or withhold rewards (or punishments) in return for the performance or non-performance of the organization's instructions. Furthermore, whenever an organization requires a group decision, as contrasted to decision by a single executive, the decisions themselves are made by communications and transactions which are roughly the same as persuasion and payoff, respectively. If these fail, the decision is made by a dominant coalition, a group which holds the largest bloc of the particular type of power relevant to the organization. The power of the dominant coalition is itself based on its internal communications, transactions, and possible subcoalitions.

By contrast, the structure of informal organization is not specified or controlled by the main system. Furthermore, its work is done exclusively by each subsystem's pursuit of its own goals by its own techniques, not on instructions from the main system. Interactions among the subsystems of informal organizations consist of communications, transactions, and suborganizations. Should the whole society prescribe some particular types of communications, transactions, or organizations, the informal organization to that extent becomes formal. *Government* itself, of course, is a formal organization.

In summary, as I see it, each different kind of system I have suggested requires a different kind of analysis, yet (except for pattern systems) an analysis which is common for all systems within each type. That is, different propositions apply to one type of system than to others. All in all, I know no better scientific basis on which to build a classification system—a particular type of pattern system to which systems analysis does not apply!

APPENDIX

Systems: A Tentative Classification Scheme with Special Reference to the Behavioral Sciences

I. Action Systems (Acting, or behaving systems): Mutual cause-effect relations between at least two elements, *A* and *B*. A change in each element, by movement of matter-energy or information, induces a change in the other(s). All action systems are real systems.

A.   Controlled (Cybernetic) Systems: Has at least one goal of the system as a unit, and engages in some coordinated activity as a unit to achieve it. (Maintains at least one variable within some limited range.)

1.   Formal Organization: (involves multiple humans), particular case of controlled interactions of controlled subsystems.

a. Traits (defining characteristics)—

(1)   All lowest level components are human beings (though some social behavior of animals partially parallels that of the formal organization).

(2)   Communications between formal organizations and among their subsystems are semantic.

(3)   Transactions (exchanges) between formal organizations and

among their subsystems are value-based, and involve mutually contingent decisions.
   b. Levels and types (examples from Western societies)—
      (1) Whole-society level: governments & controlled economies.
      (2) Parts-of-society level: firms, churches, charities, clubs, unions, professional associations, etc.

   2. **Biological and Nonliving Systems:** Includes single human and subhuman systems. (The latter may incorporate humans as components at some points, but in a technical, not social, role.)
   a. Traits—
      (1) Components may be subsystems, human or nonhuman, or non-system elements.
      (2) Communications are nonsemantic (except perhaps with computer components).
      (3) Exchanges of matter-energy are not value-based.
   b. Examples: Organisms, organs, thermostatic controls, a plane operated jointly by pilot and instruments, computerized inventory control, TVA water-level controls.

   B. **Uncontrolled (Noncybernetic) Systems:** Has no goal and no behavior as an entity; hence does not interact as an entity with any other system. All variables of the main system fall where they will.

   1. **Informal Organization:** (Involves multiple humans), the solely human parallel of the ecosystem.
   a. Traits—
      (1) All lowest level components are human beings.
      (2) Communications among subsystems are semantic.
      (3) Transactions among subsystems are value-based.

      Note: There are not communications or transactions between informal organizations, as such, since they engage in no behavior as entities.
   b. Levels and types—
      (1) Whole society level.
         (a) A laissez-faire economy.
         (b) The social system — i.e., the part, other than governmental and economic systems, studied by sociologists and anthropologists. (In primitive societies the social system in this sense approximates the controlled, formal organization.)
      (2) Parts-of-society level: groups of persons who interact through communications and/or transactions, but who hold and execute no joint goal. e.g., a cocktail party, informal groups in firms.

2. Ecosystem: A system produced by the uncontrolled interactions of its controlled subsystems, each seeking its own, not main system goals.

   a. Traits—

   (1) At least two components are organisms or species, one of which may or may not be human. Conceivable, but not probably, ecological analysis might be applied to uncontrolled interactions of controlled, nonliving systems.

   (2) Communications among components are non-semantic.

   (3) Transactions among components are not value-based.

   b. Examples: The total interactions of all organisms in a pond or forest, the interaction between a human society and its natural environment, a predator-prey relation, the "nitrogen system."

3. Wholly Nonliving Systems.

   a. Traits—

   (1) No components are living systems, though some may be controlled. Some components, and all lowest level components within the relevant analysis, are nonsystems.

   (2) Communications are nonsemantic.

   (3) Exchanges of matter-energy are not value-based.

   b. Examples: Noncybernetic man-made machines, the solar system, a natural river system, a meteorological system.

II. Pattern Systems (Nonaction systems): Relations between at least two elements, *A* and *B*, such that A and B are consistent with one another within the criteria and constraints of some action system(s), *C*. *A* does not "act on" *B*, or vice versa; only *C* acts on either. Pattern systems do not *do* anything.

   A. Real Pattern Systems—

   1. Traits: these systems take the form of spatial or temporal patterns in matter-energy, including the behavior of action systems.

   2. Examples: the relation between the shape and structural materials of a skyscraper or pottery bowl, a family structure, a style of music or painting, the pattern of any one composition or painting, the correlation between income and voting behavior, the relation between technology and economic structure, the total pattern of a personality or a culture.

   B. Analytical or Conceptual Pattern Systems—

   1. Traits: these are conceptual constructs in the heads of humans (and possible other animals) or in computers. They may or may not be constructed to represent action systems or real pattern systems. Whatever their origin, they may at times be coded into external form, such as the Tinkertoy model of a molecule, the printed drawings and propositions of Euclidean geometry, or the projective behavior of a person suffering delusions. Although in such cases they give rise to real counterparts, their essence remains that of the conceptual form.

2. Examples: logical and mathematical systems, languages, classification systems of science, the world view of a particular society or individual, capitalism (not the capitalist bloc, which is an acting system), the relation between a particular theology and its associated moral code, the total conceptual set of an individual.

> *Note:* To the extent we focus on the conceptual set as such, the conceptual content of a culture or an individual is classified as a conceptual system. But to the extent we view it as part of the behavioral pattern of an actual person or culture it is classified as a real pattern system.

References and Notes

1. Caws, P., "Science and System: On the Unity and Diversity of Scientific Theory," *General Systems*, Vol. XIII, p. 3, 1968.
2. Maruyama, Magorah, "The Second Cybernetics: Deviation-Amplifying Mutual Causal Processes," *General Systems*, Vol. VIII, p. 233, 1963.

9
Cultural Organization

LAWRENCE K. FRANK

Social Systems and Culture

For a unified theory of human behavior, we need a conceptual framework which will enable us to recognize the many dimensions of human behavior as observed in the cultural-social environment in addition to the geographic environment. This calls for a concept of the personality in terms of the varied behavior we are seeking to understand.

One promising approach to a unified theory is to follow the growth, development, and maturation of the human child as an organism-personality from conception on. In this way we may observe how a young mammalian organism, with all the wisdom of the body, undergoes successive alterations and passes through sequences of transformations whereby he learns to live in a cultural-social field which is being maintained by the transactional processes of many human beings. Such a field need not be regarded as a separate independent organization, a more or less superhuman system or mechanism, as our classical social theory has long conceived it. In such a perspective the individual is seen primarily in terms of how he adjusts to that system or mechanism. Rather, this field may be viewed as we are learning to conceive of other fields, as arising from the patterned transactional relations of all members of the cultural-social field, each of which carries on continual intercourse with other members of the group. If one views his conduct and feelings as circular, reciprocal, transactional, occurring between and among persons, all the varied patterns, rituals, institutional practices, and symbols of group life appear as so many different modes of communication in and through which each person can approach, negotiate, and seek consummation. In this way we may view the economic, political, legal, and social patterns and transactions as defined and prescribed modes of human behavior which each member of the group must utilize if he is to communicate with others. Likewise, other persons in turn must utilize these same modes of communication so that all members of the group conform with greater or less fidelity to these sanctioned patterns.

It is to be noted that this approach differs from that typically accepted in our social sciences. We have long regarded the individual participant primarily in terms of his adherence to or deviation from these modal patterns and the prescribed use of these group-sanctioned symbols. This, it will be recalled, was the model of classic physics, and has been immensely productive. But this social model, like the physical model, either ignored the individual actor or reduced him more or less to an automaton who was assumed to act always in accordance with the accepted beliefs about individual behavior. Those who deviated too far from these assumed norms were regarded as criminal or insane.

Today we find it difficult, or at least awkward, to think in terms of transactional processes through which the individual person relates himself to his environment (geographical, cultural, social, and private) and through which the environment is related to him. This conception implies not a series of different environments, but rather the idea of an organism in a geographic environment who is enculturized, and socialized, and through those processes learns to establish and maintain a number of different modes of relations and communications with different dimensions or patternings of the organism-environment field.

This point is fairly crucial since it is just here that we are most likely to create a variety of constructs which we then reify and begin to treat as if they were actual properties of the geographic environment and operate more or less independently, above and beyond human participation or intervention.

Viewed as products of transactional processes, individual members of the group must conduct all their life activities by evoking similarly patterned relations from others. It is also to be noted that using this approach we need not reify the various data on social life, such as prices, wages, votes, marriages, divorces, crimes, etc. In classical social theory, we have treated these as entities and invoked various superhuman "forces" to account for both their short term and long term alterations. If we view these data as so many categories of human behavior channelled into different modes of social, economic, political, and legal communication, we no longer need to conceive of superhuman systems or mechanisms (the economic system, the political system, the social system) which have been guiding or coercing the individual to "adjust."

We may regard the persistence and stability of the institutional practices in a group as derived from the goal-seeking and purposive striving of the many individual human actors in the group. The individuals utilize group-sanctioned symbols and practices in order to relate themselves, to carry on their varied transactions with others. In the same way we can see cultural-social change taking place as individuals with increasing frequency deviate or depart from accepted patterns and begin increasingly to explore for and utilize new patterns which supersede the older patterns.

It may be useful to recall how the individual member of a group is subject to a similar coercion by his cultural-social life when he communicates through language with others. He cannot communicate with others nor can they communicate with him unless he utilizes the group-accepted consensual patterns which are recognized, accepted, and responded to in verbal and written communications, however idiomatically he speaks. In much the same way, one can view the coerciveness of economic, political, legal and social patterns as arising from a similar dependence upon common patterns of communication.

As we attempt to formulate a field concept, we must recognize and fully account for the more or less coercive group patterns and practices in and through which each individual person relates himself to others, participates in the public world, and thereby meets its many requirements and utilizes its opportunities in his life career. Equally we must recognize the idiosyncratic organism-personality as the source or agent of all the activities observable in group life who, while participating in the consensual public world, always does so in his idiomatic, individualized manner of living as if in a private world of his own.

As pointed out earlier, we may trace the successive steps whereby the young mammalian organism is successfully inducted into the cultural environment and the social environment. In so doing the individual is transforming his basic organic needs and physiological capacities into the patterns of functioning and of activities that progressively become goal-seeking and purposive. We can also trace the process through which he becomes oriented to the symbols and through which he learns to establish an ever-widening range of transactional relations with his environment and especially with other persons. As suggested previously, we may see the personality emerging as the child learns to participate in his cultural-social world, to relate himself through all the prescribed patterns and practices, especially through language. He becomes increasingly capable of communicating with others in and through economic, political, legal, and social patterns essential to interpersonal and group relations. But insofar as each individual child is a unique organism, developing his idiosyncratic feelings, we may regard the personality as the individualized way in which each child learns to participate with others.

It seems necessary to emphasize and re-emphasize that this personality process is not a passive adjustment to or acceptance of the consensual world with its demands, restrictions and privileges. Rather, it appears to be a very active transactional process wherein the individual imposes, imputes, or invests emotional or affective significance into each situation, person and event. This means that the human personality is engaged in a continuous process of patterning his perception of whatever he selectively observes according to his cultural-social models, but always modified, often warped and distorted, by his own idiosyncratic perceptions and feelings. While we may on the one hand emphasize regularities and group-sanctioned patterns in an individual's behavior, we must, for an adequate conception of the individual personality, give equal recognition to the idiosyncratic, the idiomatic, in all the individualized ways in which the individual both conforms to and deviates from what is accepted and required by his group.

Here we should acknowledge explicitly how these deviations from modal patterns may seriously threaten the group life and at the same time lead often to tragic self-defeat. In view of the undeniable dependence of the individual upon others from the moment of birth onward, and the clearly exhibited eagerness of the child and the youth to live in the public consensual world of the adult, we may find it increasingly necessary to look more carefully at our various theories of how stunting and distortion of individual personality takes place. It may be appropriate to suggest that the denial or failure to recognize the idiosyncratic organism, and the attempt to block or to coerce that organism into conformity with patterns that are either uncongenial or incompatible with his idiosyncratic needs, capacities and rate and mode of development, may be one large source of the tragic wastage of human personality.

We are not dealing with passive individuals awaiting a stimulus in order to respond, but rather we are observing goal-seeking purposive striving. In this striving, we observe individuals scanning the world and either attempting or failing to evoke the kinds of situations and relations in and through which they can pursue their goals and attain their deferred or symbolic consummations.

It should be underscored that this conception of communication goes beyond the bare idea of sending messages. The individual member of a group must code or translate his message in such a fashion that it will be recognized, accepted, and responded to by the individual or group to whom it is addressed. This means that in all human communications the individual person is concerned not only with the selection of the appropriate mode of communication, but what he says or transmits is governed as much by the recipient as by his own intentions or purposes. Human communications, therefore, are likely to be attempts primarily to evoke responses instead of just transmitting information or sending messages.

It is of equal significance that all human communication is essentially a circular, reciprocal, and transactional relationship. Moreover, each individual is continually exposed to a large number and a considerable variety of different kinds of communications to which he may exhibit a selective reception. He may decode or translate what he does receive largely according to the meanings and the feelings which he has imposed upon the sender of such communications.

This highly complicated situation in which all human communications take place, where two or more individual personalities are involved, each with his or her own highly individualized concerns, gives rise to continual efforts to establish and maintain patterns of communication having the minimum of ambiguity. As the development of the law, especially civil law, shows it has been a constant struggle, with never a clear outcome, to establish certain practices and modes of communication regarding such important transactions as those involving land, property, and sexual relationships. The immense load of civil litigation is eloquent testimony to the great frequency of failure in communications which involve what the lawyers call rights, titles, interests, and obligations as declared by common law and by statute.

The patterns of communication utilized in economic transactions have had a similar history of repeated efforts to establish and maintain unequivocal modes of communication. With equal emphasis we might similarly describe the patterns and practices of political transactions in terms of how each group has established certain modes and patterns for individuals to relate themselves to each other and to various groups through what we call electioneering, voting, legislation, and public administration.

Clearly, much of our individual and group living takes place apart from legal, economic, and political practice, although always subject to their limitations. We should also note in this regard the immense variety and diversity of modes of communication that are carried on with limited interpersonal relations, in the family and in many small group activities, and in and through the many so-called informal relations that make up the texture of human living.

As we observe these different categories of communication, we have moved from the more rigidly prescribed modes and patterns to those where the individualized or idiosyncratic aspect of human relations is not only tolerated but may be especially prized and sought, as in friendship, in marriage, and in more intimate groups of individuals. All group-sanctioned practice and rituals and use of symbols may be considered as modes of communication which each individual utilizes in his own way, but with a sufficient degree of conformity to function as a valid communication to and from others. In all such communications, the role of language is central since these transactional relations almost always involve some form of verbal or written communication.

The adequacy and the effectiveness of modes of communication are governed not only by words but by the use of those more or less standardized ceremonies and rituals which have been established for the different transactional processes and by the complex of patterns which we call roles. It may be useful at this point to consider roles as group codified patterns for communication, since each role serves to focus and to guide the activities of individuals in such a way as to facilitate their recognition by others, and to evoke from others a readiness to receive and to respond.

Taking a role or, more precisely, patterning one's activities, verbal and otherwise, according to the prescriptions or requirements for a given kind of communications serves to reduce the inescapable individuality and ambiguity of most human communications. At the same time it serves also to channel human activities into the recurrent patterns and regularities through which the social order is maintained.

Needless to say, any individual may attempt to communicate in language and to exhibit the patterns of a role which may or may not be relevant or appropriate to what he is attempting to communicate.

Individuals may with little or no outward indications, seek certain goals or fulfillments which are considered appropriate for one mode of communication but which they may seek through another. Thus we find individuals turn alternately to economic transactions or political transactions for attaining much the same goals. Likewise, we may observe individuals relying upon all manner of verbal persuasion and seduction to obtain responses from others with little or no adequate compensation, using deceit, fraud and whatever means will enable them to exploit another individual. It cannot be denied, however, that many individuals are, so to speak, actively seeking to be thus deceived and exploited.

The foregoing may become more immediately contributory to a unified theory of human behavior if we will see each individual member of the group as existing as an organism in the geographical environment of nature, exposed to all the impacts to which organisms are subject, but living in this multi-dimensional cultural-social field where he is also exposed to all the approaches from other individuals in his group. Here we should see each individual as having developed an extensive repertory of modes of communication both for approaches to other individuals and eliciting their responses, and for responding to their approaches. This means that he is expected to receive an almost bewildering array of messages, to be able to decode or interpret them, and to reply or respond in terms of what will be meaningful to others.

To formulate this multi-dimensional situation in terms of a conceptual model that will enable us adequately to discuss these multiple channels and modes of communication, we may have recourse to a variety of analogies which may offer some illumination and at the same time may involve some unnecessary and misleading features. Thus, we may think of the individual as both a sender and receiver of messages, being tuned to a variety of wave lengths through which he both sends and receives the various kinds of communications. We may also conceive of the individual as operating much like a radar set insofar as he is continually sending out impulses which then come back to illuminate and define the cultural-social world for him, subject to the continual corrections to which he must submit in the course of his varied transactional relations with others.

Another analogy would be that of an individual growing, developing, being enculturized, and socialized, and in that process becoming increasingly engaged in various fields which operated like an electromagnetic continuum. This implies that there is one such continuum in which he is immersed and which he helps to sustain by all of his activities. Through that electromagnetic continuum, the cultural-social field, he both sends and receives diverse communications which may be regarded as so many different kinds of perturbations or waves which the cultural-social field is capable of transmitting, always with more or less noise of distortion.

Still another analogy highlights the role of the symbol and the notion that the symbol is meaningful only insofar as it is used by people. We could say that each individual in a society plays somewhat the same role as the gene in the sense that he ensures the perpetuation, with variation of the symbol patterns and practices. The personality then can be thought of as perpetuating symbols and culture patterns from one generation to another.

Returning to the child, we see how the child is inducted into a human way of living and during the first five or six years of life is expected to master extraordinarily subtle and complicated patterns of behavior and the beginnings of different modes of communications. We may say that each generation of children must learn these patterns, undergo various transformations, take on various roles assigned as masculine and feminine in all their variations, striving to master what the human race has been struggling with from the beginning of human living. All this learning takes place in the context of interpersonal relationships, through processes of communication as the organism is transformed into a personality capable of entering into and actively participating in the maintenance of the cultural-social field. This does not mean that the child recapitulates the history of culture, but rather that in each generation we see how a child is expected to learn to live in a cultural-social field at that time, always as mediated and translated by parents, teachers and other experienced adults. Thus we can focus on the recurrent patterns and regularities of the cultural-social field, or focus upon the idiomatic personality, invoking the principle of complementarity for the assertion that both statements are valid, depending upon which point of observation we may select.

For a unified theory, it seems necessary to reconcile these seemingly diverse approaches, just as physical theory has had to reconcile particle physics and quantum physics, and to accept seemingly contradictory observations. In this connection it may be appropriate to recall that earlier in the nineteenth century scientists had made many observations and some careful measurements of heat, light, electricity, magnetism, sound, mass and gravitation. Each of these different kinds of data were then reified: heat was considered a substance, electricity a fluid, and so on. Physical theory made a great advance and began to develop a more unified theory when these different data were recognized as different ways in which fundamental energy transformations were propagated and recorded so that each one could be regarded as a manifestation of the same basic event according to the kind of instrument, measurements and recordings that were employed.

It may also be pointed out that much of our thinking has been governed by the statement of problems in which we were concerned primarily with position, velocity and the impacts of seemingly inert particles. For such problems it was both necessary and desirable to develop a technique of ever more refined measurements. The basic problem was to find some order in the disorder of events, such as is shown by gas laws where a large number of convergent events average out into certain recurrent relationships for which the concept of cause and effect has been both useful and appropriate. More recently we are recognizing the problem of divergent events and we are also becoming aware of the problem or organized complexity as exhibited by those persistent configurations which are found in atoms, crystals, plant and animal organisms, ecological complexes and cultural and social organizations and the human personality. These organized complexities call for conceptual formulations and for methods of study which recognize their multi-dimensionality and attempt to reveal the dynamic processes operating in fields to produce often different products, as contrasted with the problem of the relation of two variables to be studied in an anonymous data.

SECTION III
Human Communication
In Systems Perspective

Human Communication in Systems Perspective

This section of the volume is devoted to the presentation of a variety of interpretations of general systems theory and its applicability to human communication.

In "The Systems Approach to Communication," Klaus Krippendorff presents a discussion of several concepts of systems and associated modes of inquiry, leading to the presentation of a view of information and communication in systems perspective. Krippendorff categorizes modes of inquiry into three areas: axiomatic, scientific, and praxiological. Each of these classifications is approached in terms of systems thinking. The author also discusses the differences he sees between systems approaches and non-systems approaches in communication studies, and provides insight into common abuses of the term "system."

In "Intrapersonal, Interpersonal, and Mass Communication Processes in Individual and Multi-Person Systems," Brent Ruben suggests the value of approaching human communication from a functional perspective, which Churchman and others have considered essential to the development of a system framework. Communication is defined as information metabolism, and discussed as one of two essential processes of all living systems. Ruben elaborates a paradigm for conceiving of human communication which utilizes the individual and the multi-individual levels of analysis. He focuses on intrapersonal and socio-cultural functions of human communication.

Next, in "Communication Study in System Perspective," Aubrey Fisher places particular emphasis on the notions of open systems, feedback and equifinality, in the development of a systemic concept of communication. Here, Fisher emphasizes a view of communication where causation is multiple and reciprocal, rather than unilateral and unidirectional. Fisher further criticizes what he considers to be a blind faith in the concept of scientific predictability. Predictability, in his view, has its origins in the traditions of linear, analytic thought, and needs to be reconceptualized if it is to be of use in systems perspectives on communication.

In the following chapter, John Kim explicates the concept of feedback. Originating in the hard sciences, the notion of feedback was accepted, and in Kim's view, uncritically applied, by the behavioral sciences. He argues that the original concept of feedback is cast in a mechanistic, atomistic, and analytic tradition, and tied to the notion of unilateral, although circular, causality and concepts of closed systems. He develops the concepts of morphostasis, upward morphogenesis, and downward morphogenesis—which collectively replace the earlier mechanistic feedback concept developed in closed system contexts.

James Campbell and John Mickelson present a view of communication functions in organic systems. Consideration is given to several popular assumptions about the nature of human communication toward this end. They contend that there is no such thing as a "communication breakdown," an assumption which leads, they argue, to a futile search for a cause and remedy. Another example is provided in the discussion of what the authors label as the myth of misinterpretation. They suggest that the term "misinterpretation" implies someone's value judgment about what should have been communicated, reflective of linear, rather than systemic thought. The primary focus of the chapter is on the life cycle of the communication system. Three properties are discussed: systems are viewed as open, tending toward coherence, and following laws of parsimony.

Finally, Lee Thayer in "Knowledge, Order and Communication," demonstrates the implications of a systems view of communication from his perspective. He raises for consideration fundamental questions about the nature of man and his relation to knowledge and truth, and probes for systems-oriented explanations of these issues. Emphasizing the "informing" function of communication, he suggests the social origins of human artifacts and knowledge, and in so doing emphasizes the notions of co-determinancy, mutual-causality, and interdependency so central to general systems theory.

10
The Systems Approach to Communication

KLAUS KRIPPENDORF

Before getting to the substance of this chapter, I would like to eliminate three sources of possible misconceptions.

First, the reference to *THE* systems approach might create the impression that there is only one way systems theorists and researchers approach processes of communication. This is far from being the case. The study of systems has not yet developed a unified and universally accepted body of theory and method. One has to appreciate the coexistence of several systems theories and the stubborn persistence of many methodological problems associated with systems analysis. But I do feel that a thread connects the different systems theories and what they have in common is what will be my point of departure.

Second, like systems theory and research, the study of communication processes also is fairly recent in nature. It has obtained numerous important impulses, for example, from theories in electrical engineering, linguistics, journalism, genetics, organization theory and psychotherapy, but it has mainly flourished with attempts to solve practical problems, such as optimizing information flows, finding correlations between mass media performance and the emergence of social issues, improving human relations or developing strategies for changes in individual behavior. As a consequence, its body of theory is even less matured than that of systems theory. There are disagreements as to what the field is about, as to which problems are to be tackled and as to which criteria are to be used for evaluating possible solutions. Because of this, many researchers have found it difficult to abstract the *process* of communication from such material manifestations as the senders and receivers between which it takes place, from the messages that are transformed in the process or from the behavior that results from it. Nevertheless this is what I will have to assume to be feasible.

Third, acknowledging the coexistence of a variety of different systems approaches and of a variety of problems considered in the study of communication, I cannot do anything other than to present classifications, conceptual schemes and examples which show how knowledge about systems can be transfered and utilized in studies of communication, and which methods of inquiry into systems are also of interest to communication research. Consequently, I am not concerned with reporting on or reviewing a class of studies. Rather, I shall attempt to order them so that the relations that hold between them become transparent. My aim is therefore conceptual and perhaps programatic.

In the following study I will discuss several concepts of system and associated modes of inquiry. Then I will try to relate concepts of information and communication as used by traditional communication scholars with those implied by the different systems approaches. In the course of this discussion, I hope to show how systems approaches to the study of communication may enhance knowledge about human behavior, the behavior of large scale social institutions and public welfare.

Systems

The term "system" has come to be used in so many different contexts that its meaning is quite variable. Compare the meaning of: number systems, solar systems, communication systems, open systems, sewage systems, colonial systems, nervous systems, price systems, educational systems, value systems, the periodic system, systems analysis, systems in gambling, etc. The term has become popular in everyday discourse and, even in sales arguments its use ranks regretably high. Let me try to settle the differences not by adopting one definition and implicitly excluding others from consideration, but by presenting a three-way classification of definitions of "systems"—regarding their relative rigor according to which they are distinguished as being either "hard," "soft," or "vague"; regarding their epistemological positions, that is, in reference to their implied "axiomatic," "scientific," or "praxiological" mode of inquiry and regarding whether they delineate "static" or "dynamic" systems.

The Relative Rigor of System Definitions

Rapoport[1] used a helpful distinction between "hard" and "soft" definitions of system to which I will add the category of "vague references" for reasons that will become clear below. A hard definition is one that permits an unambiguous identification of the properties according to which something does or does not belong to the class of things defined. There must be an explicit test with a yes or no outcome. A soft definition, on the other hand, provides only an intuitive approach to the definition. The recognition of the defining characteristics then depends to a large extent on the ingenuity of an observer and there may be disagreements as to how these characteristics are to be interpreted.

A hard and in a sense minimal definition of system demands the following to be present:

(1) A set of states (each of which must be individually identifiable and unambiguously distinguishable relative to each other).

(2) One or more transformations defined on at least some of the set of states.

Examples include the algebraic operation of addition: here any two real numbers are transformed into a third real number, the sum. The transformation thus remains wholly within the set of real numbers. Another example is a phrase structure grammar: here strings of symbols are generated from two sets, set of non-terminal symbols including an initial symbol and a set of terminal symbols, and the transformation takes the form of several rewrite rules which are applied on a string of symbols until it contains only terminal symbols. Transformations may be represented materially such as in the wiring of a radio receiver with inputs, outputs and internal conditions defining the states of the states of the system. Or they may be executable with the help of mental operations, pencil, and paper, such as in deriving theorems from given axioms.

A corresponding soft definition of system would stress that there must be

(1) Many constituent elements which have some property in common.

(2) A structure, i.e., recognizable relationships among the elements which are not reducible to a mere accidental aggregation of elements.[2]

Soft definitions of this kind distinguish between systems and aggregates by determining whether the properties of the whole is more than or exactly the sum of the properties of its parts. The difference lies precisely in whether there exist composition rules, laws or principles that impose an order on the variety of elements over and above the collection of individual properties. A social group provides a good example. All of its constituent members have at least the common property of belonging to the group. In addition, one should expect at least some "pecking order," some division of labor if not a network of formal roles assigned to each member that holds the group together. Social groups are probably too complex to be studied in terms of the hard definition of system because the states each can take and the transformations that account for their behavior are not easily specifiable without ambiguity. Therefore, the social sciences often rely on soft definitions of system even though the hard one would be preferable.

It should be noted that the components that go into the soft definition of system are implied by the hard definition but the inverse is not true. The soft definition recognizes many elements. By its own, each constituent element may assume any of a set of states. Their joint states would have to be described as vectors or as many-tuples. The hard definition of system now requires that a transformation be defined at least on some of the possible vectors so that some vectors imply others. The soft definition demands that the transformation be such that the resulting relationships between elements is not reducible to an aggregate. A simple example might illustrate the case. If the elements of a system are so related that the total exceeds the sum of its parts then one should expect the system to consist of some transformation θ for which

$$\theta\,(a+b+c) > \theta\,(a) - \theta\,(b) + \theta\,(c)\,.$$

This is satisfied, for example, by

$$(a+b+c)^2 > a^2 + b^2 + c^2$$

The difference lies in the interaction terms, 2ab, 2ac and 2bc which account for "recognizable relationship among the elements," that is required by the soft definition of systems. Needless to say, the hard definition permits consideration of many transformations not all of which may imply the relationships stipulated in the soft definition of system. The hard definition of systems therefore has a wider scope and includes the systems according to the soft definition as a special case. Soft definitions are more oriented towards existing complexes while hard definitions include all conceivable complexes. On the other hand, given the empirical fact that it is difficult to treat very complex objects of interest such as beehives, social institutions, international communities by mathematical models that satisfy the hard definition, soft definitions of systems open the way to methodical investigations of a class of complex objects otherwise inaccessible.

Vague references to systems prevail mostly in colloquial but also in political discourses. I think all such references intuitively recognize that there are

(1) **a large number of constituent elements (individuals, rules, institutions, etc.) not all of which are clearly identifiable.**

(2) **complex forms of interrelations among them** *which defy understanding* **in detail giving nevertheless the appearance of wholeness and unity.**

The classical notion of organism with the defining dogma that any analysis would destroy it, is a case in point. The attitude is exemplified in such assertions as "you can't change the system." The term "system" here is likely to refer to some all-powerful supra-individual complex of integrated political-social-economic behaviors which is regarded as invariant to individual actions. In most cases not even an intuitive understanding of the relationships that account for the apparent stability of the complex is attempted. Vague references to systems are common in many ideological discussions, for example, on "the communist system" or on "the class system". Such discussions recognize the unity of the complex being referred to and tend to associate it with a few abstract traits without being able to understand how both are the consequence of the transformation defined on or the interactions between the constituents of the system. Also most of these discussions take place on such a level of abstraction that it is not entirely clear what the constituent elements of the system are. Vague references to systems attest to the inability of its user to specify—even by way of a soft definition—what the system under consideration consists of. Only a feeling of some hidden complexity is thereby expressed.

Static Systems-Dynamic Systems

The systems as defined above are static and concern configurations of states and relations among constituent elements without reference to time. The examples given reflect this notion. However, the more important classes of systems involve some kind of behavior, i.e., changes over time. Accordingly, the hard definition of dynamic system requires in addition to the two requirements that

> (3) **The transformation is defined on states at different points in time so that states at a given point in time imply states at some future point in time.**

Thus the behavior of a system is specified by a succession of states.

Soft definitions of dynamic system usually emphasize three typical consequences of transformations. They recognize the fact that nearly all living things, organizations, or societies possess a structure, as in (2), and in addition

> (3) **A behavior or a function, i.e., they show efforts to maintain a short-term steady state at which some essential structure, the "identity" of the system, remains invariant (a) in spite of changes in elements, cells or membership that go on within them and (b) in spite of changes in the environment with which they interact, and**

> (4) **A history, i.e., they undergo slow, long-term changes in those structures, i.e., they grow, develop, evolve or degenerate, disintegrate, die.**

As Rapoport points out, the soft definition of dynamic system is an idealization of the concept of organism. "Organisms, ecological systems, nations, institutions all have these three attributes: structure, function, and history; or, if you will, being, acting and becoming."[3]

Static systems like a logic, a language or a geometrical figure, do not act but certainly possess structure. On the other hand, static systems rarely occur without a dynamic one: a system of logic is manipulated by a mathematician, a language evolves within a culture, certain visual configurations are created by an artistic movement. And one can at once see the possibility of studying the mechanisms that maintain consistency, correct usage and aesthetic appearance and the history that lead to the current state of affairs.

Modes of Inquiry

Systems approaches are peculiarly intertwined with epistomology, i.e., with the way knowledge is obtained and validated. There are definitions that make a system a mathematical object without explicit or implied relation to any portion of the real world. For example, a logical system, an algebra, a calculus, or a set of recursive functions. To a mathematician, such systems are acceptable as valid only if they are consistent. Whether such systems predict some behavior is quite secondary to him. Systems that are denoted by the hard definition do not require observations either, though it is entirely possible that they conform to available data. The system properties of interest to mathematicians are all implied by the transformations which are applied on some initial configuration of symbols, most of which are written on paper. The deduction of theorems from axioms, the algebraic partitioning of quantities according to a calculus, the derivation of solutions from sets of linear equations are all examples of the axiomatic mode of inquiry into systems.

On the other hand, there are definitions—and the above soft definition of system may be considered one of them—that seek to locate system in the real world. The language in terms of which such—usually material—systems are described, is then regarded as somewhat secondary to or as only an abstraction from "objectively" existing characteristics. Systems that are defined in terms of "many interacting parts, exhibiting a joint behavior that is not predictable from the behaviors of the individual parts" attest to the frequent assumption that their existence is prior to observation, description and comprehension. Also research aimed at comparing "communication systems" of different societies[4], for example, assumes that their difference will lie in the real world, not in the properties of their respective models. While there is no need to share the implied ontological claim, such operations as data processing, hypothesis testing experimentation, and model-building always make the acceptance of a system as valid, dependent on whether a particular symbolic representation, a model, is predictive of observable states of affairs however complex they may be. This is the mode of inquiry of all predictive sciences.

There is, finally, a large class of definitions that seek to identify systems not only in a portion of the real world, but stress in addition the requirement that they serve some specified purpose. For example, according to Forrester's usage, "a 'system' means a grouping of parts that operate together for a common purpose"[5] or, according to Gibson, a system is "an integrated assembly of interacting elements designed to carry out cooperatively a predetermined function."[6] Such definitions reveal the typical engineering approach to the real world. It is therefore not surprising that the Systems Science and Cybernetics Group of the Institute of Electrical and Electronic Engineers (IEEE) designates its own domain as "the scientific theory and methodology that is common to all large collections of interacting functional units that together achieve a defined purpose."[7] In the introduction of a book on systems and human engineering by DeGreene, the same definitional attitude is adopted:

> Many workers do not consider as systems those natural organizations or structures that lack purpose, where purpose is construed to be the discharge of some function. For example, minerals can be

MODE OF INQUIRY	KIND OF KNOWLEDGE PRODUCED	CRITERIA OF VALIDITY	LIKELY SYSTEM CONCEPT
Axiomatic	Formal systems, their mathematical properties and the homomorphisms between them	Consistency	Mathematical object
Scientific	System models of particular portions of the real world	Consistency predictability	Real objects that are describable in a system language and thereby subject to tests
Praxiological	Designs for material compositions, plans or strategies for purposive actions on an environment of interacting parts	Consistency predictability utility	Real objects that are describable in a system language and at least to some extent controllable or reproducible

Fig. 10-1   Three Modes of Inquiry for General Systems Analysis

classified into one of six systems (nalite into the cubic system and calcite into the hexagonal system); however some authors[8] argue that crystals cannot be said to form a system, because they perform no function, are end-products in themselves, and do not change except by application of external force (DeGreene[9]). . . .Most people will agree that a man is a system and that a submarine is a system and that each can be characterized in terms of certain properties; most also will agree that a single perceptual motor action is not a system and that an electron is not a system. On the other hand, many will disagree as to whether a crystal or a city is a system, primarily because of differing conceptions of *purpose*. . . .[10]

For man-made systems in the broader sense, i.e. when the problem is one of optimizing a given organization with respect to a certain set of variables, when the problem is one of designing novel hardware configurations or when the problem is one of linking up man, machines and administrations to form new integral units, the notion of purpose, of mission, is clearly significant. But when one tries to comprehend as systems, living organisms, large scale social organizations such as an ant hill or a government, or mechanisms of technological growth, the *a priori* imposition of a purpose may be premature. As it turns out, whenever this kind of systems concept is applied to such existing complexes as listed above, the attributed purposes are rarely free of anthropocentric attitudes or of hidden ideological commitments, neither of which serve to make the object of analysis transparent. This is, incidentally, the prime objection raised against Parson's[11] systems theory of society by his critics (e.g.Berghe[12]). Thus, this kind of systems definition puts the researcher in the epistomological position of a judge or of an acting participant whose objective is to evaluate or control a portion of the real world and who accepts knowledge as valid whenever it is not only consistent and predictive but also in conformity with his own objective. Observable complexes that do not serve a useful function or cannot be made to serve one, are, as has been pointed out by DeGreene, excluded from this typical engineering or activist approach to real world phenomena.

To put these implicit epistomological differences between the three classes of systems definitions in context, let me use a scheme (Krippendorff[13]) initially proposed by Smith,[14] for distinguishing modes of inquiry for general systems analysis. Fig. 10.1 will make the crucial differences between praxiological, scientific and axiomatic modes of inquiry clear. The formal mathematical study of systems is obviously associated with the axiomatic mode of inquiry and relies exclusively on the hard definition of system. These activities that are aimed at observing, understanding, and predicting delineated aspects of real world phenomena belong to the scientific mode. Here, purpose enters at best as an intrinsic property of the systems as described. In addition to the hard definition of system, the

	HARD DEFINITION (1) a set of states (2) one or more transformations defined in these states (3) transformation over time	
	Static Systems	Dynamic Systems
Axiomatic Mode of Inquiry	a formal language a logic an algebra a calculus	a set of linear equations recursive functions (automata theory) stochastic communica- tion theory (Shannon)
Scientific Mode of Inquiry	the periodic system a color system a system of kinship terms (Goodenough) a network of definitions (in Webster)	a model of the national economy a model of urban growth (Forrester) a simulation model of human cognition
Praxiological Mode of Inquiry	information display of early warning system a file system, a telephone book, a switching diagram a data bank	a working data retrieval system special purpose computer the components involved in satellite communication

Fig. 10-2 Examples of Objects, Viewed as Systems from Different Perspectives

SOFT DEFINITION		VAGUE REFERENCES
(1) many elements with common property		(1) a large number of constituent units
(2) a structure relating these elements		
	(3) a behavior	(2) complex forms of interaction which defy understanding in detail
	(4) a history	
Static Systems	Dynamic Systems	
natural language	the dynamics of a city, of a beehive, etc.	
a system of meanings		
	communication within a social institution	
informal rules of proper conduct		
	an ecology	
gestalts on a photograph		
a system of traffic signs	the mass media (for law makers)	a set of drawings (for the artist)
configurations of consumer attitudes	the cognitive dynamic of psychiatric patients	the audience (for the actor)
a set of verbal instructions		"Man against Systems" (A book on Soviet Russia)
	a computer center as seen by its manager	

soft definition, which is derived from the study of such integrated wholes as biological organisms and social organizations, is common to this mode of inquiry. Those activities that aim at modifying or creating a portion of the real world belong to the praxiological mode of inquiry. It is the approach taken by designers, engineers, planners, political activists etc. who may employ hard or soft definitions as well as rely on vague references to systems.

It should be appreciated that the disagreements regarding what a system is are not merely verbal but based on fundamentally different epistemological positions relative to the real world and on different objectives for research. Each has a justifiable existence of its own. To illustrate the three-way classification so far proposed, Fig. 10.2 attempts to give some examples of systems as viewed from different perspectives.

Non-Systems Approaches

I mentioned the condition under which the three epistomological positions respectively accept certain kinds of knowledge as valid and thereby exclude certain objects as unworthy of study. This seems entirely general and not a characteristic of systems approaches alone. To appreciate what distinguishes systems approaches from others let me give a few examples of research strategies that are either excluded from systems considerations or regarded as of less interest.

The first example is found in attempts *to isolate a single and often unique event* and to describe it from various different perspectives. This is the approach of those historians who contribute to knowledge by searching out the many ways a particular historical event may be interpreted or by elaborating on one such interpretation so as to gain maximum possible depth. While judgments regarding whether an interpretation makes sense is presumably cognitively linked to the interpretations of other, possibly similar, historical events, each such contribution to knowledge then stands relatively isolated. In choosing this example I do not wish to imply that historians refuse to describe successions of states and evolutionary processes as a consequence of the interaction between the components of a system. I merely argue that a confinement to the study of isolated events—however many dimensions may be considered in each case and in whichever discipline this strategy is adopted—will not aid the understanding of how such events are related to other events, how they come about, and to what they will lead in the future.

A second example is found in attempts *to single out for attention one or more observed variables* and to try to understand their variation in terms of their dependencies on another set of observed variables. This is the approach common to much of traditional sociological research with its conceptual distinction between "dependent" and "independent" variables and in much of psychological research involving experimental designs with its synonymous distinction between "criterion" and "predictor" variables. While this methodology clearly recognizes many variables and possibly many relations holding between them, by preconceiving the direction of the possible explanations, causal or otherwise, *inter*action and mutual causal dependencies can hardly be discovered and the kind of system properties which underly the observed behavior are likely to be missed. A corollary to this is the attempt in much experimental work to hold constant as many variables as possible and to vary only one at a time. This is a method which reduces the complexity of an object of study by forcing possible complex interactions out of existence.

A third example for what a systems approach would exclude or regard as of less interest is found in attempts *to reduce an obviously complex organism by analysis into certain individually comprehensible units without regard to the relationships among them.* This has been clearly observed by Ashby who writes:

> . . . for two hundred years [science] has tried primarily to find, within the organism, whatever is *simple*. Thus, from the whole complexity of spinal action, Sherrington isolated the stretch reflex, a small portion of the whole, simple within itself and capable of being studied in functional isolation. From the whole complexity of digestion, the biochemist distinguished the action of pepsin or protein, which could be studied in isolation. And avoiding the whole complexity of cerebral action, Pavlov investigated the salivary conditioned reflex - as essentially simple function, only a fragment of the whole, that could be studied in isolation. The same strategy—of looking for the simple part—has been used incessantly in physics and chemistry. Their triumphs have been chiefly those of identifying the *units* out of which the complex structures are made.[15]

Thus, we know more about the nerve fibers of which the brain is made than about the properties of the mind. We have more and clearer conceptions for dealing with human individuals than for social organizations of which they are a part and through which they derive their significance. We have mastered the design, production, and control of cars but we fail to understand the car complex which involves many industries, the network of public roads, and the masses of drivers.

It should be noted that these examples are predominantly taken from the scientific mode of inquiry as delineated above. It would be easy to do the same for the praxiological mode. Books on system engineering and management are full of illustrations for how the systemic consequences of an improvement can lead to fantastic failures, the current ecological problems caused by excessive industrialization being a case in point. These examples all boil down to the fact that whenever many componet parts are interacting with each other to form a larger whole, the complexity that does emerge can be handled neither by in depth understanding of isolated events, nor by selectively controlling the variation of a few "independent" variables, nor by functionally isolating its constituent parts. Such strategies would presumably be avoided by systems approaches.

Let me add three more negative examples of systems approaches, now more specifically from the field of communication research. Lasswell's conception of communication research may serve as a starting point, and it should be noted that he has been one of the most influential writers in the field. Lasswell argues:

> A convenient way to describe an act of communication is to answer the following questions:
> Who
> Says What
> In Which Channel
> To Whom
> With What Effect?
> The scientific study of the process of communication tends to concentrate upon one or another of these questions. Scholars who study the "who," the communicator, look into the factors that initiate and guide the act of communication. We call this subdivision of the field of research *control analysis*. Specialists who focus upon the "says what" engage in content analysis. Those who look primarily at the radio, press, film, and other channels of communication are doing *media analysis*. When the principal concern is with the person reached by the media, we speak of *audience analysis*. If the question is the impact upon audiences, the problem is *effect analysis*. Whether such distinctions are useful depends entirely upon the degree of refinement which is regarded as appropriate to a given scientific and managerial objective. Often it is simpler to combine audience and effect analysis, for instance, than to keep them apart. On the other hand, we may want to concentrate on the analysis of content, and for this purpose subdivide the field into the study of purport and style, the first referring to the message, and the second to the arrangement of the elements of which the message is composed.

This strategy proposes not only a particular unitization of the process—in terms of sender, message, channel, receiver and effects—but it also suggests that an understanding of the process is obtainable by studying each unit *separately*. From the point of view of systems theory there is nothing wrong either with a particular unitization or with studying these units independently of each other. Also that the terms refer to units on different levels of analysis (sender and receiver are the parts of a system, the channel is a binary relation between them, the effects are presumably measured on the receiver, etc.) is not objectionable. However, if the notion of communication process does have some wholistic qualities, some supra-individual properties as many communication researchers would contend, then a research strategy which observes each unit separately could not possibly gain insights into the very properties of communication processes. It would at best discover certain primitive correlates of the process without coming to grips with what in fact accounts for it.

A second negative example comes from the same school of thought. It is an attempt by Lerner[17] to compare communication systems (his term) across different societies. Instead of describing the systems either in terms of transformations, states, relations between any of their component parts or in terms of their wholistic properties, he is satisfied merely with giving names to certain units:

Units	Media Systems	Oral Systems
Channel	Media (Broadcast)	Oral (Point to Point)
Audience	Mass (Heterogeneous)	Primary (Homogeneous)
Source	Professional (Skill)	Hierarchical (Status)
Content	(Descriptive)	(Prescriptive)

This is neither to say that such comparisons would not provide interesting insights, nor is it intended to claim that communication technologies could not constitute or be constituent parts of large systems, but the way such "systems" are described does not lend itself to any study of their properties. What is described here are a few aspects or dimensions of some "system" that is vaguely conceptualized and lies outside the researcher to be discovered in the real world. The data that are gathered in such cases do not lend themselves to an analysis of the objects as systems, rather, they are at best real correlates of systems properties and are thus far removed from the systems under consideration.

A third example, also taken from Lasswell,[18] comes a bit closer to a systems approach. It is possible, Lasswell argues, to take acts of communication as the units of analysis—thereby rendering the constituent components as less important—and to study the functions of these acts within the context of a society. Just as particular organs of an organism are assigned several roles or are specialized to perform certain tasks, so can acts of communication be assigned certain responsibilities. This interpretation comes closer to a systems approach because at least an attempt is made to relate various units of analysis, here acts of communication involving senders and receivers, and certain other social activities with each other. However it differs from a systems approach because these relations are specified not in terms of interactions from which some behavior may be concluded, not in terms of transformations which would specify how some events imply others, etc. These relations have primarily *cognitive significance.* They render the existence of each unit meaningful to the observer or to the participant of the social process by the assumption of a shared purpose. Lasswell takes for granted, for example, that something like "rationality in society" is a value toward which communication is to be employed. He assumes that communication is to serve "the maintenance of cultural heritage" and "the correlation of the various units of society with each other." He thereby ignores the possibility that communication may also highten emotionality, selectively destroy such heritage, or contribute to conflicts all of which may well be socially creative.

It is not the issue here to question the ideological underpinnings of Lasswell's conceptual frames of reference, rather, the example is chosen to demonstrate that this form of integrating the units of analysis is merely cognitive and derived from some purpose superimposed upon the whole. The explanation, while subjectively highly meaningful, has neither formal logical implications nor predictive value.

Systems Approaches to Information

After giving a few examples of research strategies that systems approaches would presumably avoid, I would like to take a more positive stance and show the kind of knowledge that such approaches could conceivably provide. Let me start by illustrating how various systems approaches would conceptualize information. Deutsch provides a particularly clear description.

> Generally, information can be defined as a patterned distribution, or a patterned relationship between events. Thus the distribution of lights and shadows in a landscape may be matched by the distribution of a set of electric impulses in a television cable, by the distribution of light and dark spost on a photographic plate, or on a television set, or by the distribution of a set of numbers if a mathematician had chosen to assign coordinates to each image point. In the case of photography or television the processes carrying this information are quite different from each other: sunlight, the emulsion on the photographic plate, the electric impulses in the cable, the television waves, the surface of the receiving screen. Yet each of these processes is brought into a state that is similar in significant respects to the state of the other physical processes that carried the image to it.
>
> A sequence of such processes forms a channel of communication, and information is that aspect of the state description of each stage of the channel that has remained invariant from one stage to another. That part of the state description of the first stage of the channel that reappears invariant at the last stage is then the information that has been transmitted through the channel as a whole.[19]

From a mathematical point of view, this concept of information is equivalent to a particular state of a static system, i.e., a configuration of elements, a pattern or a set of relations which is invariant over time under the repeated application of some transformation. Deutsch thereby emphasizes implicitly what communication theorists often wish to make explicit, that the concept of information is related to a variety of possibilities, for example, a selection of one message out of several conceivable ones, one linguistic expression out of several logically acceptable ones, one of several possible states. In other words, only in the context of several possible patterns is the one actually sent, transmitted, received or stored meaningful. Deutsch also defines a channel of communication as a transformation maintaining at least the principal features of information. He thereby recognizes the empirical fact that information rarely exists in isolation from processes that may alter the pattern, whereby destruction or maintenance are but special cases. But it is possible to abstract from such processes and to describe as static systems the complex patterns that are subjected to such transformations and this is what the systems approach to information essentially entails.

Actually, the axiomatic mode of inquiry into information is so highly developed that it defies a complete account. It has at its disposal virtually all moderately complex mathematical structures. Let me mention just two, graph theory and stochastic information theory as examples of an algebra and a calculus respectively.

In graph theory, the basic elements are nodes and the relations are links between any two such nodes. Often depicted as lines between two points, a collection of such links is called a graph and can have the appearance of all kinds of networks, trees, lattices, chains, circles, etc. When the links are asymmetrical, often depicted by arrows, the graph is called directed, when the links are assigned values (numbers, positive or negative signs, etc.) the graphs are called signed. A large number of theorems have been developed, exhibiting various properties of graphs, or mathematical operations that hold between them. Each graph can be regarded as information provided that the restrictions accepted for the particular mathematical structure allows variation, i.e., more than one graph is well formed.

Stochastic information theory is essentially a calculus of variation which allows to algebraically decompose a quantity, called entropy. Entropy is directly related to the variety of possible elements. More specifically, it is a function of the probability of such elements and thereby measures that property of information, which may be interpreted as the average number of decisions needed to specify a particular element or the average number of yes and no questions that need to be answered by a message in order to reduce a given uncertainty, etc.

In offering interpretations of this kind we leave the domain of pure syntactical concerns with consistency as sole criteria of validity, and enter the scientific mode of inquiry which seeks explanations and prediction of observable phenomena. Graphs can represent the logical structure of arguments with nodes interpreted as statements and the asymmetrical links interpreted as implications. Graphs can represent the tree structures that underlie the generation of a sentence for non-terminal to terminal symbols by rewrite rules. Graphs can represent the list structure memory of a computer. Graphs can represent the network of sociometric choices among friends. Graphs can represent associative or dissociative connections between attitudes, etc. All these examples are treated as static systems with many elements and some transformation, the set of links, defined on them. Once information is cast in those terms a host of systems properties may be found, for example, density of connection, completeness, clusters, connection between clusters, "bottle necks," circularities (tautologies), balance-imbalance. I will refrain from listing examples of uses of the stochastic theory of information. This calculus is well known in management sciences, psychology, electrical engineering, and very many other scientific endeavors.

On the praxiological level one emphasizes successful manipulation, measurable improvement or new designs over and above considerations of prediction. Thus the objects of concern can be to make more efficient such "memories" as materialized in public libraries, in the file organization of bureaucracies, in the forms that circulate within a social organization, in data banks accessible by computer or in neuronal configurations of the human brain. The design of facilities for the recording, storing, processing and displaying of information is another aim of praxiological modes of inquiry. A direct result of developments in stochastic information theory is the availability of theorems according to which efficient codes for transforming information can be constructed. The theory also suggests certain absolute limitations for manipulating information which has considerable implications for praxiology in general. The use of graph theory in constructing data storages and in evaluating search processes relative to informational pattern could provide an even more impressive list of examples of systems approaches to information.

Thus, in contrast to research strategies that focus on a single message or that measure some overall quality of several messages (and thereby deal with them as one undifferentiated unit), systems approaches to information are more inclined to look at the possible connections between a number of units. Such connections may be · specified algebraically, algorithmically or probablistically and on the basis of such relations overall systemic properties may well be deduced. Of particular interest are languages. Languages impose complex constraints on the configuration of symbols and the legitimate expressions of language are equivalent to the states of a static system. Data languages, for example, in terms of which scientific data are recorded and stored for further analysis are usually formal languages and thus conform to the hard definition of static systems. But it might well be possible to store data in the non-formal language of a source and later formalize the available information by means of some kind of content analysis. Here then one is concerned with coding a relatively rich, possibly ambiguous, and usually incompletely specifiable natural language (which can be regarded as a system according to the soft definition of system at best) into a selectively simple, hopefully unambiguous but computable formal language. The specification of successful coding instructions is a typical praxiological aim of research. The comprehension of how various people would accomplish this task is a typical scientific aim, whereas the mere study of the syntactical or semantical homomorphisms between the two languages may be an aim of the axiomatic mode of inquiry into information.

I should like to emphasize again that the mere recognition that certain messages, objects or markers constitute "a complex interlinked whole" is not sufficient for systems approaches to provide significant insights. For example, when it is the task to study the coordination across different communication channels of the contents in an advertisement campaign, then the researcher cannot just analyze each channel separately or count particular symbols as if they could be treated as independent units. He needs a representational device, formal or at least somewhat formalized to record the phenomena in their actual complexity. Otherwise references to information systems, message systems, etc. become vague and in the end indefensible. It is one thing to intuitively recognize a gestalt in a set of colored dots and quite a different thing to spell out and to describe the order that accounts for this perception. Mixing up the colored dots (or equivalently, counting their relative frequencies) would certainly not help the understanding of an apparent wholeness.

Systems Approaches to Communication

The above quotation by Deutsch indicates the intricate relation between information and communication. In fact, when one speaks of information systems one rarely excludes from consideration those transformations or hardware configurations which decompose, recombine, maintain, delete, retrieve, or recode information from larger storages—from the circulation within confined boundaries or from past records. These transformations involve time, describe behavior over time and thereby constitute dynamic systems. Deutsch labeled those transformations that maintain patterns of events, channels of communication. Generalizing the idea, we can interpret all transformations of information involving time (and possibly space) as processes of communication, whether they occur within one (e.g., thinking, memorizing) or between different organisms (e.g., transmission, dynamic interdependence), whether they maintain information or alter it, whether they involve human beings, machines, or societies.

From a mathematical point of view, communication is a property of dynamic systems. While one can, according to Deutsch, interpret any transformation of information as a channel of communication, what makes the axiomatic mode of inquiry into dynamic systems particularlv powerful is that such a transformation may be decomposed without loss into partial transformations within and among the component parts of a system, i.e., into a set of dynamic subsystems *and* into a network of communication channels among them which, taken together, account for the behavior of the whole system. If the transformation of the whole can be regarded as a mere aggregate or composite of the transformations within its parts, then communication between these parts is absent. As a primitive example, consider the transformation defined on the values of Z:

$$z_{t+1} = z_t^2$$

If the system is composed of three parts, A, B, and C, and their respective values are related to the whole by:

$$z = a + b + c$$

and if it can be shown that:

$$a_{t+1} = a_t^2$$

$$b_{t+1} = b_t^2$$

then A and B are independent from each other and from C, while both communicate with the latter. The communication implied by this transformation can be depicted as in Fig. 10.3.

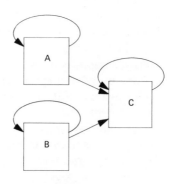

Fig. 10-3

The arrows to C represent the remaining partial transformation:

$$c_{t+1} = c_t^2 + 2(ab + bc + ac)_t$$

Incidentally, as a channel of communication, the system has two points of stability, at $z=0$ and at $z=1$, where it reliably maintains the pattern (a,b,c): (0,0,0,), (0,0,1), (0,1,0), (1,0,0). And it might be noted that the mathematical theory of communication would assess this channel to have a transmission capacity of two bits of information.

An example of a system without communication among its component parts is given in the following transformation of values of Z:

$$z_{t+1} = 2z_t$$

Provided that, when references to the three components are introduced as before, it can be shown to be fully decomposable into three summatively equivalent transformations of values of A, B, and C:

$$a_{t+1} = 2a_t$$
$$(a+b+c)_{t+1} = 2(a+b+c)_t \text{ implies } b_{t+1} = 2b_t$$
$$c_{t+1} = 2c_t$$

If this were to be the case then it must be concluded that the components are isolated from each other, nothing is transmitted across, all effects remain within each component, and consequently communication is absent.

Although this example is too simple to lend itself to interesting real life interpretations, it serves to demonstrate how the mathematical idea of communication emerges in the process of decomposition. Whenever it can be shown that effects between a set of components at one point in time and that set of components at another point in time are confined within each component, no evidence for communication exists. Conversely, when an attempted decomposition would result in losses of specificity, communication as an explanatory construct is indispensable. When such transformations are interpreted as channels of communication—as Deutsch is suggesting—one can say that the axiomatic systems approach provides rigorous procedures to decompose a complex channel of communication into the channels within and among each component part of the system. Systems theory and communication theory are thereby shown to be coextensive.

In the scientific mode of inquiry, with its emphasis on predictability and adequate representation of real world phenomena, communication is likely to be conceptualized in terms of the conditionality over time of one part of an observable complex on another. Thus, when the ideas that someone possesses can only be explained by recourse to someone else's prior linguistic behavior, then communication must be said to have taken place. When no such explanation is justified, the relation of communication is empty. When the presence or absence of an event at one point in space imposes some constraint on the subsequent occurence of events at another point in space, then communication is the suitable basis for explanation, its direction being the direction of time as well as that in space. In its most simple form, the answer to the question: "Who says what to whom, in which channel and with what effect" involves the account of a communication process provided that the answers to all of the question's components are conjoined.

What the systems approach to communication adds to this elementary notion of communication is a methodology for dealing not with one communication link at a time but with a large number of them simultaneously, not with binary communication relations between a single sender and a single receiver but with many-valued relations among a possibly large number of communicators, not with one-way processes of communication but with interaction and complex circular flows. Once it is established that a particular system is a model of a portion of the real world, the system can be analyzed and subjected to numerous formal tests. Communication is just one of many properties of dynamic systems.

The significance of communication as an explanatory construct for complex social systems has been expressed by Wiener:

> The existence of Social Science is based on the ability to treat a social group as an organization and not as an agglomeration. Communication is the cement that makes organizations. Communication alone enables a group to think together, to see together, and to act together. All sociology requires the understanding of communication. What is true for the unity of a group of people, is equally true for the individual integrity of each person. The various elements which make up each personality are in continual communication with each other and affect each other through control mechanisms which themselves have the nature of communication.
>
> Certain aspects of the theory of communication have been considered by the engineer. While human and social communication are extremely complicated in comparison to the existing patterns of machine communication, they are subject to the same grammar; and this grammar has received its highest technical development when applied to the simpler content of the machine.[20]

But in spite of this agreed upon significance, one cannot hide the fact that the complexity of observable situations often exceeds the capacity of available mathematical systems methodology. And in the face of this methodological lag, scientists who wish to understand at least something about social organization have chosen different strategies, of which I will discuss three. The first one is the attempt to isolate units that can be conveniently studied. I have criticized this strategy earlier and I am afraid to say that communication research has largely resorted to this approach by assuming the basic unit to be a binary communication relation between sender and receiver. The study of mass communication as a one-way flow of messages from an institutionalized source to a mass audience is a prime example of isolating an object of study for the sake of convenience with little regard for the systemic context of the process. What is needed in such a situation are studies that look simultaneously at many channels of communication and deduce some interesting system properties from it, one of which may well be the purpose toward which the whole system seems to be oriented, regardless of the will of the human components of the system.

The second strategy of coping with unmanageable complexity is to abandon the idea of detailed predictions and thereby gain models of certain abstract parameters of the observable complexes. Statistical characterizations of communication processes provide typical examples for this strategy. The stochastic theory of communication can be interpreted as a calculus for multivariate causes. On the basis of their distributions, predictions regarding quantitative limitations of channel of communication and control, regarding time required for processing particular forms of information, regarding tolerable levels of noise within a channel, etc. can be ascertained. I should mention that contrary to common applications this calculus is not limited to binary communication. As Ashby[21] has shown, quantities of multivariate transmission provide very powerful concepts for analysing information flows in complex systems.

Another example of this strategy is to develop indices of a variety of measurable properties and observe, and describe or postulate the transformation that these indices might follow over time. Economic models take this approach quite explicitly. Recently, Rapoport[22] suggested this strategy to account for the behavior of the large corpora of verbal output that societies produce. Presumably one would find that such corpora respond to social changes or slowly evolve over time as a consequence of interaction within a corpus. Clearly there are many problems to be solved: how the component parts of such corpora are to be identified, what the interaction laws will look like, to what extent such corpora are in fact distinguishable from their social environments. In the context of this strategy of systems research in communication, I might add numerous attempts to develop indices for systems properties such as the communication density, the stability of a behavior, and the mobility of members. These are defined over relatively complex forms, behave like variables, and may be used as the components of an abstract system to be specified.

A third strategy of systems approaches to communication in complex situations is to develop a set of analytical concepts which are in principle derivable from mathematical systems models but are—because of the difficulty of their formulation—measured directly on the object under study. This approach is promoted by what Rapoport calls soft definitions of system. In terms of this approach, one could study evolution, i.e., the slow higher order changes in organizational structure, as a communication channel between parent and offspring generations of a species which takes place in the face of interaction with an environment. Mutations can be interpreted as noise. Based on common experiences, one can say that all forms of organization interact with their respective environments so as to maintain certain essential variables such as temperature or self-identity. It has been shown that this property is related to circular flows of information. A usual problem is to delineate the boundary between an organization, and its environment. But once this is accomplished, numerous hypotheses can be tested in those terms. For example, as the size of a social organization increases, its boundary processes proportionally less information than is processed internally. Carried to its logical conclusion, such an inverse relationship would presumably shed light on optimal sizes of social organization as a function of data processing facilities available to them. Cells, organs, organisms, groups, organizations, and societies are said to form hierarchies of subsystems. This concept leads to the study of various abstractions from information penetrating an organism at its boundary and on the lowest level of abstraction. One can assess the decoding capabilities of the boundaries of various organisms and test hypotheses as to which quantities of information would result in information overload and how each level of organization reacts to this event. Such questions are very much associated with the work of Miller [23,24,25] in whose systems approach the concepts of information and communication play the most important roles.

The praxiological mode of inquiry into systems is focused on the manipulation and control of a portion of the real world. When we talk loosely about communication systems, we usually refer to some piece of technology which is designed to mediate between certain selected parts of society that would otherwise be independent or not interacting so strongly. The implementation of communication technology—whether it be the postal service, the mass media, or the communication satelite—creates complex dynamic interdependencies which are increasingly difficult to study. Another important communication system is created by the use of computers in social organizations, for storing large amounts of data or for decision-making. Clearly, such technology is. designed and ultimately evaluated by someone according to some criteria of utility. But there are also other objects of praxiological concern for communication: studies aimed at improving human relations by opening up certain channels of interpersonal communication among the employees of a company; studies aimed at relieving people of their poverty by bringing them into contact with work opportunities and knowledge about their behavior relative to each other; studies aimed at making education in the classroom more efficient; and, finally, studies in psychotherapy aimed at eliminating mental illness. Knowledge about communication is here evaluated primarily according to whether it allows an actor to influence a process in question, whether "it works," whether the objective would be obtained as a consequence, i.e., according to a criterion of utility.

On the praxiological level, available knowledge about communication is even more limited. The scope of mathematical models of communication is currently quite narrow and the conceptual frameworks implied by soft systems definitions do not always lend itself to accurate predictions and control. In the face of the need to act upon a complex environment, the strategy that has been followed usually involves, as a first step, the isolation and precise definition of a problem. The communications engineer could not start until the range of possible inputs and the transformation which he is to realize materially are well specified. Similarly, a psychotherapist could not start the treatment until he accepts a definition of himself, of the patient's problem and of what constitutes his success. It follows that the current state of praxiological knowledge about communication often optimizes communication locally while creating unmanageable complexity globally. For example, the installation or improvement of mass communication technology is certainly enjoyed by a majority, for whatever reason. But this relatively simple one-way communication technology also links up with or influences other communication patterns of society which relate individuals in ways that had been evolved slowly before the excessive use of such technology. In addition to creating large publics and to coordinating—knowingly or not—the behavior of many individuals towards specific topics, objects or people, complex webs of institutional and interpersonal feedbacks are created which are not yet fully understood. We do not even know the ultimate danger of reorganizing society around the invention of such communication technologies. By way of analogy, I would like to point to the ecological problems we face today which are caused by a technological development that started a long time ago. In the last analysis, the reliance on communication technology is probably more consequential than the use of chemicals which has polluted our water and the atmosphere as well as poisoned our food. Therefore, unless we learn to cope with large scale systems of which such technology is a part we may well face a crisis that is more disastrous than what we have experienced so far.

It should be noted that definitions of communication which link the concept to some intentionality of the sender are wholly consistent with the praxiological mode of inquiry into communication. The scientific mode of inquiry would regard this as a special case of the transmission of information, one that is presumably explainable in terms of circular flows of information of which the actor, claiming an intention, is a part. In terms of systems theory, it is easily seen that the praxiological mode of inquiry always has some built-in narrowness, it sacrifices understanding the large context in favor of controlling a small part. Perhaps this narrow focus is necessary for rational action. But, particularly when the inquiry concerns complex processes of social communication, a consideration of systems that are as large in scope as possible might be the only way of comprehending how we live.

References and Notes

1. Rapoport, Anatol, "Modern Systems Theory—An Outlook for Coping with Change," *General Systems*, Vol. 15, 1970, pp. 15-25, included in chapter 3 of this volume.
2. Piaget, Jean, *Structuralism*, New York: Harper & Row, 1970.
3. Rapoport, Anatol, "Modern Systems Theory—An Outlook for Coping with Change," *General Systems*, Vol. 15, 1970, pp. 15-25, included in chapter 3 of this volume.
4. Lerner, Daniel, "Communication Systems and Social Systems," *Mass Communications*, Wilbur Schramm (ed.) Urbana, Ill.: University of Illinois Press, 1960, pp. 131-140.
5. Forrester, Jay W., *Principles of Systems* (2nd Preliminary Edition), Cambridge, Mass.: Wright-Allen Press, 1968.
6. Gibson, Ralph E., "A Systems Approach to Research Management," Part I, *Research Management*, Vol. 5, No. 4, 1962, pp. 215-228.
7. Rowe, W. D., "Why Systems Science and Cybernetics," *IEEE Transactions on Systems Science and Cybernetics*, SSC-1 No. 1, 1965, pp. 2-3.
8. Gerardin, Lucien, *Bionics*, New York: McGraw-Hill, 1968
9. DeGreene, Kenyon B., *Systems Psychology*, New York: McGraw-Hill, 1970.
10. *Ibid.*
11. Parsons, Talcott, *The Social System*, Glencoe, Ill.: Free Press, 1951.
12. Berghe, Pierre L. van den, "Dialectic and Functionalism: Toward a Synthesis," *American Sociological Review*, Vol. 28, 1963, pp. 695-705.
13. Krippendorff, Klaus, "Values, Modes and Domains of Inquiry into Communication," *Journal of Communication*, Vol. 19, No. 2, 1969, pp. 105-133.
14. Smith, Nicholas M., *The Role of Intuition in the Scientific Method*. A paper presented to the 8th Conference on the Design of Experiments in Army Research, Development and Testing, sponsored by the Army Mathematics Steering Committee, conducted at the Walter Reed Institute of Research, Walter Reed Army Medical Center, Washington, D.C.: October 26, 1962.
15. Ashby, Ross W., "General Systems Theory as a New Discipline," *General Systems*, Vol. 3, 1958, pp. 1-6.
16. Lasswell, Harold D., "The Structure and Function of Communication in Society," *Mass Communications*, Wilbur Schramm (ed.), Urbana, Ill.: University of Illinois Press, 1960, pp. 117-130.

17. Lerner, Daniel, "Communication Systems and Social Systems," *Mass Communications,* Wilbur Schramm (ed.), Urbana, Ill.: University of Illinois Press, 1960, pp. 131-140.
18. Lasswell, Harold D., "The Structure and Function of Communication in Society," *Mass Communications,* Wilbur Schramm (ed.), Urbana, Ill.: University of Illinois, pp. 117-130.
19. Deutsch, Karl W., *The Nerves of Government:Models of Political Communication and Control,* New York: Free Press, 1963.
20. *Ibid.*
21. Ashby, Ross W., "Two Tables of Identities Governing Information Flows within Large Systems," *Communications of the American Society for Cybernetics,* Vol. 1, No. 2, 1969, pp. 3-8.
22. Rapoport, Anatol, "A System-Theoretic View of Content Analysis," *The Analysis of Communication Content: Development in Scientific Theories and Computer Techniques,* George Gerbner, Ole R. Holsti, Klaus Krippendorff, William J. Paisley, Philip J. Stone (eds), pp. 17-38.
23. Miller, James G., "Living Systems: Structure and Process," *Behavioral Science,* Vol. 10, No. 4, 1965, pp. 337-411.
24. Miller, James G., "The Nature of Living Systems," *Behavioral Science,* Vol. 16, No. 4, 1971a., pp. 227-301.
25. Miller, James G., "Living Systems: The Group," *Behavioral Science,* Vol. 16, No. 4, 1971b., pp. 302-398.

11

Intrapersonal, Interpersonal, and Mass Communication Processes in Individual and Multi-Person Systems

BRENT D. RUBEN

For communication study, one of the particularly significant contributions of C. West Churchman is his application of the concept of functionality. In *The Systems Approach,* Churchman differentiates between what might be termed *functional analysis,* which he contends is essential to the development of a systems orientation, and *descriptive analysis* which he believes is antithetical to system thinking. To make clear the difference, Churchman uses the automobile as an example. Where a descriptive analysis of an auto begins by listing the parts: wheels, axles, alternator, frame, and so on, analysis of function proceeds instead by considering how automobiles are used—what they are for.[1] The strength of this paradigm when applied to human communication study is that it draws one's attention to the predominantly descriptive traditions reflected in the majority of definitions of communication, while at the same time suggesting an alternative approach.

Descriptive Analysis in Human Communication Thought

That communication has been conceived of primarily in terms of "how-it-works," becomes apparent from even a most cursory consideration of the history of thought about the phenomenon. Since Aristotle set forth his concept of rhetoric, communication has primarily been examined in descriptive, component-oriented fashion:

> Since rhetoric exists to affect the giving of decisions. . . the orator must not only try to make the argument of his speech demonstrative and worthy of belief, he must also make his own character look right and put his bearers, who are to decide, into the right frame of mind.[2]

With his concern for a person who speaks, the speech to be given, and the person who will listen, Aristotle underscored in *Rhetoric* the same elements of communication as do most contemporary descriptions.

The descriptive mode of analysis was also evident in the classical portrayals of communication advanced by Lasswell,[3] Shannon and Weaver,[4] and Schramm,[5] whose models focus generally upon the same components as did Aristotle.[6] Lasswell,[7] of course, posited the well-known "*Who* said *what* in *which channel* to *whom* with *what effect,*" and Shannon and Weaver[8] listed source, transmitter, signal, receiver, and destination as primary ingredients in their analytic scheme which was intended to characterize communication in mathematical terms. Similarly, Schramm[9] referenced the elements of source, encoder, signal, decoder, destination.

The more elaborate "two-step flow" paradigm advanced by Katz and Lazarsfeld[10] evidenced a similar descriptive focus. In that definition, communication was conceived of in terms of messages flowing from impersonal sources to opinion leaders who in turn influenced non-leaders through interpersonal means. Riley and Riley[11] provided a scheme which integrated aspects of previous models yet maintained a primarily descriptive component orientation, though giving some attention to sociological processes, structures, and functions.

The models provided by Westley and MacLean,[12] and Berlo[13] were intended to focus more upon communication as a *process*,[14] and particularly the Westley-Maclean[15] model better accommodated the communicative implications of non-purposive behavior than had previous characterizations. Broadened in application and increased in sophistication, these two pervasive models further reflected, and no doubt contributed significantly to, the penchant for descriptive portrayal of communication.

Speech-communication schemes, while often considering more elements, have maintained a predominantly descriptive focus. Barker and Kibler[16] provide a useful compilation of the variety of dimensions in terms of which writers in speech communication have chosen to characterize and examine communication. Their list includes: verbal and nonverbal communication; interpersonal, intrapersonal, group, mass and cultural communication; oral and written communication; formal and informal communication; intentional and unintentional communication; and logical and emotional communication.[17]

Brooks,[18] in like manner, presents a taxonomy of communication which focuses upon verbal, interpersonal, nonverbal, dyadic, and small group communication, and utilizes the basic Lasswellian paradigm of an initiator, message, and recipient(s). Samovar and Mills[19] offer a model which also stresses the elements of encoder, message, channel, and receiver. Miller,[20] Becker,[21] and Hasling[22] similarly conceptualize communication descriptively in terms of a speaker, messages, and listener(s).

In mass communication, descriptive analysis and consequent emphasis upon specific components has perhaps been more pronounced than in the writings on speech-communication.[23] The "how-it-works" orientation has been manifest in the tendency to focus upon the technology of the mass media as if it were the same as the mass communication *phenomenon*. One finds, for example, the terms mass media and mass communication used more or less interchangeably in Barnouw,[24] Stephenson,[25] and DeFleur.[26] This same descriptive focus leads other popular authors to fail to differentiate conceptually between mass communications (messages), and mass communication. This is the case, for example, in Schramm;[27] Emery, Ault and Agee;[28] and Rivers, Peterson and Jensen.[29]

Typically stressing *channel*—and sometimes *message*—as opposed to *source* and *receiver,* such schemes for conceiving of communication (and mass communication) have both reflected and reinforced the descriptive orientation.

The writings of journalism, taken to a generic level of analysis, indicate a similar proclivity for descriptive analysis, although the focus is generally more upon the *message* than *source, channel,* or *receiver.* Hohenberg,[30] Brown,[31] and Charnley[32] are examples. The literature of persuasion, whether approached from speech, social psychology, or mass communication evidences this pattern also, as Miller and Burgoon[33] suggest by implication. The works of Rosnow and Robinson,[34] Bettinghaus,[35] and Rogers and Shoemaker[36] are illustrative.

Clearly, there has been a great deal of attention devoted to models explaining how *communication works*. Like the definition of the automobile in terms of its parts and how they work together, communication has been characterized largely by focusing upon *source, message,* √*channel,* and *receiver* and operational interactions between them.

What is noticeably lacking are models of the phenomenon which utilize functional analyses of the sort Churchman suggests. Few researchers who conceive themselves (and are conceived by others) to be in the field of communication appear to be focusing their efforts in any direct fashion toward an exploration of the *functions* of communication— what it is for, and how it is used.

Functional Analysis in Human Communication Thought

There are no doubt various explanations for this imbalance. Some would argue that the attention given to descriptive analysis indicates the lack of appropriateness, validity, and/or utility of functional modes of characterization. Others would point out that findings of descriptive analysis seem to have a clearer relevance for communication practitioners (e.g. journalists, speakers, librarians, writers, announcers, managers, information system managers, counselors, etc.) and that directions of scholarship in the field have been impacted centrally by a desire for findings which will help the practitioner on an operational level. Others have suggested that the shape and direction of scholarship in communication has come about more by default—through socialization and homogenization of individuals entering the field—than by conscious choice.

For these and perhaps other reasons many—if not most—of those contributions which are most central to characterizing human communication in functional terms, have been provided by individuals whose work falls outside the boundaries of "the field" as it is generally defined in reviews of the literature in many major journals and volumes.

One such source of analysis of function in human communication is provided in the works of Berger,[37] Luckman,[38] Holzner,[39] and McHugh,[40] whose research focus upon the social origins of information and knowledge and functions of the informational relationships between the individual and social reality.

Other sociologists, including Goffman,[41] Duncan,[42] and Blumer,[43] have provided particularly useful analysis for understanding communication in terms of its social functions.

Another pertinent area is general semantics with its focus upon the functions of information for science and reality mapping. The work of Korzybski,[44] Johnson,[45] and Brown,[46] are especially relevant here.

Additionally, the general semanticists' interest in human information ecology has in many respects been complimented by work on the role of communication in human adjustment of Rogers;[47] Ruesch;[48] Bateson;[49] Watzlawick, Beavin, and Jackson;[50] Grinker,[51] Shands,[52] Speigel,[53] and Quill.[54]

Still another source of input for functional research on human communication and individual behavior comes from a group of scholars with a psychological background. The writings of Thayer;[55] Allport;[56] Church;[57] Kelley;[58] Maslow;[59] Schroder, Driver and Streuffert;[60] and Lindsay and Norman[61] are among these contributions.

Other works, by individuals often not centrally associated with communication, and yet expecially useful for conceiving of communication in functional terms, have been provided by Delgado,[62] Young,[63] Laszlo,[64] and Smith,[65] relative to the neurophysiological, biological, epistemological, and cultural functions of information for man.

Given this wide-ranging diversity, it is apparent that a functional approach to human communication would have, of necessity, a multidisciplinary heritage. And to the extent that one seeks to develop a system paradigm that meets the criteria suggested by von Bertalanffy, Boulding, and Rapoport, as well as by Churchman, the framework must be valid and useful in cross-disciplinary application.

As a foundation for such a conceptualization of communication and communication systems, J. G. Miller's [66] view of information processing as one of two basic processes of living systems is especially valuable. Building on this notion, communication can be meaningfully defined as *the process of information metabolism,* and understood to be of parallel importance to living organisms as the processes involved in the metabolism of matter-energy. In this light, communication can be regarded as essential to the birth, growth, development, change, evolution, and survival or death of all that is human.[67]

To further refine one's scheme for categorizing the processes of information metabolism, and hence communication, the concept of *symbol* is important.[68] There are, for man, but two sorts of possible exchanges with the environment: those involving bio-physical transactions and those involving symbolic transactions. And in a number of instances the two operate conjunctively. While man is clearly not the only living organism that processes information about his milieu, nor is he the only animal who can be said to utilize language, man alone has the capacity for inventing, accumulating, and attaching meanings and significance—through symbols—to the entirety of his biophysical and social environment and to himself.

Unlike other non symbol-using animals, man uniquely has the capacity and the necessity of accumulating information cast in the form of knowledge, behavior and culture for diffusion to and inculcation among his contemporaries and members of subsequent generations. Further, unlike other non-symbol-transacting animals, man alone has the capacity and therefore the necessity of acquiring membership in the various social collectivities upon which he depends solely through the identification and internalization of the significant symbols of the social unit.

The study of communication systems is, therefore, logically understood as the study of the role of symbols, symbolization, and symbol internalization in the creation, maintenance, and change of all human individual and multi-individual organization.

In order to develop a communication system paradigm, it is therefore necessary to develop a scheme for categorizing information-metabolizing structures in terms of the symbolic processes involved. For present purposes, the first such classificatory unit will be labelled the *individual system* and the second, the *multi-individual system.*[69] In considering the former, the focus of this chapter will be upon what can be termed the *intrapersonal functions of human communication.* Examination of the multi-individual system will center on the *interpersonal and socio-cultural functions of human communication.* The processes at the first of these levels of analysis will be termed *personal communication,* and those at the second level, *social communication.*

Personal Communication

Personal communication can be thought of as sensing, making-sense-of, and acting toward the objects and people in one's milieu. It is the process by which the individual informationally fits himself in (adapts to and adapts) his environment.

As the individual organizes himself in and with his milieu, he develops ways of comprehending, seeing, hearing, understanding, and knowing his environment. Largely as a consequence of this process, no two individuals will view the objects or people in their environment in the same way.

What an individual becomes is therefore a function of having organized himself in particular ways with the objects and people in his milieu. Allport[70] describes this fundamental process of personality development as becoming. General semanticists refer to this process as abstracting and speak of it in terms of a mapping of the territory.[71] Thayer refers to this as in-formation.[72] In a neuro-physiological context one could think of personal communication as a process of intracerebral elaboration of extracerebral information.[73] Berger[74] characterizes the process as internalization.

From a variety of disciplinary viewpoints then, personal communication can be conceived of as that active process by which the individual comes to know and be in relationship in his world. Unlike lower animals who are genetically organized with their environments in relatively fixed and determinant ways, man must organize himself.[75] He can and must invent his rules for attaching significance and meaning to his milieu and the people in it. It is man's organize-ability which would seem to most clearly distinguish him from lower organisms, and which here serves to clarify the nature of *personal* communication.

The necessary condition for these complex adaptive functions may be termed *reality integration*, and understood to be a most basic and essential information metabolizing function of personal communication. It is simply that function which allows and compels the individual to organize himself with—to come to know, to map the territory—his milieu, and therefore to become what he is and will be.

Personal communication, and the *reality integration function* can be categorized based upon the particular adaptive functions subserved. Such a classification includes: 1) Biological adaptation; 2) Physical adaptation; 3) Interpersonal adaptation; 4) Sociocultural adaptation.

Biological Integration

Through personal communication an individual develops, maintains, and alters the knowledge and "maps" necessary for his biological functioning. He comes to understand procreation and with whom, where, when, and under what circumstances it is appropriate. With regard to the processes involved in the metabolism of matter-energy, he comes to know what, when, where, and how to eat and excrete wastes. Through personal communication the individual learns about those aspects of his physical and biological environment which may threaten his well-being as a living system. He also comes to understand what data he must gather, how the data are to be processed, and how decisions are to be made in order to avoid collision with other structures; some of which are stationary, and others having patterns and rates of movement he must discern.[76] Personal communication functions also to enable the development and assertion of the individual's identity and territoriality as a human creature distinct from, and yet dependent upon, all others of the species. This occurs through the use of symbolic and geographical distancing utilizing a wide range of symbolic markers such as beach blankets, houses, autos, clothes, perfumes, hair stylings, and so on.

Physical Integration

Personal communication also functions to enable the individual to develop, maintain, and alter his explanations of the *non-human objects* in his environment. For present purposes, it is meaningful to distinguish between physical matter which is contrived and that which is non-contrived. Within the category of contrived objects are those non-living things which man has created, like cars, tools, buildings, furniture, and processes like sawing, lawn-mowing, writing, and so on. Personal communication also enables the individual to develop and maintain understandings of physical properties and processes such as the atmosphere, metabolism, geological structures, evolution, rivers, communication, plants, animals, living/dying as well as other substances and processes generally assumed not to be human in origin.

Interpersonal Integration

One increasingly popular research area regards the functions of personal communication through which the individual comes to conceive of people—himself and others. It is this function of personal communication that enables the individual to know who he thinks he is, what he is like and who and what others in his milieu are about.

Sociocultural Integration

One of the least familiar, yet centrally important functions of personal communication, relates to the symbolic reality systems of the various multi-person organizations in which all individuals operate. It is through personal communication that the individual comes to know what is informationally and behaviorally expected of him if he is to participate in such collectivities as friendships, passengers on an elevator, families, clubs, fraternities, religious sects, political parties, professional and vocational groups, societies, and so on.

Personal communication functions to enable the individual to internalize, symbolically, the accepted organizational truths, operating

principles, habits, norms, rituals, protocol, conventions, explicit and implicit goals, required competencies, ethical standards, laws, rules, and so
on. He learns what most people seem to say, what most people seem to
do, how they dress, and where he fits.

Of particular importance also is the learning personal communication affords relative to the accepted modes of explanation. In an organization of social scientists, for example, "science" provides the explanatory
framework which one must learn. In another organization, a "religious"
mode of explanation may be more popular, etc.

A related function of personal communication regards an individual's
symbol internalization of prescribed and prohibited behaviors, which are
both implicit and explicit in nature. The individual learns the nature and
price of membership, "the coinage of the realm,"[77] the significant and
sacred symbols, flags, words, behaviors and the consequences of failure
to posture oneself in an organizationally consistent manner.

At the level of analysis of the individual system then, personal communication operates such that the individual is able to identify and internalize through symbolic information processing those biological,
physical, interpersonal, and sociocultural realities necessary for him to
adapt in his environment.

Social Communication

Social communication is the process underlying *intersubjectivization,*
a phenomenon which occurs as a consequence of public symbolization
and symbol utilization and diffusion. It is through this information
metabolism process that the world we know is defined, labeled, and
categorized, our knowledge of it shared and validated, and our behavior
toward it and one another regularized and regulated. It is through this
same process that multi-person organization, social order, control and
predictability are achieved.[78] The most basic transaction of social communication is two or more individuals organizing with one another, knowingly or not, in an effort to adapt to or adapt their environment.[79]

Because of the nature of human communication—and personal communication—achieving this goal requires active participation in the invention, construction, and maintenance of a plethora of overlapping and
non-overlapping organizations.[80] Organization through social communication varies from the relatively simple informational-behavioral interdependency patterns man creates and perpetuates with other
passengers riding an elevator, to the extremely complex and varigated organization necessary to the emergence, continuity, and evolution of a
society.

Clearly then, the specific consequences of social communication may
vary greatly from one multi-person organization to the next in terms of
complexity and function. The basic information metabolizing processes

by which these organizations are initiated and maintained, however, do not. When people organize with one another, in an elevator, a friendship, or a society, they discover, create, and share informational and behavioral realities.[81] In so doing, the whole they define together becomes more than a simple sum of the parts. This discovery, creation, sharing, socialization process can be termed intersubjectivization. Were there no intersubjective reality structures, there could be no multi-person organization. Thus "values," "norms," "knowledge," and "culture" may all be viewed as instances of intersubjectivated realities, defined and diffused through social communication.

Considered in this light, reality definition, standardization, and diffusion can be viewed as both necessary and sufficient conditions for social organization and joint-adaptation, and may be understood to be the primary function of social communication. The process of social communication can be further delineated in terms of particular biological, physical, and socio-cultural functions.

Biological Definition

Through social communication, multi-individual organizations define, label, and standardize information-behavior patterns relative to a wide range of human biological functions. Intersubjectivizations, variously termed knowledge, norms, and rituals that relate to sexual and reproductive practices, food consumption and excretory functions, medical care and medication are exemplars. It is not the intention to detail specifics in each case here, and it is adequate simply to note the rather obvious point that within multi-person systems rather specific socially defined legal, medical, and normative guidelines are constructed and shared with regard to where, under what conditions and with whom sexual relations are appropriate. Similarly, conventions are created and maintained with regard to conventions of food procurement, preservation, and preparation as well as excretion. It is also clearly through social communication that both organic and psychological illness and health are defined, and labels created, agreed upon and attached to what are conceived to be maladies.[82] It is this same process by which strategies for treatment are invented, tested, applied or discarded, and validated.

Additionally, it is through social communication that both explicit and implicit rules for locomotion—time-place movement—are developed, standardized, and diffused. Rules for passing oncoming pedestrians and cars on the right rather than left, and vice versa, as well as conventions governing "right-of-way," pedestrian cross-walks, red lights on street signs, and so on provide examples.

It is also through social communication that the concepts of personal space and protection and differentiation from the environment are defined and institutionalized, and methods for marking and separating territories invented and regularized.[83] Architecture plays a central role with regard to the institutionalization of this social communication function. The nature and placement of construction, size, accessibility, and location of boundaries within physical structures exemplify the process and consequences of intersubjectivization.[84] Related also are multi-individual system conventions as to whom and under what conditions several persons can appropriately inhabit a single structural domain, and customs developed pertaining to the use of boundaries (e.g., walks, windows, doors) to isolate or protect individuals within one dwelling (or portion of a dwelling) from individuals in another portion of that dwelling or another structure.

Physical Definition

Intersubjectivization with regard to geophysical and biophysical substances is an important function of social communication. It is through social communication that informational-behavioral orientations relative to substances like granite, telephones, water, and books, as well as plants and animals are defined, standardized, classified, and those intersubjectivizations perpetuated and validated.

Social communication functions such that biophysical and geophysical substances and processes are classifiable in a systematic taxonomical framework in which each substance is defined in terms of constituent sub-classes and is itself categorized as one component of the next larger encompassing classification.[85] It is through these same processes that biophysical and geophysical phenomena like evolution or metabolism are discovered, defined, and shared. It should be noted also that the instruments by which these and other biophysical and geophysical definitions are validated are themselves products of social communication and standardization, as with the rock hardness scale or the Richter Scale.

A distinct function of social communication is the invention, production, marketing, utilization, and validation of technological devices, manufactured products, and consumer goods in general.[86] Thus, social communication is as critical to the production and definition of books, automobiles, or typewriters as it is to systems for the metaorganization of information about them.[87]

Sociocultural Definition

It is through social communication that sociocultural patterns essential to the functioning of all multi-person systems are defined, standardized, and diffused. While specific consequences in terms of complexity and goals will vary from one multi-person unit to the next—from an organization consisting of passengers on an elevator, to a friendship, family, club, business organization, professional group, or society—the fundamental information metabolizing processes and often the functions subserved remain constant. Informational-behavioral patterns related to roles, rules, language use patterns, values, habits, norms, appropriate jargon, protocol, ethics, aesthetics and even requisite vocational competencies are created, shared, and perpetuated through social communication.

Social communication performs another critical socio-cultural function involving the establishment and maintenance of particular organizational truths, operating principles, or belief structures around which a multi-person system is formed. It is also through social communication that a characteristic mode of explanation for the events that beset members of the collectivity are created, implemented, and validated. Religion and science each exemplify the notion of mode of explanation in the sense suggested here.[88] For each multi-person system, social communication allows for the creation, utilization, and institutionalization of significant symbols such as flags, trademarks, political campaign posters and buttons, dress or any organization-specific insignias which function to identify and differentiate one multi-person system from another.

Another critically important sociocultural function of social communication relates to the enabling of transactions between members of a system. It is through social communication that social currency, and hence an economy, becomes possible. Without intersubjectivization and hence shared concepts of intrinsic value, comparative value, and symbolic value, neither a barter system nor a token-utilizing economic system is achievable. Further, these same economic functions may be said to be subserved in even the simplest multi-person systems such as friendships, where the coinage of the realm—the means of transaction—may be understood to be language and non-verbal symbols rather than more familiar monetary markers.

Mass Communication

The institutionalization, by multi-person systems, of the processes by which informational-behavioral patterns are diffused and perpetuated, may be termed *mass communication*. Such a definition, it should be noted, suggests that the mass communication process is neither media centered, nor purposive in the sense most definitions imply. Rather, mass communication is conceptualized in terms of function served rather than mode of transmission, size or nature of an audience, or goals of a communicator.

Thusly viewed, mass communication is an aspect of social communication; it serves the diffusion function necessary for intersubjectivization. By this definition, restaurants, schools, churches, supermarkets, highways, the clothing industry, and political campaigns are defined as mass communication institutions along with the mass media, theatre, museums, art galleries, and libraries in that all serve a reality diffusion and intersubjectivization function. A related function of mass communication pertains to the perpetuation function, which may be thought of in terms of time and space binding.[89] Through the institutionalization of diffusion processes, informational-behavioral realities are perpetuated across time, geographical distances, new members of multi-person systems, and new generations.

Transactions

Social communication, it has been said, is fundamental to the definition, categorization, and standardization of information-behavioral patterns; mass communication is essential to their diffusion; personal communication to the manner in which they are sensed, made sense of, and acted upon by the individual. Clearly, these three functions are not ac-

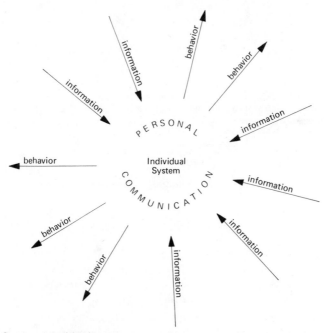

Structures: Individuals
Processes: 1) Matter-energy metabolism
             2) Information metabolism: Personal Communication—sensing, making-sense, acting toward
Information Metabolizing Functions: Adaptation—reality integration
                        1. Biological integration
                        2. Physical integration
                        3. Interpersonal integration
                        4. Sociocultural integration

Fig. 11-1   Individual Systems

Structures: Social Organizations (two or more individuals)
Processes: Information Metabolism: Social Communication—intersubjectivization
Functions: Joint Adaptation—reality definition, standardization, diffusion (mass
             communication)

        1. Biological definition
        2. Physical definition
        3. Sociocultural definition

Fig. 11-2   Multi-Person Systems

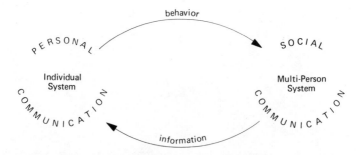

Personal communication consists of individual reality integration serving the ends
of individual adaptation. The primary reality with which the individual adapts is
informational, and a product of the social organizing and hence social communication processes of the multi-person system. The multi-person system takes its
definition from the behaviors of the individuals who compose it.

Fig. 11-3   Human Communication System

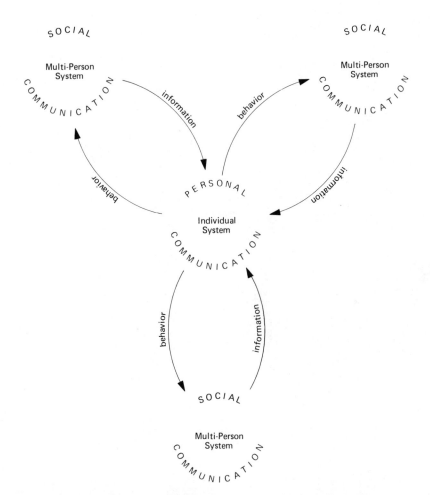

Personal communication consists of individual reality integration—sensing, making sense of, and acting toward. The information with which the individual organizes himself is largely a consequence of social communication processes of a variety of multi-person communication systems.

Fig. 11-4   Individual Communication System

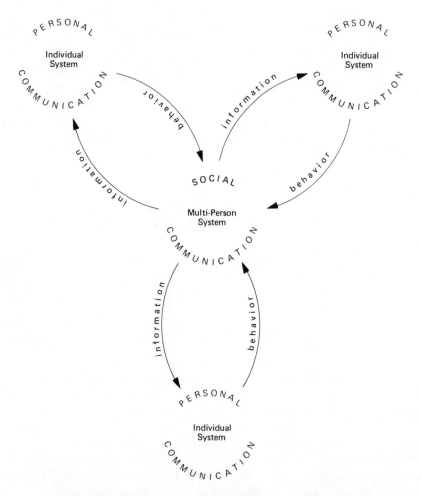

Through serial communication the multi-person communication system is defined, standardized, and perpetuated by the behaviors of the constituent individual systems, who in turn through social communication, are provided with information about the multi-person system.

Fig. 11-5 Multi-Person Communication System

complished by independent activities, but rather operate in a continuous, interpenetrating, transactional fashion as suggested in a cumulative fashion in Figures 11.1 through 11.6.

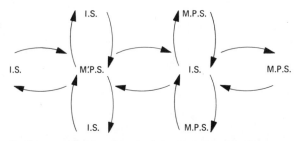

The figure provides a two-dimensional characterization of the transactional, interpenetrating, mutually-defining, and co-determinant relationship which exists between individual and multi-person communication systems.

Fig. 11-6 Transactional Communication System Networks

The information metabolizing functions of informational-behavioral *definition, standardization, diffusion,* and *integration* are as basic to the *individual-multi-individual suprasystem,* as sensing, making sense of, and acting toward are to the individual system and defining, standardizing, and diffusing are to the multiperson system. Implied is that what an individual becomes and can become is largely a consequence of how he or she organizes with the informational-behavioral patterns and demands of his or her milieu. Implied also is that the patterns with which the individual organized are consequences of the activities of multi-person system information metabolizing processes, which in turn, are a consequence of the social synthesis of the individual behaviors of its constituent members. Thus, as suggested in Fig. 11.7, society can be viewed as a multi-person communication system and understood to be defined and perpetuated by the behaviors of citizens. Information necessary for the individual citizens to adapt is provided by the multi-person system and digested and acted upon by the individual citizens, such as to continually redefine the society for themselves and one another. Fig. 11.8 provides still another example of this transacting relationship.

Conclusion

This, then, is the basic paradigm. In sum, the perspective developed provides a view of human enterprise as a complex network of functionally interrelated individuals in multi-individual systems, who, through the information metabolizing processes of intrapersonal, interpersonal and mass communication, enable and constrain, satisfy and frustrate, create and destroy, change and not, in all that is human.

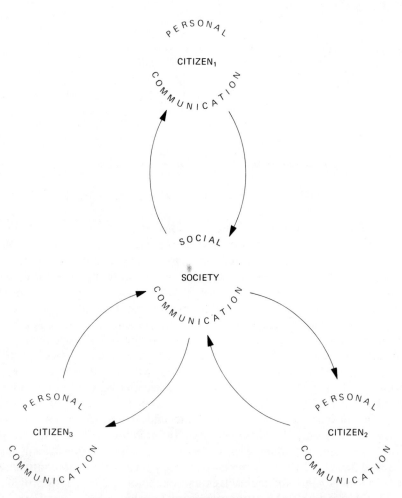

Society can be viewed as a multi-person communication system and therefore is defined and perpetuated by the behaviors of the citizens. Information necessary for the individual citizens to adapt is provided by the multi-person system and is therefore a social communication function.

Fig. 11-7   Transactional Communication Systems (Example 1)

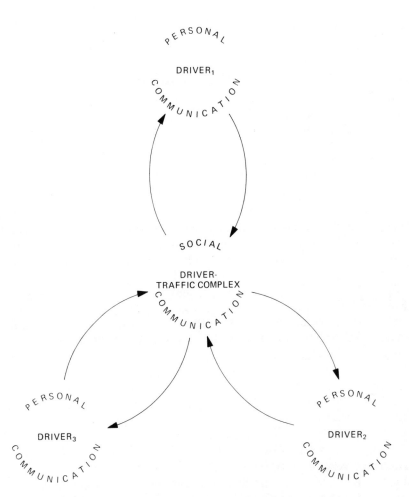

The Driver-Traffic Complex on any segment of a turnpike or freeway may be viewed as a multi-person communication system defined by the behaviors of the individual drivers who are a part of the pattern. Information necessary for any of the individual systems to adapt to that pattern is provided by the multi-person system and is therefore a social communication function.

Fig. 11-8 Transactional Communcation Systems (Example 2)

The view of communication systems which emerges draws heavily on many fundamental open systems concepts, particularly multi-lateral causality, equifinality, multi-finality, functionality, dynamic stabilization, organic growth and change, and interdependent, hierarchically ordered levels of organization. Basic notions of symbolic interaction, general semantics, transactional psychology, and sociology of knowledge are also heavily utilized.

While far from comprehensive in its present form, the paradigm would seem also to satisfy the systems criteria of cross-disciplinary validity and interdisciplinary applicability, and in this sense may serve as an outline for the subsequent development of more elaborate and detailed operational models.

References and Notes

1. Churchman, C. West, *The Systems Approach*, New York: Delacorte, 1968.
2. This point is presented and discussed by Richard F. Hixson, "Mass Media: An Approach to Human Communication," *Approaches to Human Communication*, Richard W. Budd and Brent D. Ruben, eds., Rochelle Park, N.J.: Hayden Book Co. (Spartan), 1972.
3. Lasswell, Harold D., "The Structure and Function of Communication in Society," *The Communication of Ideas*, Bryson Lyman, ed., Institute for Religion and Social Studies, 1948. Reprinted in *Mass Communications*, Wilbur Schramm, ed., Urbana, Ill.: University of Illinois Press, 1960, 1966, pp. 117-130.
4. Shannon, Claude, and Warren Weaver, *The Mathematical Theory of Communication*, Urbana, Ill.: University of Illinois Press, 1949.
5. Schramm, Wilbur, "How Communication Works," *The Process and Effects of Mass Communication*, Wilbur Schramm, ed., Urbana, Ill.: University of Illinois Press, 1960, 1966, pp. 3-26.
6. This point is discussed by John Hasling, *The Message, The Speaker, The Audience*, New York: McGraw-Hill, 1971, pp. 2-3
7. Lasswell, Harold D., "The Structure and Function of Communication in Society," p. 225.
8. Shannon, Claude, and Warren Weaver, *The Mathematical Theory of Communication*, Urbana, Ill.: University of Illinois Press, 1949. *See also* Donald K. Darnell, "Information Theory: An Approach to Human Communication," *Approaches to Human Communication*, Rochelle Park, N.J.: Hayden Book Co. (Spartan), 1972.
9. Schramm, Wilbur, "How Communication Works," *The Process and Effects of Mass Communication*, Wilbur Schramm, ed., Urbana: University of Illinois Press, 1960, 1966, pp. 3-26.

10. Katz, Elihu and Paul F. Lazarsfeld, *Personal Influence,* New York: Free Press, 1960. *See also* earlier work of Paul Lazarsfeld, Bernard Berelson, and Hazel Gaudet, *The People's Choice,* New York: Columbia University Press, 1944, 1948. Discussion by Bernard Berelson, "Communication and Public Opinion," *The Process and Effects of Mass Communication,* Wilbur Schramm, ed., 1954, 1965, pp. 343-356, and Elihu Katz, "The Two-Step Flow of Communication," *Mass Communications,* Wilbur Schramm, ed., pp. 346-365.
11. Riley, John W. Jr. and Matilda White Riley, "A Sociological Approach to Mass Communication," *Sociology Today,* Robert K. Merton, Leonard Broom and Leonard S. Cottrell, Jr., eds., Basic Books, 1959. *See* "Sociology: An Approach to Human Communication," *Approaches to Human Communication,* Rochelle Park, N.J.: Hayden Book Co. 1972.
12. Westley, Bruce H. and Malcolm S. MacLean, Jr., "A Conceptual Model for Communication Research," *Journalism Quarterly,* Vol. 34, 1957, pp. 31-38.
13. Berlo, David K., *The Process of Communication,* New York: Holt, Rinehart and Winston, 1960.
14. An excellent discussion of the status of "process" in conceptualizations of communication is provided in "Communication Research and the Idea of Process," by David H. Smith, *Speech Monographs,* August 1972. Smith argues that most models of communication which have purported to integrate the process concept have generally failed in their attempts.
15. The Westley-MacLean model is referenced in most contemporary communication volumes. *See* for example, discussion in *Communication— The Study of Human Interaction,* C. David Mortensen, New York: McGraw-Hill, 1972. An excellent critical discussion of the Westley-MacLean, Berlo, and other popular models of communication provided by John Y. Kim in "Feedback and Human Communication: Toward a Reconceptualization," an unpublished doctoral dissertation, University of Iowa, 1971.
16. Barker, Larry L. and Robert J. Kibler, *Speech Communication Behavior,* Englewood Cliffs, N. J.: Prentice-Hall, 1971.
17. *Ibid.* pp. 3-8.
18. Brooks, William D., *Speech Communication,* Dubuque, Iowa: W. C. Brown, 1972.
19. Samovar, Larry A. and Jack Mills, *Oral Communication,* Dubuque, Iowa: W. C. Brown, 1968, 1972, pp. 3-5.
20. Miller, Gerald R., *An Introduction to Speech Communication,* Indianapolis, Ind.: Bobbs-Merrill, 1972, p. 58. *See also* Gerald Miller, "Speech: An Approach to Human Communication," *Approaches to Human Communication,* Rochelle Park, N.J.: Hayden Book Co., 1972.
21. Becker, Samuel L., "What Rhetoric (Communication Theory) Is Rele-

vant for Contemporary Speech Communication?'' presented at the University of Minnesota, 1968, Spring Symposium on Speech-Communication.

A presentation of the model with discussion is also provided in C. David Mortensen, *Communication—The Study of Human Interaction,* New York: McGraw-Hill,1972, pp. 46-48.

22. Hasling, J., *The Message, the Speaker, The Audience,* New York: McGraw-Hill, 1971, pp. 3-5.
23. It is interesting to note that although descriptive component-oriented analysis predominates in both speech and mass communication, there is remarkably little evidence of conceptual cross-fertilization between these disciplines despite some rather obvious philosophical and operational similarities.
24. Barnouw, Erik, *Mass Communication,* New York: Holt, Rinehart and Winston, 1956.

That mass communication is understood to be defined in terms of the mass media (channel component) is suggested by the subtitle of this volume: ''Television, Radio, Film, Press.'' The point is underscored in Section 1 entitled ''The History of Mass Communication,'' which consists of the following chapters: ''The Paper Tide,'' ''The Moving Image,'' ''Signals in the Air,'' and ''Of Words and Mousetraps.''
25. Stephenson, William, *The Play Theory of Mass Communication,* Chicago: University of Chicago Press, 1967.

Stephenson begins Chapter 1, ''Two New Theories of Mass Communication Research,'' as follows:

''From its beginnings, in 1924 or so, mass communication theory has concerned itself primarily with how the mass media influence the attitudes, beliefs, and actions of people. There was little evidence up to 1959, however, that the mass media had any significant effects on the deeper or more important beliefs of people. . .''

''. . .it is the thesis of this book that at its best mass communication allows people to become absorbed in *subjective play.* People read newspapers, magazines, and paperbacks in vast numbers, and there are ever increasing audiences for movies, radio, records, and television.''
26. DeFleur, Melvin L., *Theories of Mass Communication,* New York: McKay, 1966, 1970.

While DeFleur argues initially that mass communication is a special case of communication, five of the eight chapters in the volume focus on the mass media.
27. Schramm, Wilbur, *Mass Communication,* Urbana, Ill.: University of Illinois Press, 1960, 1966.

On page 3, Schramm says:

''When did mass communication begin? The date usually given is that of the beginning of printing from movable metal type, in Western Europe in the fifteenth century, but the roots are much earlier and the flowering much later.''

''The *mass media* are the resultant forces set in motion when groups of manlike animals first huddled together against the cold and danger of primitive times. . . . In Korea, where they had paper, ink and metal type first, conditions were not ripe for the growth of *mass communication*; in Western Europe, when Gutenberg began to print, society was more nearly ready to develop *the new device.* ''(italics added)

The volume includes sections on ''The Structure and Function of Mass Communications'' which consists of articles by Lasswell, Lerner, Breed, and others about the structure and function of *mass communication* as a process.

In other sections, such as ''The Development of Mass Communications,'' Schramm seems clearly to be referring to the development of the *mass media*. In yet another section, ''Responsibility for Mass Communication,'' references are to *messages*.

28. Emery, Edwin, Philip H. Ault, and Warren K. Agee, *Introduction to Mass Communications,* New York: Dodd, Mead, 1960, 1965, 1970.

Of the 18 chapters in the volume, 13 are devoted to the mass media.

29. Rivers, William L., Theodore Peterson, and Jay W. Jensen, *The Mass Media and Modern Society,* New York: Holt, Rinehart, and Winston, 1971.

On page 16, the authors state:

''Today one can more correctly speak of 'mass communications' than of 'journalism' when referring to media other than newspapers and magazines. In a sense, of course, every *communication* uses some medium, is committed to some channel for transmission. The letterhead or sheet of notepaper in correspondence, the sound waves utilized in conversation—these are channels or media. But in *mass communication,* a whole institution becomes the message carrier—a newspaper, a magazine, a broadcasting station. . .''

''The term *mass communication* has sometimes been defined in two ways: *communication by the media* and *communication for the masses. Mass communication,* however, does not mean communication for everyone.'' (italics added)

The term ''mass media'' is used in the book to refer to channel, source, message, and sometimes receiver(s), as well. Included in the volume, for example, are chapters entitled ''The Media as Persuaders'' and ''The Media as Informers and Interpreters.''

30. Hohenberg, John, *The Professional Journalist,* New York: Holt, Rinehart, and Winston, 1960, 1969.

31. Brown, Lee, ''Journalism: An Approach to Human Communication,'' *Approaches to Human Communication,* Rochelle Park, N. J.: Hayden Book Co. (Spartan), 1972.

32. Charnley, Mitchell V., *Reporting*, New York: Holt, Rinehart, and Winston, 1959,1966.
33. Miller, Gerald R., and Michael Burgoon, *New Techniques in Persuasion*, New York: Harper and Row, 1973, pp. 1-3.
34. Rosnow, Ralph L., and Edward J. Robinson, *Experiments in Persuasion*, New York: Academic Press, 1967.
35. Bettinghaus, Erwin P., *Persuasive Communication*, New York: Holt, Rinehart, and Winston, 1968.
36. Rogers, Everett M., and E. Floyd Shoemaker, *Communication of Innovations*, New York: Free Press, 1971. A related discussion is provided by Everett Rogers in *Communication and Social Change*, Rochelle Park, N.J.: Hayden Book Co.
37. Berger, Peter L., and Thomas Luckmann, *The Social Construction of Reality*, Garden City: Doubleday, 1966 and Peter L. Berger in *The Sacred Canopy*, Garden City: Doubleday, 1969.
38. Berger, Peter L. and Thomas Luckmann, *The Social Construction of Reality*, Garden City: Doubleday, 1966.
39. Holzner, Burkart, *Reality Construction in Society*, Cambridge, Mass.: Schenkman, 1966.
40. McHugh, Peter, *Defining the Situation*, Indianapolis, Ind.: Bobbs-Merrill, 1968.

    The central concepts undergirding the frameworks of Berger Luckmann, Holzner, and McHugh are reflective of the contributions of Schutz, Sorokin, Scheler, Mannheim, and Durkheim to the study of epistemology and the "sociology of knowledge."

    A discussion of their work and of the sociology of knowledge in general, is provided by Robert Merton in *Social Theory and Social Structure*, New York: Free Press, 1949, 1957, 1968, pp. 510-562. *See also* Werner Stark, *The Sociology of Knowledge*, London: Routledge and Kegan Paul, 1958, 1960, 1967, and W.J.H. Sprott, *Science and Social Action*, London: Watts, 1954, 1961.
41. Of the contributions of Erving Goffman, *Relations in Public*, New York: Basic Books, 1971; *Interaction Ritual*, Garden City: Doubleday, 1967; *The Presentation of Self in Everyday Life*, Garden City: Doubleday, 1959; and *Strategic Interaction*, Philadelphia: University of Pennsylvania, 1969, are most particularly relevant.
42. Duncan, Hugh D., *Symbols in Society*, London: Oxford University, 1968; *Communication and Social Order*, Oxford University, 1962; and *Symbols and Social Theory*, New York: Oxford University, 1969.
43. Blumer, Herbert, *Symbolic Interactionism*, Englewood Cliffs: Prentice-Hall, 1969. Portions appear as "Symbolic Interaction: An Approach to Human Communication," *Approaches to Human Communication*, Rochelle Park, N.J.: Hayden Book Co., 1972.
44. Korzybski, Alfred, *Science and Sanity*, Lakeville, Conn.: International

Non-Aristotelian Library, 1933, 1948. *See also* discussion by Richard W. Budd, in "General Semantics: An Approach to Human Communication," *Approaches to Human Communication,* and *Communication: General Semantics Perspectives,* Lee Thayer ed., Rochelle Park, N.J.: Hayden Book Co., 1970.

45. Johnson, Wendell, *People in Quandaries,* New York: Harper, 1946 and *Coping With Change* (Wendell Johnson and Dorothy Moeller), New York: Harper and Row, 1972.

46. Brown, Roger, *Words and Things,* New York: Free Press, 1958,1968.

47. Of Carl Rogers many contributions, *On Becoming a Person,* Boston: Houghton-Mifflin, 1961, and *Encounter Groups,* New York: Harper and Row, 1970, are particularly relevant as input for analysis of function in communication.

48. Major summary contributions of Jurgen Ruesch include *Communication: The Social Matrix of Society* (with Gregory Bateson), New York: Norton, 1951, 1968; *Nonverbal Communication* (with Veldon Kees), Stanford: University of California, 1956, 1972; *Therapeutic Communication,* New York: Norton, 1961; and *Disturbed Communication,* New York: Norton, 1957, 1972.

49. Major summary contributions of Gregory Bateson include *Communication: The Social Matrix of Society* (with Jurgen Ruesch), New York: Norton 1951, 1968; and *Steps to an Ecology of the Mind,* New York: Ballantine Books, 1972.

50. Watzlawick, Paul, Janet Beavin, and Don D. Jackson, *Pragmatics of Human Communication,* New York: Norton, 1967.

51. Grinker, Roy R. Sr., *Toward a Unified Theory of Human Behavior,* New York: Basic Books, 1956, 1967.

52. Shands, Harley C., *Thinking and Psychotherapy,* Cambridge, Mass.: Harvard University Press, 1960.

53. Spiegel, John, *Transactions,* New York: Science House, 1971.

54. Quill, William G., *Subjective Psychology,* Rochelle Park, N.J.: Hayden Book Co., 1972.

55. Major summary contributions of Lee Thayer especially relevant for functional analysis of communication: *Communication and Communication Systems,* Homewood, Ill.: Irwin, 1968; "Communication—*Sine Qua Non* of the Behavioral Sciences," *Vistas in Science,* D. L. Arm, ed., Albuquerque: University of New Mexico, 1968; *Communication: Concepts and Perspectives,* Rochelle Park, N. J.: Hayden Book Co. 1967; *Communication: Theory and Research,* Springfield, Ill.: Thomas, 1967; "Communication and the Human Condition," prepared for the VII Semana de Estudios Sociales "Mass Communication and Human Understanding" Instituto de Siencias Sociales, Barcelona, Spain, November, 1969; "Communication and Change," *Communication and Social Change,* Rochelle Park, N.J.: Hayden Book Co., "On Communication

and Change: Some Provocations," *Systematics,* Vol. 6, No. 3, December, 1968; "On Human Communication and Social Development," presented at the first World Conference on Social Communication for Development, Mexico City, March, 1970.

56. Allport, Gordon W., *Becoming,* New Haven: Yale University, 1955.
57. Church, Joseph, *Language and the Discovery of Reality,* New York: Vintage Books, 1961.
58. Kelly, George A., *A Theory of Personality,* New York: Norton, 1955, 1963.
59. Maslow, Abraham H., *Toward a Psychology of Being,* New York: Van Nostrand, 1968, and *Motivation and Personality,* New York: Harper and Row, 1954, 1970.
60. Schroder, Harold M., Michael J. Driver, and Seigfried Streufert, *Human Information Processing,* New York: Holt, Rinehart, and Winston, 1967.
61. Lindsay, Peter H., and Donald A. Norman, *Human Information Processing,* New York: Academic Press, 1972.
62. Delgado, José M. R., *Physical Control of the Mind,* New York: Harper and Row, 1969, portions of which appear as "Neurophysiology: An Approach to Human Communication," *Approaches to Human Communication,* Rochelle Park, N.J.: Hayden Book Co., 1972.
63. Young, J. Z., *Doubt and Certainty in Science,* Oxford University, 1970, and "Biology: An Approach to Human Communication," *Approaches to Human Communication,* Rochelle Park, N.J.: Hayden Book Co., 1972
64. Particularly relevant contributions of Ervin Laszlo include *System, Structure and Experience,* New York: Gordon and Breach, 1969, *The World System,* New York: Braziller, 1972, and "Basic Concepts of Systems Philosophy" in this volume.
65. Of the numerous contributions of Alfred G. Smith, *Communication and Culture,* New York: Holt, Rinehart, and Winston, 1966, "Anthropology: An Approach to Human Communication," *Approaches to Human Communication,* Rochelle Park, N.J.: Hayden Book Co. and "Change, Channels and Trust," *Communication and Social Change,* Rochelle Park, N.J.: Hayden Book Co. (in preparation) are especially relevant.
66. Miller, James G., "Living Systems," *Behavioral Science,* Vol. 10, 1965, p. 338.
67. *Cf.* Lee Thayer, *Communication and Communication Systems,* Homewood, Ill.: Irwin, 1968, p. 17.
68. *Cf.* Kenneth Boulding, "General System Theory—Skeleton of Science," *Management Science,* Vol. 2, 1956, edited and included as Chapter 2 of this volume.
69. Additional discussion of the concepts of individual and multi-person systems is provided on pp. 137-140 "General System Theory: An Approach to Human Communication," *Approaches to Human Communication,* Rochelle Park, N.J.: Hayden Book Co., 1972.

0. Allport, Gordon W., *Becoming,* New Haven: Yale University, 1955.

1. Korzybski, Alfred, *Science and Sanity,* Lakeville, Conn.: International Non-Aristotelian Library, 1933, 1948; Wendell Johnson, *People in Quandaries,* New York: Harper, 1946 and Richard W. Budd, "General Semantics: An Approach to Human Communication," *Approaches to Human Communication,* Rochelle Park, N.J.: Hayden Book Co., 1972.

2. Thayer, Lee "On Human Communication and Social Development," a paper presented at the first World Conference on Social Communication for Development, Mexico City, March, 1970.

3. Delgado, Jose M.R., *Physical Control of the Mind,* New York: Harper and Row, 1969 especially Ch. 5-7. *See* "Neurophysiology: An Approach to Human Communication," *Approaches to Human Communication,* Rochelle Park, N.J.: Hayden Book Co., 1972.

4. Berger, Peter, and Thomas Luckman, *The Social Construction of Reality,* Garden City: Doubleday, 1966; and Peter Berger, *The Sacred Canopy,* Garden City, Doubleday 1969, Ch. 1.

5. *C.f.* Rapoport, Anatol, "Man—The Symbol-User," *Communication: Ethical and Moral Issues,* Lee Thayer, ed., New York: Gordon and Breach, 1973.

6. *Cf.* Goffman, Erving, *Relations in Public,* New York: Basic Books, 1971, Ch. 1.

7. A phrase for which I am indebted to David Davidson.

8. *Cf.* Duncan, Hugh D., *Symbols in Society,* London: Oxford University, 1968, *Communication and Social Order,* Oxford University, 1962, and *Symbols and Social Theory,* New York: Oxford University, 1969.

9. *Cf.* Rapoport, Anatol, "Man, The Symbol-User," *Communication: Ethical and Moral Issues,* New York: Gordon and Breach, 1973.

30. Lower-order animals function in some rather sophisticated multi-individual collectivities, but the nature of those organizations and the requisite individual roles are usually genetically predetermined and highly predictable. In contradistinction, human communication makes possible—in fact requires—active participation in these processes.

31. *Cf.* Blumer, Herbert, *Symbolic Interactionism,* Englewood Cliffs: Prentice-Hall, 1969 and "Symbolic Interaction: An Approach to Human Communication," *Approaches to Human Communication,* Rochelle Park, N.J.: Hayden Book Co.

32. *Cf.* Watzlawick, Paul, et al., *Pragmatics of Human Communication,* New York: Norton, 1967; R. D. Laing, *The Politics of Experience,* London: Penguin, and Thomas Szasz, *The Manufacture of Madness,* New York: Harper and Row, 1970. An interesting example of the point was provided at an annual conference of the American Psychological Association, held in April 1974, where by a majority vote, it was determined that homosexuality is no longer an illness.

83. *Cf.* Goffman, Erving, *Relations in Public*, New York: Basic Books, 1971, Ch. 2.
84. *Cf.* Norberg-Schulz, Christian, *Existence, Space and Architecture*, New York: Praeger, 1971 and *Shelter: The Cave Re-examined*, Don Fabun, Beverly Hills: Glencoe Press, 1971.
85. *Cf.* Upton, Albert, *Design for Thinking*, Stanford: Stanford University Press, 1961 and *Creative Analysis* (with Richard W. Samson), New York: E.P. Dutton, 1961.
86. *Cf.* Smith, Alfred G., in "Anthropology: An Approach to Human Communication," and Bent Stidsen, "Economics: An Approach to Human Communication," *Approaches to Human Communication*, Rochelle Park, N.J.: Hayden Book Co., 1972.
87. *Cf.* Maruyama, Magorah, "Metaorganization of Information," *General Systems Yearbook*, Society for General Systems Research, Vol. XI, 1966.
88. *Cf.* Johnson, Wendell, and Dorothy Moeller, *Coping With Change*, New York: Harper and Row, 1972 pp. 3-55, a discussion of "scientific" versus "magic" explanation. For an exploration of religious explanations, *see* Peter Berger, *The Sacred Canopy*, Garden City: Doubleday, 1969.
89. *Cf.* Budd, Richard W., "General Semantics: An Approach to Human Communication," *Approaches to Human Communication*, Rochelle Park, N.J.: Hayden Book Co., 1972.

12

Communication Study in System Perspective

B. AUBREY FISHER

Few terms in our language command as much respect and popularity as "communication." Commonly used in everyday conversation and the object of thousands of scholarly research studies, communication may be the most widely discussed and least understood phenomenon of academia. There exists little agreement among scholars concerning the boundaries of communication, its components, or, indeed, even the very definition of the term. Many scholars, however, have agreed on a probable cause of this perplexing state of affairs—despite the proliferation of the term, "communication theory," no unified theory of communication exists at the present time.

A basic assumption underlying this chapter, then, is that the study of communication needs a theory. This assumption does not imply that no "theories" exist. Indeed, the literature is filled with models, philosophies, and constructs—among them, role theory, personality theory, graph theory, innoculation theory, learning theory, exchange theory, game theory, and a seemingly infinite list of balance theories (e.g., dissonance, congruity, equity, consistency, etc.). Nor do I imply that these "theories" are not true. But the truth of a theory is of little importance. The more important question to ask of a theory is "What does it do for you?"

I shall take the position that barriers now exist which mitigate against the development of communication theory. These barriers are of two types—assumptions about theory and research practices. In the absence of these barriers, a theory of communication based on modern systems theory can be developed. Suggesting guidelines for such a theory and depicting human communication as an open system, constitutes the primary goal of this chapter.

Limiting Assumptions

The first assumption about theory of communication is the omnipresent emphasis on linear causality. Ludwig von Bertalanffy has suggested that social and behavioral sciences have been victimized by this theoretical perspective of their predecessor—the physical sciences.[1]

Given this inherited perspective of linear causality, one seeks to explain an existing phenomenon by searching backward for its primal cause, or one seeks to establish conditions and observe the effects of those antecedent conditions. A typical communication research design, then, is to establish "pure" conditions, inject an antecedent variable or two, and measure their causal reaction on another variable or two. For example, the researcher specifies an ego-involved attitude, injects a treatment condition of high source credibility, and observes the factor-analytic effect on a series of SD scales.

But antecedent conditions do not always lead to the same consequent. Nor does the same consequent always result from similar antecedent conditions. The late eminent psychiatrist, Don Jackson, explains this characteristic of the open system—equifinality:[2]

> Specifically, our traditional model of causality does not encompass those feedback processes of a system which *achieve outcomes.* The problem of like causes which do not produce like results (or conversely, identical results from unlike antecedents) has been analyzed in cybernetics in terms of positive and negative feedback mechanisms. A random event introduced into a system with deviation-amplifying tendencies, for instance, will produce a final result quite different from the same event in a system with deviation-counteracting processes. Thus the study of single elements or static "before and after" situations will not be too enlightening. . . . Adopting the premise of. . . a system requires us to *attend only to present (observable) process,* that is, to ecology rather than genesis.

The principle of equifinality is, allegedly, not controversial in the study of communication, yet our journals are replete with reports of research claiming that one or two independent variables directly affect the outcome as measured by one or more dependent variables. If the concept of equifinality were accepted, however, the research problem would change from measuring effects of antecedent conditions in pre-, post-test fashion to observing the process of how that injected variable affects the operation of the system.

Jackson also suggests, "the circular, or feedback, model of causality is a necessary corollary to our basic axioms of communication."[3] However, the attempt to isolate the linear impact of one or more variables on another variable or group of variables appears to characterize the bulk of our present communication research. Our theory should rather treat communication as an ongoing process free from the limitations of linear causality. As van den Berghe writes, "Societies must be looked at holistically as a system of interrelated parts. Hence, causation is multiple and reciprocal."[4] This rejection of linear causality in favor of mutual causal systems (i.e., positive and negative feedback sequences) is incorporated in the guidelines which follow.

A second assumption about theory may be a source of considerable controversy. For some reason we have insisted that a theory have, above all else, predictive linear causality necessitating overemphasis on the structure of a system and subsequently de-emphasizing the system's function.

At this point a digression is in order to clarify three basic elements of systems—structure, function, and evolution.[5] The structure of a system has typically been defined as the pattern of matter in space—the relationships among the components, holding time as a constant. To the extent that a system is structured, it possesses order. The function of a system, then, is the pattern of relationships among components in time. A system functions with repetitive, transient, and reversible patternings of events. To the extent that the patterning is transient and reversible, the system possesses complexity. Those enduring (i.e., slow to change), irreversible, and progressive relationships among components over both time and space may be considered the evolution of the system. Unlike structure (order) and function (complexity), the principles of systemic evolution are axiomatic across all systems—human and mechanical. (The nature of structure and function typically conceived as bounded by time and space will be discussed later.)

To return to the point at hand, insisting that a theory be predictive may be natural consequence of linear causality but is incongruent with the current state of our understanding. Prediction of outcomes is possible only under highly controlled conditions. More importantly, prediction of outcomes demands information that we just don't have in the real world. Game research has demonstrated that human behavior becomes predictable only as the game approaches perfect information. Machlup makes the point for the social sciences.[6]

> We must not be too sanguine about the success of social scientists in making either unconditional forecasts or conditional predictions. Let us admit that we are not good in the business of prophecy and let us be modest in our claims about our ability to predict. After all, it is not our stupidity which hampers us, but chiefly our lack of information. . . .Social scientists, for some strange reason, are expected to foretell the future and they feel badly if they fail.

Nothing is inherently harmful about prediction, but our worship of prediction above all else is delimiting to theory development. I do not reject prediction out of hand, but I do reject the insatiable demand that theory and research must predict outcomes in order to be labeled theory and research. The problem lies in utilizing the concept of prediction to develop theory and research and not utilizing theory and research to develop prediction.

The question is not *whether* our theory of communication is able to predict but *how* and *in what form* prediction should be included in the theory. Buckley provides some direction as he discusses the nature of systemic structure and function:[7]

> But for the sociocultural system, "structure is only a relative stability of underlying, ongoing, micro-processes. Only when we focus on these can we begin to get at the selection process whereby certain interactive relationships become relatively and temporarily stabilized into social and cultural structures.
>
> The unit of dynamic analysis thus becomes the systemic *matrix* of interacting, goal-seeking, deciding individuals and subgroups— whether this matrix is a part of a formal organization or only a loose collectivity.

Note that Buckley's systemic perspective rejects only the overwhelming demand that a theory be ultimately predictive. Thus, predictiveness is changed from predicting consequent effects from antecedent conditions to the discovery of probabilities of occurrence of a subsequent state from an earlier state or sequence of states. Buckley continues:[8]

> Newer analytical tools being explored to handle such processes include treatment of the interaction matrix over time as a succession of states described in terms of transition probabilities, Markoff [sic] chains, or stochastic processes in general.

Buckley thus advocates the understanding of "transactional processes as they operate" in an ongoing process.[9] But he firmly states, ". . . we cannot hope to develop our understanding much further by speaking of one 'structure' determining, 'affecting,' or acting upon another 'structure.' "

For Buckley's "process focus," prediction is not the primary goal even though predictions, in the form of transitional probabilities are possible in the short term. The more important goal at present is a thorough description and understanding of the system's structure and function.

Closely related to the problem of forsaking function for structural predictability is an emphasis on structural interaction rather than transaction. Without notable exception, all "models" of communication are structurally based on transceiving messages through space unidirectionally—either "one way" or "two way." Brodey believes a structural perspective may have been "made necessary by our subject-predicate language, as if there is a 'doer' of the action and 'one done to'—a receiver. The loop concept has been subverted. . . . Now there may be moments when the action is more unilateral, but the information exchange is the freshening of changings responsively timed to each other's changings. Who is father to the child fits the cause-effect model, but the evolution of the child and his family are a matter of dialogue."[10]

If communication is viewed transactionally, structure and function merge inseparably blurring the distinction between time and space. With a focus on transactive relationships, "information," according to Buckley, "in its most general sense is seen, not as a thing that can be transported, but as a selective interrelation or mapping between two or more subsets of constrained variety selected from larger ensembles."[11] The later theoretical propositions adopt the transactional perspective of communication.

Research Practices

Shifting the viewpoint from theoretical assumptions to research practices, one can also find communication scholars being victimized assuming the perspective of previous researchers. The bulk of communication research is indistinguishable from psychology in that both use the human system as the basic model from which to draw variables. Components of the human system are people—individual human beings. Thus, a human system is organized through cognitive and affective relationships among people. As a result, variables chosen for communication study are typically those hypothetical constructs which are embodied within the "black box" of an individual's central nervous system—e.g., attitude, value, cognitions, self-esteem, perceptions, ego-involvement, etc. A common research practice may select a variable from the physical environment and determine its effect on one of those constructs. Even a term which has been uniquely associated with communication such as ethos or communicator credibility remains within the individual. While Aristotle conceptualized ethos as embodied within the source (possessed), the modern conceptualization of credibility places it within the perception of the receiver (attributed). The principle of embodying ethos within the individual remains constant. Only the placement of which individual has changed in 2000 years. The research practices may have changed over the centuries, but the theoretical rationale is incredibly similar.

Communication research practices are natural consequences of viewing the human system as the model from which to conduct research. Communication has been little more than a necessary evil—a vehicle for the more important variables of the human system model. For example, communication is often not observed directly. That is, communication research has become a science of the independent variable. Witness the multitude of "effects" studies—typically in persuasion and attitude change research. Secondly, communication is often emasculated by manipulation and tight laboratory controls. For example, the bulk of negotiation and bargaining studies restricts communication to exchanging written messages selected from a predetermined list or exchanging dollars-and-cents offers which can only be accepted or rejected without communication. Thirdly, communication is observed structurally without consideration of process. The denial of communication as a process is epitomized by the studies of networks which count the number of messages sent and received along certain channels.

My final criticism of research practices involves the use of the experimental design. To avoid being misunderstood, I must emphasize that the fault is not necessarily inherent in the experimental design, but lies primarily with its overly restricted use by researchers. While the experimental design encourages "effects" studies, the more important problem resides in conceptualizing time. All too often, time is treated unidimensionally as simple duration—the length of time required for treatment, the length of time between pre-test and post-test and delayed post-test. But simple duration may be the least important and certainly the least sophisticated dimension of time. Ornstein, for example, notes several more important dimensions of time experience including temporal perspective. simultaneity, succession, rhythm, intervals, and information time.[12] Jaffe and Feldstein, while not epitomizing a breakthrough in communication research, at least consider the rhythmic aspects of time in their research on conversations.[13] Brodey discusses time graining and time driving as integral to communication in the time dimension.[14] Yet experimental research in communication has virtually ignored time dimensions other than duration.

But my primary concern is not to denegrate past research. Rather, it is to develop guidelines for a theory of human communication based on modern systems theory. Of course, my systems perspective may be quite different from those of others. The communication system which follows is, for example, only vaguely similar to Berrien's black box conceptualization[15] while in more substantial agreement with Watzlawick, Beavin, and Jackson[16] and particularly Scheflen.[17]

The first step in theory development is to enumerate some basic principles of systemic behavior adapted to communication systems. These principles are intended not as *technical* rules but as *basic* rules of every communication system—that is, not merely useful techniques employed by communicators to obtain desired goals but axiomatic expressions of *how* individuals *do* organize their behaviors. That is, a communication system is based on how communicative behaviors are organized in a social setting rather than how content—the "what" of the transactions—is organized by each individual. The second step in this proposal is to add to the life of tentative axioms of communication theory begun by Watzlawick, Beavin, and Jackson.[18]

Principles of Behavior in Communication Systems

1. *Communicative behavior is purposeful.* Rosenblueth and Wiener provide criteria of purposeful behavior—an actor who is part of a larger system, goal direction, and sequential progression.[19] But, as they had pointed out earlier, purpose is not to be confused with causal determinism—"a one-way, relatively irreversible functional relationship."[20] Rather, purpose is associated with behavior constraints. Nor is the goal of behavior necessarily external to the individual or high in his awareness field. Churchman and Ackoff observe, ". . . the individual has choices all of which potentially produce (make possible) some *future* action.[21] The machine may go through certain adjustments that enable it to solve a different kind of problem, the person may eat so that he can work, and so on." In any case, the emphasis of purpose remains on behavior and the function of behavioral constraints—not on cause and goal.

2. *Purposeful behavior is a natural and inevitable result of adaptation through directive correlation.* Sommerhof has explained the process of adaptation through directive correlation, and I will not dwell on explicating his model.[22] In summary, Sommerhof emphasizes the theoretical significance of a future goal or focal condition linked inextricably to present behavior and prior conditions (the coenetic variable). Most importantly, he emphasizes the rightful place of causality in the system model. His model does not contradict "efficient causation" but actually presupposes it within the concept of purpose. Sommerhof considers "final causes" and "teleogical causation" to be "superfluous" and dismisses them as "scientifically sterile."[23] They are thus not central to either the model or its theoretical basis. For those readers who remain confused as to the nature of presupposed causality, Dore provides an excellent discussion of how functionalism, for example, presupposes causality without necessitating an empirical search for causes and thereby creating the theoretical problem of reductionism.[24]

Osgood discusses adaptation similarly from the viewpoint of sensory and motor integration and states, "even the crudest observations of behavior reveal that certain patterns and sequences of responses are more readily executed than others and that certain patterns and sequences of stimuli have priority over others."[25] McHugh has demonstrated empirically the natural phenomenon of adaptation via directive correlation.[26] He placed subjects in an environment of controlled anomie in which he randomly ordered responses to their behaviors. Even in this totally unstructured environment, McHugh discovered that humans consistently and persistently strived through a patterned sequence of behaviors to endow the transactions with some order or structure.

3. *Communication serves the purpose in the system of reducing equivocality of information.* In Weick's terms, communication serves to reduce equivocality.[27] Ashby concurs in different terms—communication

constrains possibilities in a system's product-space which thus reduces uncertainty.[28] A natural result of communication, then, is to reduce ambiguity by constraining the behaviors of individuals in the system by limiting the range of choices available to them. Ashby notes that constraining ambiguity is a natural phenomenon similar to the process of natural selection in biology.[29] Thus, the number of possible interaction sequences for structuring the system (reducing equivocality of information) are reduced through communication so that certain selected sequences have significantly greater frequency and, therefore, priority over others. Those characteristic sequences, then, epitomize the structure (information) of the system.

1. Tentative Axioms of a Developing Theory of Communication

1. The Communication Process Occurs in a Social System. This axiom implicitly identifies the individual as the component of a communication system. That is, the individual is the enduring element of a communication system—the element that carries the history of the system through its developing stages in time.[30]

2. The Structure and Function of a System are Visible in the Behaviors Performed by Individuals. While individuals are components of the system, they are not the units of interest or analysis. This unit is the act—an instance of discriminable and observable behavior performed by an individual. Since transactive relationships are important in the process focus, the more important unit of analysis is the combination of contiguous acts, i.e., the interact and double interact. The importance of interaction sequences to define interpersonal relationships has been stressed by numerous others including Weick,[31] Scheflen,[32] McGrath and Altman,[33] and Brodey.[34]

3. The Structure-Function Complex of a Communication System may be Wholly Observed in Time-Space. The blurring of distinctions between space and time—structure and function—in a process perspective is now complete. Behaviors are inherently transient and have no existence in space. The structure of a communication system, unlike a physical system, cannot be described in spatial terms. Parsons, recognizing the importance of events, also defines social structure in terms of time, i.e., action:[35]

> The concept of structure focuses on those elements of the patterning of the system which may be regarded as independent of the lower-amplitude and shorter time-range fluctuations in the relation of the system to its external situation. It thus designates the features of the system which can, in certain strategic respects, be treated as constants over certain ranges of variation in the behavior of other significant elements of the theoretical problem.

Since events serve to characterize the components of the system and events have existence only in time, the typical notion of structure as a physical spatial phenomenon is not applicable. Ashby further explains this apparent paradox between the limitations of time and space.[36]

> . . . two factors must be *excluded as irrelevant*. The first is "materiality"—the idea that a machine must be made of actual matter. . . . This is wrong, for examples can readily be given showing that what is essential is whether the system . . . behaves in a law-abiding and machine-like way. Also to be excluded as irrelevant is any reference to energy, for any calculating machine shows that what matters if the *regularity* of the behavior—whether energy is gained or lost, or even created, is simply irrelevant.

The structure of a system, then, may be defined as the interaction sequences which characterize the relationships among individuals at any given point in time.

The function of the system already exists in time as reversible and transient relationshops which are also characterized by interaction sequences. (The system's function would also include phases and cyclical transformations, too; but this discussion will focus on only one level of function-complexity—the interaction sequences.) But since systemic functioning may possess some degree of complexity, it remains to be seen how complexity can be defined and measured through interaction sequences. Pringle indicates:[37]

> If order. . .can mean order in time as well as order in space, then the hypothesis must be extended to include, the concept of complexity in time as well as complexity of form. . . .
>
> The establishment of an orderly relationship between two events, one of which is new, increases the complexity of the system, in contra-distinction to the continuation of a pre-existing relationship. . . .the final state in which the response does not occur is different from a state in which the response never occurs, since the habituation it has occurred and may recur again in the course of time. The absence of a single event in a sequence is thus a more complex state than its presence.

An example may serve to clarify Pringle's point. If the interact (act_1 act_2) always—or never—signposted the subsequent act (act_3) in a double interact sequence, the communication system is not very complex since "act_1 act_2" is—or isn't—the antecedent of "act_3" with 100% reliability. On the other hand, if "act_1 act_2" is sometimes followed by "act_4" or "act_5," the system increases in complexity. Perhaps "act_3" is the subsequent of "act_1 act_2" only 85% of the time. It is the state in which "act_3" does not occur—the absence not the presence of the single event in the sequence of "act_1 act_2 act_3" which gives the system its complexity.

Brodey reiterates the point of complexity. "The dialogue of an interdependent system is maintained by growing and evolving, for simple repetition does not easily persist when there is adequate complexity."[38]

Implicit in this axiom is the primary importance of the time dimension in locating and defining the structure and function of a communication system. And equally important is the revelation that not only can the structure of a communication system be defined and measured—so too can its complexity and its evolutionary changes.

4. The Order (structure) of a Communication System is Defined by Basic Interaction Sequences which Recur Predictably According to Rules of Empirical Redundancy. Information theorists have provided rules of empirical redundancy which explain and measure the organization of a system. Frick writes, ". . . information theory offers a ready-made tool for the description of behavior patterns and the analysis of sequential behavior. . . . in application to response sequences, redundancy may be used as a measure of the degree of stereotypy, or organization, of the observed behavior."[39] Miller makes a similar point: "If the course of action is coherent in such a way that future conduct depends upon past conduct, we say the behavior is predictable or, to some degree stereotyped. In such cases, the redundancy . . . can be used to measure the stereotypy."[40]

Systemic order is observed as regularity of behavior brought about by the operation of feedback loops. When the system is characterized in a steady state of order or increasing order, negative feedback (deviation correcting) loops are predominant. In a period of growth or change, positive feedback (deviation amplifying) loops are predominant. In interaction terms, Scheidel and Crowell define a potential feedback loop as a self-reflexive double interact.[41] Too commonly, communication researchers have considered feedback only the reflex action in response to some received act. For example, Leathers cites Scheidel and Crowell and still falls into the trap of defining feedback as a simple reaction—a single act.[42] Information theorists emphatically disagree: "Obviously, the reflex is not the unit we should use as the element of behavior: the unit should be the feedback loop itself."[43] Defined as double interact, the feedback loop emerges from direct observation of communicative behavior and, as sequences which characterize the system, serves to regulate the structure of the communication system.

5. The Complexity (function) of a Communication System Exists in Two Forms: (a) The Degree of Probability that Subsequent Events in the Behavioral Sequences will Occur in the Presence of Antecedent Events, and (b) a System in Flux — Evolution of Growth or Change in the System Responding to Positive Feedback. In the first case, discussed earlier, complexity is normal and may increase or decrease independent of an increase in order. That is, a system may increase its order without a corresponding increase in complexity, or *vice versa*. In the second case, complexity is abnormal and increases contingent upon a decrease in order.[44] A system responding to positive feedback is a system in a period of change. When deviation in the system is amplified, the system suffers a decrease in structural order and, for the time being at least, is not adequately self-regulated. Of course, if deviation continues indefinitely unchecked, complexity increases to a point of virtual random patterning—systemic destruction. An evolving and healthy system, however, will experience periods of increased complexity and decreased order, but those periods will be temporary as negative feedback loops are reasserted.

Guidelines for Future Research

An appropriate question to ask at this point is, "So what?" How do these abstractions serve to further the development of communication theory? The answer to this question lies in future communication research. All research is inevitably based on some theoretical perspective whether the researcher is aware of it or not. The source credibility researcher using SD scales and factor analysis, for example, utilizes a theory based on intrapersonal phenomena—possessed or perceived— which bears an amazing similarity to Aristotelian ethos, i.e., focus is on antecedent conditions producing similar outcomes in a linear causal chain. To adopt the present theoretical perspective from general system theory would guide the researcher in rather specific directions.

1. The Researcher Should Select Variables for Study From the Communication System Paradigm. The paradigm, as suggested, would necessitate direct observation of behavior and deny the significance of internalized and abstracted psychological characteristics of individuals.

2. The Model for Communication Research Should Embody a Process Focus. The static design of pre-test, treatment, and post-test considers time only grossly as simple duration. More specific dimensions of time, such as simultaneity, sequence, and succession must not be overlooked. Brodey, for example, stresses the importance of a commonly ignored aspect which he calls "information time"—setting two time periods as equivalent when the same amount of data is processed." Some empirical evidence in group communication suggests that information is processed more quickly in the latter stages of a group's task accomplishment than in the early stages of orientation—indicating that the unit of information time early in a group's history is longer in simple duration than the unit of information time near task completion. Probably our language embodies simple duration within its structure, in Sapir-Whorfian tradition, and encourages us to conceptualize time in a rather unsophisticated manner. Thus, to consider time differently in communication research may be the most difficult guideline to follow.

3. Inherent in Communication Research from the System Model is a Search for Interactive Features which Characterize Communicative Behavior. As a logical corollary, research with the process focus virtually eliminates simple effects studies in favor of observing communicative behavior directly. Such a guideline does not eliminate an experimental design as such, but it de-emphasizes "effects" as the key feature of the experiment. Thus, whether the design is experimental or not, observable and discriminable communicative behavior should always serve as one of the dependent variables rather than merely a mediating variable. If the researcher claims to be engaged in communication research, it does not seem unreasonable to expect him to observe communication.

4. Communication Researchers Should Consider Interaction Analysis their Primary Measurement Technique. The natural outcome of measuring observable communicative behavior, rules out internalized abstracted qualities of personality which are susceptible only to inferential behavior measures. Then, too, isolated units of communicative behavior yield little research information when observed outside the context of the entire interaction sequences. Scheflen explains:[46]

> Since behavior is patterned in larger and larger levels and contexts, thereby deriving its meaning, the study of behavioral isolates out of context [of the program] cannot take us to meaning, purpose, significance in the system, and explanation. When we study behavioral isolates, we may unwittingly rely upon some preconception or metacommunicational myth about their actual context to make inferences about their implications.

When, however, we do isolate elements of behavior as a step in their analysis, we can discover and identify naturally occurring structural units, rather than relying on abstracted qualities such as the usual variables of personality. Scheflen goes on to emphasize that shifting from material systems to behavioral systems even requires the shift in units of analysis—from personality variables to behavioral transactions.

5. Essential to Future Communication Research are Methods of Qualitative Analysis. Unfortunately, qualitative analysis is often misconstrued as any form of analysis which does not use statistics or numbers. Rather, the difference between qualitative and non-qualitative analysis is the difference in emphasis upon linear causality and predictability. Lofland clarifies the nature of qualitative analysis by listing three questions as basic to inquiry and analysis.[47] What are the *characteristics* of a social phenomenon? What are its *causes*? While non-qualitative analysis addresses itself primarily to the last two questions—causes and effects, qualitative analysis pursues answers to the first question—forms, variations, structures, classifications, etc., of the phenomenon under investigation.

Churchman and Ackoff make essentially the same distinction between physical (non-qualitative) and morphological (qualitative) analysis.[48] Lofland's qualitative analytical method involves searching for specific characteristics under the general classes of *static* analysis, *phases,* and *cycles*—concepts readily amenable to communication and, in fact, previously suggested as guidelines for communication research in small groups. The importance of qualitative analysis cannot be overestimated if research is to provide insights into process and avoid the restrictions inherent in linear causality.

Goals of Future Communication Research

(a) An Exhaustive Morphological Classification of Communicative Situations. David Smith has suggested one list of morphological classes. Although his classification scheme is based on function performed and may be too limiting, it can certainly be utilized as a springboard to further study.[49]

(b A General Category System for Interaction Analysis. In developing a category system to analyze communicative behavior, the emphasis must be on discovering commonalities of categories across situations and levels. Although categorical differences across situations will undoubtedly be discovered and will serve to characterize different situations, finding similarities should remain the goal. In essence, research should pursue a taxonomy of communicative behaviors to correlate with the morphology of communicative situations.

(c) Cross-level Propositions which Characterize Interactive Features of Two or More Morphological Classes. Such a goal is consistent with the search for commonalities and for theoretical generality. And the goal is consistent with James G. Miller's implied suggestion that research probably needs to discover structure (characteristic features of communication at a given moment in time) before a full-blown study of process (including changes of communicative features across time) can be meaningful.[50] That is, knowledge of structure and order of a communication system is a logical first step. Research into the system's function and complexity then follows quickly.

Necessary throughout any research program is an awareness of the theoretic basis which prompts the research and a striving to increase the generality of research findings. Consistency of research perspective and generalizability of results are the essence of any sound theory. We may safely conclude that past research has not been guided by any general theory and that we still have no theory, *per se.* But now, despite the rather high level of abstraction, guidelines are available to make some progress toward that goal. And that is what research should be about—progress.

References and Notes

1. Bertalanffy, Ludwig von, *General System Theory: Foundations, Development, Applications,* New York: Braziller, 1968, p.45.
2. Jackson, Don, "The Individual and the Larger Context," *General Systems Theory and Psychiatry,* William Gray, Frederick J. Duhl, and Nicholas D. Rizzo, eds., Boston: Little, Brown, 1969, p. 390.
3. *Ibid.*
4. Berghe, Pierre van den, "Dialectic and Functionalism: Toward a Theoretical Synthesis," *American Sociological Review,* 1963, Vol. 28, 1963, pp. 695-705.
5. Gerard, R. W., "Units and Concepts of Biology," *Modern Systems Research for the Behavioral Scientist,* Walter Buckley, ed., Chicago: Aldine, 1968, pp. 51-58.
6. Machlup, Fritz, "Are the Social Sciences Really Inferior?" *Philosophy of the Social Sciences: A Reader,* Maurice Natanson, ed., New York: Random House, 1963, pp. 158-180.
7. Buckley, Walter, "Society as a Complex Adaptive System," *Modern Systems Research for the Behavioral Scientist,* Walter Buckley, ed., Chicago: Aldine, 1968, pp. 490-513.
8. *Ibid.,* p. 449.
9. *Ibid.,* p. 511.
10. Brodey, Warren M., "Information Exchange in the Time Domain," *General Systems Theory and Psychiatry,* William Gray, Frederick J. Duhl, and Nicholas D. Rizzo, eds., Boston: Little, Brown, 1969, pp. 239-240.
11. Buckley, Walter, "Society as a Complex Adoptive System," *Modern Systems Research for the Behavioral Scientist,* Walter Buckley, ed., Chicago: Aldine, 1968, p. 509.
12. Ornstein, Robert E., *On the Experience of Time,* Baltimore: Penguin, 1969.
13. Jaffe, Joseph, and Stanley Feldstein, *Rhythms of Dialogue,* New York: Academic Press, 1970.
14. Brodey, Warren, "Information Exchange in the Time Domain," *General Systems Theory and Psychiatry,* William Gray, Frederick J. Duhl, and Nicholas D. Rizzo, eds., Boston: Little, Brown, 1969, pp. 239-240.
15. Berrien, F. Kenneth, *General and Social Systems,* New Brunswick, N.J.: Rutgers University Press, 1968.
16. Watzlawick, Paul, Janet Helmick Beavin, and Don D. Jackson, *Pragmatics of Human Communication: A Study of Interactional Patterns, Pathologies, and Paradoxes,* New York: Norton, 1967.
17. Scheflen, Albert E., "Behavioral Programs in Human Communication," *General Systems Theory and Psychiatry,* William Gray, Frederick J. Duhl, and Nicholas D. Rizzo, eds., Boston: Little, Brown, 1969, pp. 209-228.

18. Watzlawick, Beavin, and Jackson, *Pragmatics of Human Communication: A Study of Interactional Patterns, Pathologies, and Paradoxes,* New York: Norton, 1967, pp. 48-71.
19. Rosenblueth, Arturo, and Norbert Wiener, "Purposeful and Non-Purposeful Behavior," *Modern Systems Research for the Behavioral Scientist,* Walter Buckley, ed., Chicago: Aldine, 1968, pp. 236-237.
20. Rosenblueth, Arturo, Norbert Wiener, and Julien Bigelow, "Behavior, Purpose, and Teleology," *Modern Systems Research for the Behavioral Scientist,* Walter Buckley, ed., Chicago: Aldine, 1968, p. 225.
21. Churchman, C. W., and R. L. Ackoff, "Purposive Behavior and Cybernetics," *Modern Systems Research for the Behavioral Scientist,* Walter Buckley, ed., Chicago: Aldine, 1968, p. 249.
22. Sommerhof, G., "Purpose, Adaptation, and Directive Correlation," *Modern Systems Research for the Behavioral Scientist,* Walter Buckley, ed., Chicago: Aldine, 1968, pp. 281-295.
23. *Ibid.,* p. 295.
24. Dore, Ronald Philip, "Function and Cause," *American Sociological Review,* 1961, Vol. 26, 1961, pp. 843-853.
25. Osgood, Charles E., "A Behavioristic Analysis of Perception and Language as Cognitive Phenomena," *Modern Systems Research for the Behavioral Scientist,* Walter Buckley, ed., Chicago: Aldine, 1968, p. 188.
26. McHugh, Peter, *Defining the Situation: The Organization of Meaning in Social Interaction,* Indianapolis, Ind.: Bobbs-Merrill, 1968.
27. Weick, Karl E., *The Social Psychology of Organizing,* Reading, Mass.: Addison-Wesley, 1969.
28. Ashby, Ross W., "Principles of Self-Organizing Systems," *Modern Systems Research for the Behavioral Scientist,* Walter Buckley, ed., Chicago: Aldine, 1968, p. 109.
29. *Ibid.,* pp. 115-116.
30. Gerard, R. W., "Units and Concepts of Biology," *Modern Systems Research for the Behavioral Scientist,* Walter Buckley, ed., Chicago: Aldine, 1968, pp. 51-58.
31. Weick, Karl E., *The Social Psychology of Organizing,* Reading, Mass.: Addison-Wesley, 1969, p. 33.
32. Sheflen, Albert E., "Behavioral Programs in Human Communication," *General Systems Theory and Psychiatry,* William Gray, Frederick J. Duhl, and Nicholas D. Rizzo, eds., Boston: Little, Brown, 1969, pp. 209-228.
33. McGrath, Joseph E., and Irwin Altman, *Small Group Research: A Synthesis and Critique of the Field,* New York: Holt, Rinehart and Winston, 1966, p. 74.
34. Brodey, Warren M., "Information Exchange in the Time Domain," *General Systems Theory and Psychiatry,* William Gray, Frederick J. Duhl, and Nicholas D. Rizzo, eds., Boston: Little, Brown, 1969, p. 234.

35. Parson, Talcott, "A Paradigm for the Analysis of Social Systems and Change," *System, Change, and Conflict*, J. J. Demerath II and Richard A. Peterson, eds., New York: Free Press, 1967, p. 190.

36. Ashby, Ross W., "Principles of Self-Organizing Systems," *Modern Systems Research for the Behavioral Scientist*, Walter Buckley, ed., Chicago: Aldine, 1968, p. 111.

37. Pringle, J. W. S., "On the Parallel between Learning and Evolution," *Modern Systems Research for the Behavioral Scientist*, Walter Buckley, ed., Chicago: Aldine, 1968, p. 264-265.

38. Brodey, Warren M., "Information Exchange in the Time Domain," *General Systems Theory and Psychiatry*, William Gray, Frederick J. Duhl, and Nicholas D. Rizzo, eds., Boston: Little, Brown, 1969, p. 234.

39. Frick, F. C., "The Application of Information Theory in Behavioral Studies," *Modern Systems Research for the Behavioral Scientist*, Walter Buckley, ed., Chicago: Aldine, 1968, p. 185.

40. Miller, George A., "What is Information Measurement?" *Modern Systems Research for the Behavioral Scientist*, Walter Buckley, ed., Chicago: Aldine, 1968, p. 128.

41. Scheidel, Thomas M., and Laura Crowe, "Feedback in Small Group Communication," *Quarterly Journal of Speech*, Vol. 52, 1966, p. 274.

42. Leathers, Dale G., "The Feedback Rating Instrument: A New Means of Evaluating Discussion," *Central States Speech Journal*, Vol. 23, 1971, pp. 32-42.

43. Miller, George A., Eugene Galanter, and Karl H. Pribram, "Plans and the Structure of Behavior," *Modern Systems Research for the Behavioral Scientist*, Walter Buckley, ed., Chicago: Aldine, 1968, p. 371.

44. Maruyama, Magorah, "The Second Cybernetics: Deviation-Amplifying Mutual Causal Processes," *Modern Systems Research for the Behavioral Scientist*, Walter Buckley, ed., Chicago: Aldine, 1968, pp. 304-313.

45. Brodey, Warren M., "Information Exchange in the Time Domain," *General Systems Theory and Psychiatry*, William Gray, Frederick J. Duhl, and Nicholas D. Rizzo, eds., Boston: Little, Brown, 1969, p. 241.

46. Schflen, Albert E., "Behavioral Programs in Human Communication," *General Systems Theory and Psychiatry*, Gray, Duhl, and Rizzo, eds., Boston: Little, Brown, 1969, pp. 223-224.

47. Lofland, John, *Analyzing Social Settings: A Guide to Qualitative Observation and Analysis*, Belmont, Calif.: Wadsworth, 1971, p. 13-14.

48. Churchman, C. W., and R. L. Ackoff, "Purposive Behavior and Cybernetics," *Modern Systems Research for the Behavioral Scientist*, Walter Buckley, ed., Chicago: Aldine, 1968, p. 246.

49. Smith, David H., "The Classification of Communication: Problems and a Proposal," *Pacific Speech*, Vol. 2, 1968, pp. 15-24.

50. Miller, James G., "Living Systems: Structure and Process," *Behavioral Science*, Vol. 10, 1965, p. 337.

13
Feedback in Social Sciences: Toward a Reconceptualization of Morphogeneses

JOHN Y. KIM

The accepted value of the feedback concept in social sciences is evidenced by the ubiquitous use of the term feedback in theoretical literature. The term has become a cliche in the field of communication in particular. Recently, however, a growing number of scholars have expressed concern over the abuse or misuse of the term feedback in human and social inquiries. Walter Buckley has stated that the term feedback has simply become "vulgarized."[1] Magoroh Maruyama also criticizes wide-ranging abuse of the term in biological and social sciences.[2]

The core problem is that the feedback concept originating in hard sciences is typically cast in linear, unidirectional, and mechanistic terms. In contrast, human communication is conceived to be multilateral, organic, and mutual causal in nature. Thus, although the notion of feedback has been expounded by systems-oriented social scientists,[3] a problem arises owing to the incompatibility between the mechanistic conception of feedback and the systemic conception of human communication processes.

This chapter attempts to explicate this problem by providing a reconceptualization of the feedback concept.[4] It does so in two stages: first, it elaborates the basic premises of the feedback concept as understood in the physical sciences; and second, it attempts to derive new systemic feedback constructs that would provide alternatives to the traditional scheme of negative feedback and positive feedback.

The Traditional Feedback Concept

Although feedback has been credited with resolving the classical problem of linear causality by introducing the circularity in the causal chain, it still is based upon the mechanistic and closed-system premises, as Ludwig von Bertalanffy pointed out.[5] The mechanistic bias of the feedback concept may be best demonstrated by the simple example of the thermostat. The room temperature at any point of time is regarded as an output. If the output (room temperature) is lower than the reference input—or the goal (as set on the thermostat)—set by a human agent, an apparatus is actuated to increase the flow of heat into the room so that the output is brought to the goal level. On the other hand, if the output level (room temperature) reaches the reference input (as set on thermostat) this information is fed back to the input process, and the apparatus shuts off the flow of the heat, thus maintaining the goal level of temperature. In this respect, regulators and servomechanisms which work on the feedback principle are characterized as self-regulating, self-organizing, goal-oriented or the goal-directed mechanisms.

Thus, first characteristic of the mechanistic feedback concept is that feedback behavior is held to be *teleological*. Previously, teleology had been dismissed by the classical physics as a misconception of reality. As Bertalanffy maintains, it was identified as the "playground of mysterious, supernatural or anthropomorphic agencies. . .a misplaced projection of the observer's mind into a nature governed by purposeless laws."[6] Thus the scientist had to reduce the properties of teleological phenomena to the level where the language of the mechanical thinking of physics would fit.

Now, the cyberneticist claims that the mysterious phenomena of teleology are amenable to scientific treatment. Rosenblueth, Wiener and Bigelow, in one of the early papers on cybernetics, identified as teleological the behavior of feedback systems implying that the behavior shows purposefulness.[7] To them, the term purposeful indicated that "the act or behavior may be interpreted as directed to the attainment of a goal." But, they also argued that *not all* purposeful behaviors are teleological—*only* the behaviors of feedback systems. Therefore, according to Rosenblueth and his colleagues, there are two kinds of purposeful behaviors: feedback (teleological) and non-feedback (non-teleological).

The cybernetic redefinition of teleology, nevertheless, appears to be limited in the same sense as classical physics, which simply concluded that there were no teleological phenomena in reality. For the cyberneticist, certain "non-feedback"—yet obviously purposeful—behaviors are simply understood to be "outside the scope of science," so to speak, by being defined out of the realm of teleological behavior. Thus, if the cyberneticist wants to study these categories of purposeful behaviors, they have to be reduced either to the language of feedback or that of the classical mechanical theories.[8]

The second characteristic of the mechanistic feedback concept is the premise of *unidirectionality* as exemplified by the several parts in the thermostat: a receptor, a control agent, and an effector, and so on. The control agent compares the output message relayed from the receptor with its image of the desired goal, finds the deviation and commands the effector to take an action to eliminate the deviation. Then the consequence of the effector's action is monitored by the receptor which feeds the information back to the input process, etc.

Such an explanation of feedback implies two important closed system properties: the causal relationship between the component units is one-way, and the relationship of the whole system with its environment is an independent one. Thus, one finds that feedback at its basic level is a closed system concept.

Systems: Degrees of Openness

Depending upon one's immediate goal, one may define a system as closed or open, so that only certain relevant variables are observed and measured, *purposefully* ignoring other variables and their mutual relationships that might characterize the system otherwise considered from another perspective. One may think of a continuum of systems. At each of the two extremes are systems which are "completely open" and "completely closed" respectively. At these extremes, the concept of system itself seems to disappear, for if a system is completely open, its boundaries would be hard to define and hence there would be no system at all. On the other hand, there is no system which is not in certain kinds of interaction with its environment. Thus, as Kenneth Berrien observes, "we are compelled to view all real systems as open, recognizing that the degree of openness may vary among systems."[9] This view seems to be in line with the wider perspective of systems theory, which defines systems as "a set of objects together with relationship between the objects and between their attributes."[10] Since systems theory also defines environment as "the set of all objects a change in whose attributes affect the system and also those objects whose attributes are changed by the behavior of the system,"[11] one can safely conclude that *all systems are necessarily open.* Given such a view, a useful approach to systems categorization is provided by Laszlo, who proposes that systems be categorized by three levels of organization: *suborganic, organic* and *supraorganic.*[12]

Once we consider systems as organic and open, W. Ross Ashby's notion of coupling machines as feedback systems takes on particular value for the social scientist.[13] Ashby maintains that two or more whole machines can be coupled to form one. Any one machine as a system can be regarded as being formed by coupling of its parts, which can themselves be thought of, in turn, as subsystems. In this context, Ashby explained what is meant by *input:* when the systems are coupled in such a way as to maintain each one's wholeness without "violence," one affects the other by affecting its input. This occurs, Ashby pointed out, when there is "feedback."

Feedback, then, is fundamentally a phenomenon where *two* or *more* systems couple with one another, not a unilateral state of affairs. Thus, in this concept of coupling systems, one system's input is another system's output, and *vice versa,* and the model becomes one of multilateral mutual causality.[14]

Criteria for Negative-Positive Feedback

The reconceptualization of feedback as coupling systems behavior provides us with a clear-cut criterion for the discrimination between "negative feedback" and "positive feedback" in human domain, where it is more difficult to quantify variables in a reliable manner than in hard sciences. A generally accepted description says that if feedback operates to *counteract* differences it is negative; if it involves *amplifying* differences it is positive. It is clear, in this description, that whether feedback is held to be negative or positive depends upon the concept of difference or deviation.

However, deviation implies at least two points of reference; difference or deviation between what and what? Depending upon what reference points one utilizes, one may reach different conclusions as to whether feedback is negative or positive.

First, in the case of the thermostat, which has been described as negative feedback system, the two reference points for deviation are undoubtedly the value of the goal and the value of the output. The deviation here is viewed to be counteracting (difference reducing) as the system attains the goal, and therefore the feedback is termed negative. Label this *goal-output* deviation concept *deviation Criterion 1*. According to this criterion, if deviation amplifies between the goal value and the output, the feedback is positive.

Second, certain social scientists have utilized "initial kick" as a reference point for identifying deviation, although not always explicitly stated. For example, the phenomenon of *growth* is described in terms of positive feedback.[15] Maruyama relies upon G. Myrdal's economic theory that what may be termed the initial kick of an economic plan determines the direction of the subsequent economic growth, in the sense that the resulting development (final output) would be far greater than the investment. Therefore, "once the economy is kicked in a right direction, and with a sufficient initial push, the deviation-amplifying mutural positive feedbacks take over the process, and the resulting development will be proportionately large as compared with the initial kick."[16]

Obviously, the reference points for deviation here are the values of the *initial kick* and that of the *output*. In general, the initial kick would be the first input value in a series of input-output sequences. Returning to the example of the thermostat, the initial kick would be the initial room temperature when a human sets the thermostat at a specific goal. It is interesting to note that if the room temperature is low and the goal is high, the feedback behavior between the initial kick and the goal would be viewed as one of deviation-amplifying, and thus would be defined as positive rather than negative feedback according to this criterion:[17] Let us label this *intial kick-output* deviation concept *Deviation Criterion II*.

Third, the coupling of feedback systems imply still another set of possible reference points. As an example, in the social domain, consider a static economy where the poor are presumed to stay poor and the rich understood to stay rich. Here, the wealth level of the poor at a given point of time would be one reference output, and the wealth level of the rich, the other reference output. Maruyama points out that economies, especially in underdeveloped countries, are dynamic in nature in that the rich get richer and the poor get poorer in mutual interaction.[18] If one assumes that there is mutual causal relationship between these subsystems of an economy, then, the deviation between the output values of the two is viewed as mutually amplifying, and on this basis, Maruyama terms the economic model whereby "the rich get richer, etc.,"an instance of positive feedback.

This example suggests a third kind of deviation criterion, involving a comparison between the value of one output and that of the other. Let's refer to this state of affairs as *Deviation Criterion III*.[19] Thus, as it turns out, there are at least three criteria for deviation, implicit but never explicitly articulated in the literature dealing with feedback in human-social phenomena. To summarize them:

1) Deviation Criterion I—deviation between the values of the *goal* and of the *output*,

2) Deviation Criterion II—deviation between the values of the *initial kick* and of the *final output*, and

3) Deviation Criterion III—deviation between the values of the *output* of one subsystem and of the *output* of another.

Morphostasis and Morphogenesis

The discussion thus far has pointed up two problems relating to the social scientist's attempt to directly apply the mechanistic concept of feedback. First, many social phenomena described as feedback may not be feedback phenomena at all, in that feedback concept is fundamentally a closed-system property. Human interactions are conceived to be processes of dynamic wholes more relevantly explained by the concept of coupling systems. Secondly, the concept of positiveness and negativeness of feedback has no clear referents. There are at least three different, and often conflicting, criteria implicit in the concept of deviation, on which the concept of feedback hinges. Thus, depending on what criterion one uses, feedback in human and social domains may be defined as either positive or negative.

These problems emphatically suggest a need for a new set of concepts that would better highlight the phenomena which the terms negative feedback and positive feedback are intended to refer to.

The concepts of *morphostasis* and *morphogenesis* have been suggested as alternatives.[20] According to Maruyama, morphostasis refers to deviation-counteracting multilateral mutual causal processes, and morphogenesis to deviation-amplifying multilateral mutual causal processes. Maruyama's examples for these concepts are two economic models: "the poor stay poor, the rich stay rich" as morphostasis and "the poor become poorer, and the rich become richer" as morphogenesis.[21]

However, Maruyama's dichotomous conceptualization disregards a *third* possibility—that "the poor become less poor (relatively rich) and the rich become less rich (relatively poor)." According to *Deviation Criterion III*, then, this state of affairs exemplifies the *truly deviation-counteracting* multilateral mutual causal process, while Maruyama's "the poor stay poor, etc.," which he termed deviation-counteracting, is better described as *deviation-maintaining*.[22]

Consider the two-nation arms race system as another example.[23] The phenomenon of nations engaged in competitive armament has been conceptualized as positive feedback—as a phenomenon of deviation-amplifying multilateral mutual causal process. Careful study reveals that there is more than one possible kind of multilateral mutual causal process involved in this context. Suppose that two nations suddenly begin expanding their individual military powers through mutual interaction. One of the following three possibilities would occur:

1) Nation A stays strong and Nation B stays weak, maintaining a constant level of deviation between the military output levels, although both nations' armament levels increase in absolute terms. This is a *deviation-maintaining* phenomenon.

2) Nation A becomes less strong (relatively weak) and Nation B becomes less weak (relatively strong), as Nation B catches up with Nation A's strength. This is a *deviation-counteracting* phenomenon.

3) Nation A becomes ever stronger and Nation B becomes ever weaker, whereas the arms levels of both nations still increase together in absolute terms. This is a *deviation-amplifying* phenomenon.

The first instance exemplifies *morphostasis*, because it is a "deviation-maintaining" phenomenon. The third instance obviously implies *morphogenesis*, since the deviation is amplified. The question that arises relates to categorization of the second instance. Is this "deviation-counteracting" phenomenon an instance of morphostasis or morphogenesis?

Structure, Organization and Negentropic Deviation

In order to answer this question, one needs to explicate further the concepts of morphostasis and morphogenesis. The prefix *morpho* in these terms is taken to mean *structure* of a system, according to Maruyama.[24] He identified morphostasis as "the process of maintaining the structuredness of a structure," and morphogenesis as "the process of generating, or increasing, the structuredness of a structure." Since Maruyama also conceptualized morphostasis as deviation-counteracting process and morphogenesis as deviation-amplifying process, as noted earlier, the concepts *structure* and *deviation* are closely related to one another. Anatol Rapoport defined structure as "the totality of relations" of a thing.[25] As such, the terms denote an arrangement or pattern of component units of a system—pattern not as static configuration but as dynamic process of internal arrangement. The concept structure can, then, be equated to that of *organization,* for, as Wiener indicated, organization is something in which there is an *interdependence* (relation) between parts.[26] Similarly, Ashby viewed organization in terms of constraint: "as soon as the relation between two entities A and B becomes conditional on C's value or state, then a necessary component of 'organization' is present."[27]

In cybernetics, organization is held to be the opposite of entropy, a functional measure of disorder within a closed system. It follows that the concept of morphostasis and morphogenesis may be reinterpreted in light of entropy-organization.[28] Information theory, further, implies that entropy is actually a measure of our *ignorance* of a system's internal organization, rather than a measure of physical states of the system. Thus, Claude Shannon explained entropy by such notions as "uncertainty" on the part of the information-receiver and "freedom of choice" on the part of the information-sender.[29] Entropy is "information in reverse gear" to borrow from Jagjit Singh's terminology.[30] Leon Brillouin coined the term *negentropy* to refer to this same phenomenon: "The connection between entropy and information was rediscovered by Shannon, but he defined entropy with a sign just opposite to that of the standard thermodynamic definitions. Hence what Shannon calls entropy of information actually represents negentropy."[31]

In a similar vein, O.C. deBeauregard argued that negentropy and information are transformable into one another, i.e., *negentropy $\rightleftarrows$ information.* His interpretation is that the transformation of negentropy into information signifies "acquisition of knowledge"; the transformation of information into negentropy signifies "power of organization."[32]

Particularly relevant to the present discussion of feedback is the notion of the transformation of *information into negentropy as power of organization.* If, for example, the multi-nation arms race system is approached as a whole system, it would be considered in a state of constant reorganization as each strives for superiority in arms whether individual subsystems purposefully seek this state of affairs or not. In this system, then, one of the three possibilities would occur. While the absolute level of armament in the entire system might go up:

1) the degree of organization (of structure) would stay at a constant level as the deviation between the output levels is maintained. This is a *negentropy-maintaining* multilateral mutual causal process;

2) the balance of power may change as the degree of organization (of structure) decreases. This is an instance of *negentropy-decreasing* multilateral mutual causal process;

3) the complexion of balance of power may change, as the degree of organization (of structure) increases. This is an instance of *negentropy-increasing* multilateral mutual causal process. This categorization indicates still a fourth criterion for deviation, in which the two points of reference are *degrees of negentropy*. This we will term *Deviation Criterion IV*.

Reconceptualization: Three Processes of Morphogenesis

The foregoing suggests three instances of morphogenesis. *Deviation Criterion IV* identifies the two-nation arms race in which the balance of power is maintained at a certain level although the arms levels may constantly go up in absolute terms as an example of negentropy-maintaining multilateral mutual causal processes. This may be described as a system with a steady state of negentropy,[33] a characteristic of living (organic and supraorganic) systems.

That living systems are capable of maintaining a steady state of negentropy is due to the system's multilateral mutual causal relationship with its environment. As Erwin Schrodinger so cogently noted, a living organism "feeds upon negative entropy, attracting, as it were, a stream of negative entropy upon itself, to compensate the entropy increase . . . and thus to maintain itself on a stationary and fairly low entropic level."[34]

It is in this sense that I conceptualize the negentropy-maintaining multilateral mutual causal process as *morphostasis,* as Maruyama did, but for different reasons. Implied in morphostasis (in the present context) is a system's "struggle to stay alive," so to speak, by fighting the downstream of entropic tendency. Thus, this structure-maintaining process turns out to be a *structure-generating* process also, because, to "stay alive" means to constantly create the structure in order to replace the portion of structure lost through increasing entropy. It follows that morphostasis denotes a superficially static structure which in fact goes through a dynamic process of multilateral mutual causal interactions that produces structure. In this sense, morphostasis indeed is a kind of *morphogenesis!*

Next, *Deviation Criterion IV* identifies as a phenomenon of negentropy-decreasing multilateral mutual causal process, the two-nation arms race in which the deviation between the output levels counteracts. This model was entirely ignored by Maruyama, as noted earlier. Also, the question of whether this phenomenon represents morphostasis or morphogenesis was left unanswered. In terms of the Second Law of Thermodynamics, this process of decreasing negentropy would represent the natural tendency of closed systems. However, the seemingly similar process occuring in organic and supraorganic systems are not the result of the law of closed systems in many cases. They are the result of conscious and multilateral mutual causal interactions between subsystems, whereas a closed system tends to increase entropy *without* such multilateral mutual causal interactions.

Thus, the negentropy-decreasing process, which is also a structure-decreasing process, may be construed as a *structure-generating* process, for the same reasons as with the structure-maintaining process. Whatever level of structure the system may contain at a given moment of time, it is a result of conscious *creation* through the multilateral mutual causal relationship among its component parts. Also, that negentropy goes down from a high level to a lower level implies that, based upon *Deviation Criterion IV*, the deviation *amplifies*, from high to low. Thus, paradoxically, what I have called negentropy-decreasing process turns out to be a *deviation-amplifying* process, and in this sense, it is an instance of *morphogenesis.*

However, such an amplification of deviation is in effect toward a downward direction (from high to low), and this phenomenon is conceptualized as *downward morphogenesis.*

The third possibility of the two-nation arms race system, in which the deviation between the output levels amplifies, is identified as a phenomenon of negentropy-increasing multilateral mutual causal process according to *Deviation Criterion IV.* In this system, the deviation between the negentropy levels is viewed as amplifying toward an upward direction (from low to high). That is, the system generates enough structure to compensate the increasing entropy, *and* to increase the level of structure. Accordingly, this structure-increasing process is no doubt a structure-generating process. Since this phenomenon shows exactly the opposite characteristics of the entropy-increasing tendency of closed systems, it is obviously unique to living systems. Therefore, it is clearly an instance of *morphogenesis.* Since the direction of deviation-amplification is upward, it is termed *upward morphogenesis.*

Table 1 presents a summary of the framework presented in this section.

Conclusions and Implications

The reconceptualization suggests three different kinds of multilateral mutual causal processes involving "feedback," reconceptualized as coupling systems: morphostasis, downward morphogenesis and upward morphogenesis. The categorization is based on *Deviation Criterion IV*, which refers to levels of negentropy within a coupling system.

The maintenance or decrease of a level of structure within living systems (organic and supraorganic) are construed to be results of conscious multilateral mutual causal process, not as results of the natural law of increasing entropy. Thus, these two phenomena are reinterpreted as *structure-generating.* Since the increase of structure also involves structure-generating multilateral mutual causal process, all the three

_____

Table 1: Summary of Reconceptualized Morphogeneses

_____

Feedback Systems: Coupling Phenomena

1. *Morphostasis*

   a. deviation-maintaining multilateral mutual causal process (Deviation Criterion III)*
   b. deviation-maintaining multilateral mutual causal process (Deviation Criterion IV)†
   c. steady level of structure
   d. negentropy-maintaining (steady state of negentropy)
   e. "two nations build up or reduce arms levels, but power balance is maintained at a constant level"

2. *Downward Morphogenesis*

   a. deviation-counteracting multilateral mutual causal process (Deviation Criterion III)
   b. deviation-amplifying multilateral mutual causal process (Deviation Criterion IV)
   c. decreasing level of structure
   d. decreasing level of negentropy
   e. "two nations build up or reduce arms levels, and the gap between the power levels decreases"

3. *Upward Morphogenesis*

   a. deviation-amplifying multilateral mutual causal process (Deviation Criterion III)
   b. deviation-amplifying multilateral mutual causal process (Deviation Criterion IV)
   c. increasing level of structure
   d. increasing level of negentropy
   e. "two nations build up or reduce arms levels, and the gap between the power levels increases"

_____

*In *Deviation Criterion III* the two reference points are two output values of two subsystems within a coupling system.

†In *Deviation Criterion IV* the reference points are the two levels of negentropy of a system when the system moves from a high negentropy state to a low negentropy state or vice versa.

phenomena are held to be structure-generating multilateral mutual causal processes, although, for terminological purposes, they are called, respectively, structure-maintaining, structure-decreasing, and structure-increasing processes.

For an example of the implications of these concepts, let me refer to the international arms competition again. As noted, the upward spiral of arms competition has been universally described as "positive feedback," while it has been noted here that more than one kind of multilateral mutual causal processes are present. The arms buildup is viewed as positive feedback, apparently in the sense that "growth" in general is so viewed. The reference points for deviation implied in this interpretation are the initial kick and the output (Deviation Criterion II). Then, applying the same criterion, the downward spiral of competitive disarmament would be viewed as a phenomenon of *negative* feedback, since the deviation between the initial kick and the output would counteract. Such an interpretation, in turn, would leave one with no alternative but to conclude, by analogy, that the phenomenon of the thermostatic system also should be construed as both positive and negative feedback. While the room temperature goes up toward a goal, it would be a positive feedback phenomenon; and while the room temperature cools off toward a goal, it would be a negative feedback phenomenon.[35]

In this regard, it appears that the concept of "growth" is equated with "positive feedback" to denote generalized "increase." It should be noted, however, that "increase" in structure of a system does not imply the increase of the system's "size," but rather, an increase in the level of organization-negentropy. Therefore, the two-nation arms race system, in which both countries raise military strength but the level of structure remains constant, is appropriately categorized as an instance of morphostasis, although the system "grows" in its overall size. The new framework proposed here also is useful in conceiving of the *downward* spiral of disarmament. In the present context there are three different possibilities in the mutual disarmament system, interpreted in terms of negentropy. As nations reduce arms levels in mutual response, the whole system:

1) would maintain the steady state of negentropy;
2) would move from a high negentropy state to a low negentropy state;
3) or, would move from a low negentropy state to a high negentropy state.

Each of these state of affairs is very well explained by morphostasis, downward morphogenesis, and upward morphogenesis, as were the three possibilities in the phenomenon of upward spiral of arms race.

References and Notes

1. Buckley, Walter, *Sociology and Modern Systems Theory,* Englewood Cliffs, N.J.: Prentice-Hall, 1967, p. 52.
2. Maruyama, Magoroh, "Morphogenesis and Morphostasis," *Methods,* 1960, pp. 251-295.
3. Deutsch, Karl, *The Nerves of Government,* New York: The Free Press, 1963; Deutsch and Richard Meritt, "Effects of Events upon National and International Images," *International Behavior: A Social-Psychological*

Analysis, Herbert D. Kelman, ed., New York: Holt, Rinehart, and Winston, 1965, pp. 132-187; Deutsch, *The Analysis of International Relations,* Englewood Cliffs, N.J.: Prentice-Hall, 1968; David Singer, "Escalation and Control in International Conflict: A Simple Feedback Model," *General Systems,* 1970, pp. 163-173.

4. Explication of theoretic concepts is imperative in the sense that concepts are basic building blocks in the construction of scientific theories. James Conant observes that science is an interconnected series of concepts and conceptual schemes. *See* James B. Conant, *Science and Common Sense,* New Haven, Conn.: Yale University Press, 1951, p. 25. Also, in Lee Thayer's terms, the basic problems of social sciences in their efforts toward theory-building are *conceptual,* hence *prototheoretical,* since "one's conceptual tools are his terms for what he believes to be going on 'out there.'" *See* Lee Thayer, "On Theory-Building in Communication, I: Some Conceptual Problems," *Journal of Communication,* December, 1963, pp. 217-235.

5. To quote Bertalanffy on this point: ". . .dynamics in open systems and feedback mechanisms are two different model concepts, each in its right in its proper sphere. The open-system model is basically non-mechanistic, and transcends . . . one way causality as is basic in conventional physical theory. The cybernetic (feedback) approach retains the Cartesian machine model of the organism, uni-directional causality and closed systems." *See* Ludwig von Bertalanffy, *General System Theory,* New York: George Braziller, 1968, p. 163.

6. Bertalanffy, *General System Theory,* New York: George Braziller, 1968, p. 45.

7. Rosenblueth, Arturo, Norbert Wiener, and Julian Bigelow, "Behavior, Purpose, and Teleology," *Philosophy of Science,* 1943, pp. 18-24.

8. In fact, this is exactly what has been done in, especially, social sciences. Practically all the cyclic, circulatory or mutual response relationships are now explained in the parlance of feedback. Some may be truly feedback, but some are not. In this connection, consider Walter Buckley's strong argument for the necessity of *control center* in a feedback system. He comments that certain examples of the circular causal chain, such as ecological interrelations between population size and food supply, and the "vicious circle" of racial discrimination, are not "truly" feedback phenomena "inasmuch as there are no internal mechanisms which measure or compare the feedback input against a goal and pass the mis-match information on to a control center which activates appropriate system counter behavior." *See* Buckley, *Sociology and Modern Systems Theory,* Englewood Cliffs: N.J.: Prentice-Hall, 1967, pp. 69-70.

9. Berrien, Kenneth, *General and Social Systems,* New Brunswick, N. J.: Rutgers University Press, 1968, p. 16.

10. Hall, A. D., and R. E. Fagen, "Definition of System," *General Systems,* 1956, p. 83.
11. *Ibid.* p. 83.
12. Laszlo, Ervin, *The Systems View of the World,* New York: George Braziller, 1972.
13. Ross, Ashby, W., *An Introduction to Cybernetics,* New York: John Wiley and Sons, 1963.

    In fact, this necessity of multilateral mutual causality in feedback systems was very implicit in the original definition of the goal of a feedback system, provided by none other than Arturo Rosenblueth, Norbert Wiener, and Julian Bigelow: "A final condition in which the behaving object reaches a *definite correlation* in time or in space with respect to another object or event" [*emphasis added*]. *See* Rosenblueth, Wiener, and Bigelow, "Behavior, Purpose, and Teleology," *Philosophy of Science,* 1943, pp. 18-24. *See also* Richard Taylor, "Comments on a Mechanistic Conception of Purposefulness," *Philosophy of Science,* 1950, pp. 310-317. What seems to be missing in this definition, however, is that the system *always* exists in definite correlation with another, not necessarily only in its final condition. In this sense, Rosenblueth and his colleagues implied that a feedback system cannot be conceived to be existing in an environmental vacuum, although they might have not made it explicit.

    The point that the system exists always in definite correlation with another, not necessarily only in its final condition, was also pointed out by Richard Taylor, a critic of Rosenblueth and Wiener. Rosenblueth and his colleagues defined "purposive behavior" (teleological) as a behavior "directed to the attainment of a goal." Thus, according to Taylor, even a clock, for instance, seems to show such purposive behavior since its breaking down at a certain point of time may be thought a final correlation in time and space with respect to another object or event.

15. Milsum, John, ed., *Positive Feedback,* New York: Pergamon Press, 1968.
16. Maruyama, Magorah, "The Second Cybernetics: Deviation-Amplifying Mutual Causal Processes," *American Scientist,* 1963, pp. 164-179.
17. Such an interpretation of positive and negative feedback, in fact, is not merely hypothetical. Certain social scientists have characterized feedback *literally* in this fashion. For example, I recently have had an opportunity to review a manuscript for a book titled "Communication Theory: A Systems Approach," authored by two California communicologists. Their interpretation of positive and negative feedback is quoted here:

    "*Positive* feedback accentuates or possibly speeds up direction of behavior in a constant direction. This is comparable to thermostatic control employing information to increase heat level toward the set 'norm' (70 degrees). *Negative* feedback decreases speed or degree of direction, or may alter or even reverse the direction in a different line of adaptation. This would be comparable to thermostatic control employing information to shut off the heat and thereby reduce temperature back to the set norm.''

What is interesting in this interpretation is that the authors of the book use the thermostat as an example of *both* negative and positive feedback.

18. Maruyama, Magorah, "Morphogenesis and Morphostasis," *Methods,* 1960, pp. 251-295.

19. Recall that one subsystem's input is another's output and *vice versa,* in the whole coupling system, and therefore the two reference points implied in *Deviation Criterion III* are merely the input and the output of a subsystem when our focus is microscopically placed upon the internal relationships of this subsystem.

20. Buckley, Walter, *Sociology and Modern Systems Theory,* Englewood Cliffs, N.J.: Prentice-Hall, 1967, p. 52. *See also* Maruyama, "Morphogenesis and Morphostasis," *Methods,* 1960, pp. 251-295.

21. Although Maruyama never specified what is his criterion for deviation here, it is strongly implied that our *Deviation Criterion III* is what he had in mind.

    For, the morphostatic model of "the poor stay poor, etc." is viewed as one of deviation-counteracting process, and here the deviation concept clearly hinges upon two output values of the subsystems.

22. We may imagine an expanding or shrinking economy in which both the rich and the poor, gain or lose economically, but the distance between the levels of output maintains a constant rate.

23. Although we speak easily of the two economic subsystems, the rich and the poor, it is unclear exactly what we mean by them. How do we divide the whole economy into these two? What is each one's output levels? Therefore, the economy as an example of our purpose here seems to be of little value, especially if we wish to compare the two subsystems with each other in terms of their output levels and the deviation between them.

24. Maruyama, Magorah, "Morphogenesis and Morphostasis," *Methods,* 1960, p. 256.

25. Rapoport, Anatol, *Operational Philosophy,* New York: Harper and Row, 1953, p. 163.

26. Wiener, Norbert, *I Am a Mathematician,* New York: Doubleday and Co., 1965, p. 322.

27. Ross, Ashby, W., "Principles of the Self-Organizing System," *Principles of Self-Organization,* Heinz Foerster and George Zopf, eds., New York: Pergamon Press, 1962, p. 255.

28. One seeming conflict between the concepts of morphostasis and morphogenesis *and* that of entropy should be resolved before further discussion. While morphogenesis in particular involves increasing structure, and therefore increasing organization (decreasing entropy), the Second

Law of Thermodynamics states that entropy of an isolated system never diminishes, it increases all the time. This law, then, specifies a *deterministic irreversible*, transformation, that is, entropy *must* increase. However, as Hans Reischenbach never failed to note, entropy has been reinterpreted in light of *probability*, an interpretation that renders decrease of entropy in a system possible. Reischenbach said: "We should not say, 'Entropy must become larger,' in the way that we say, 'Entropy must remain constant.' We should say, 'It is highly probable entropy will become larger.' In other words, the reverse process of a thermodynamical occurrence is not physically impossible; it is merely very improbable." *See* Hans Reischenbach, *The Direction of Time*, Berkeley, Calif.: University of California Press, 1956, p. 54.

29. Shannon, Claude E., and Warren Weaver, *The Mathematical Theory of Communication*, Urbana, Ill.: University of Illinois Press, 1949.

30. Singh, Jagjit, *Great Ideas in Information Theory, Language and Cybernetics*, New York: Dover Publications, 1966, p. 77.

31. Brillouin, Leon, *Science and Information Theory*, New York: Academic Press, 1961, p. 161.

32. The idea of O.C. de Beauregard ("Sur l'equivalence entre information et entropie," *Sciences*, 1961, p. 51-58) quoted here is based upon James Miller's translation from the French text and discussion on it. *See* James Miller, "Living Systems: Basic Concepts," *Behavioral Science*, July, 1965, p. 194.

33. To quote James Miller regarding this idea: "They [*living systems*] maintain a steady state of negentropy even though entropic changes occur in them as they do everywhere else. This they do by taking in inputs of matter-energy higher in complexity of organization or in negative entropy, i.e., lower in entropy, than their outputs. Thus they restore their own energy and repair breakdowns in their own organization." *See* Miller, "Living Systems: Basic Concepts," *Behavioral Science*, July 1965, p. 203.

Miller also says that steady state of negentropy is different from the state of equilibrium: in a closed system, an equilibrium can be reached; it is always approached but never reached in an open system.

34. Schrödinger, Erwin, *What is Life?: The Physical Aspect of the Living Cell*, Cambridge: Cambridge University Press, 1946, p. 74.

35. For acutal interpretation such as this by social scientists, see Note[17] above.

14

Organic Communication Systems: Speculations on the Study, Birth, Life, and Death of Communication Systems

JAMES H. CAMPBELL
AND
JOHN S. MICKELSON

General systems theory proposes for us a style of thinking, an approach to research in human communication, more relevant than more traditional styles and approaches. Centrally, we are led to look upon communication as an organic process. By this is meant, communication is best studied and understood by refraining from extensive partitioning of the process. Further, following Ashby[1] we suppose that operation of communication systems at one level (say the biological) should be consistent with their operation at other levels (say the behavioral). In other words, attitude theory should be consistent with what is known of biological brain capability. Whereas, for some, this reflects a reductionist philosophy, we agree with K.J.W. Craik[2] that as scientists we have little choice but to adopt this view. Knowledge and education have been partitioned beyond what is necessary. This partitioning is in large measure what leads people, scientists, and societies to manage outdated models of reality.[3]

This chapter proposes to examine several strategies for applying elements of general systems thinking to study of human communication processes. In one area, traditional concepts for communication study are reexamined from a systems view. In a second area, we speculate about the life cycle of communication systems demonstrating the dynamic/organic nature of the system. Finally, in a third area some questions designed to get at the importance of human information generation/creation are explored. Because much of the material presented is speculative, we have avoided use of numerous references within the text. We provide instead a relevant selected bibliography.

The Exchange

The critical requirement for life, the *sine qua non* for life, is the organism's capacity/ability for exchange. This exchange capacity makes possible an organism's interdependence with, not independence of, its internal and external physical environments. One significant example of this interdependence exists in the mutual exchange requirement between plant and animal life for O_2CO_2 cycle. One might also observe, it is the capacity for exchange that permits living organisms to exert some control (though only in a limited time frame) over the second law of thermodynamics. Living organisms only have the capability for increasing or reducing or redistributing natural entropy production. This control is exhibited by technological processes which combine naturally occurring elements, so the combination is more resistant to processes like oxidation (e.g., composite materials science). Naturally, many of these technological processes only redistribute entropy production. Slowing the rate in one area increases it in others—e.g., noise, air, and water pollutants.

The exchange concept, then, is a critical one for the existence of life. Especially, this capacity/ability for exchange makes communication possible. In fact, it may be useful to view exchange processes between organisms and their physical, internal and external enviroments as communication.

We are not suggesting that behavioral scientists do not look upon communication as a process of exchange. We only suggest the usual view is narrow. Were biologists prone to view exchange processes such as food processing and sexual reproduction in a manner similar to how many behavioral scientists look upon communication process, we would understand litte of eating or reproduction. The behavioral scientist when investigating the communication process observes a message event (exchange) and a consequent (observable) behavior. Controlled manipulation and rigorous observation of these events has and will continue to produce knowledge and information necessary for understanding communication. Fuller control will be achieved only as underlying processes are encompassed. The biologist when investigating a dietary process observes not only the message event (food consumption) and the consequent behavior (increased activity or whatever) but also follows the food transformation into energy, stored energy, waste, and so on throughout the biological system.[4] Because biologists understand the nature of a variety of biological transformations they are capable of exerting more extensive, more effective control over dietary and nutritional problems. The significance in this is the *requirement* that to achieve effective control the nature of the integrated system must be encompassed. Control for the biologist requires knowing not only that food consumption is required but also how the food is processed/synthesized and what effects are produced upon the biological/neural/physiological states of the organism. The more narrow-view of many behavioral scientists results in less understanding and considerably less control.

Suppose, then, the communication scientist modifies his view to account for the more complete organic nature of the system he wishes to understand. This modification of view need be little more than recognition that communication exchange is dependent and interdependent with the organization and operation of the biological equipment which is the organism. This recognition leads to removal of several dysfunctional ways for thinking about communication; the removal of myths.

The Myth of Communication Breakdown

Communication breakdowns never occur. The concept of breakdown results from a continuing observation that we do not always achieve our goals through communication. Though this concept may be a useful one relative to a simple problem-oriented view of the communication process, it is less useful in providing any complete theoretic view for explaining communication behavior. More pointedly, when powerful theories are produced it becomes possible to deduce from the theory the answers to specific problems. Problem orientations, on the other hand, tend to produce quasi-theory or *ad hoc* theories.

The concept of breakdown leads one to examine communication transactions in an effort to determine why they don't work. When taking this approach one often fails to recognize that communication (exchange) did occur. Though the exchange may not have been effective for the goal we had in mind at the time, it may well have been effective for some goal. Further, in the same vein, because we create the concept of communication breakdown out of failure to satisfy a goal (usually the goal of the source), we often fail to recognize that communication is purposive for the receiver as well.[6]

In contrast, when a biologist creates some chemical mixture with the intent of controlling disease X and it doesn't prove effective, he does not out of hand either discard the chemical or fail to examine to the extent possible how the chemical did work. It may well be the chemical will control disease Y.

The Myth of Misinterpretation

The concept of misinterpretation is only another perspective on breakdown. Again, we are making an effort to understand not what happened in the transaction, but why what we wanted to happen—didn't. Again, as one follows this kind of strategy, one becomes too much problem oriented. Though, perhaps, we solve the problem (somewhat serendipitously), we fail to uncover very much of the process (or operating basis) of the organic system.

Communication scientists argue (correctly) that people create meaning. Granted the truth of the proposition, one wonders why the same communication scientists continue concentrating study so heavily upon breakdowns and misinterpretations? The more critical question from a process, system, or theoretic view is "How does this creation process work?" Though the collection of problem-oriented information is useful, a too narrow, highly partitioned system view emerges. Frequently, one fails to recognize the critical questions, discovers only the bits and pieces of the system, and fails to learn much of the total fabric.

Conscious and Unconscious as Overlapping Regions

The area of conscious vs. unconscious behavior is usually considered the realm of the psychologist, and viewed distinguishing two independent (or nearly so) realms of behavior. However, it should be noted that both realms of behavior are tied to the biological structure of organisms. Both are functions of the same substrate of biological/physiological mechanisms.

Communication exchanges occur between areas of conscious and unconscious areas of the brain. As one learns some kind of skill area, the learning takes place initially at a high level of consciousness. As the skill becomes learned (or overlearned), the conscious level of behavior becomes less necessary and the exhibition of the behavior is taken over at a less conscious level. Consider the process one goes through learning to

Fig. 14-1

play a musical instrument. Initially, a very conscious effort is made to map the communication symbols of music onto the motor/nervous system. Once this mapping is done, playing the instrument is taken over by the nervous system out-of-awareness. A musician is not aware of the precise movement of his hands as he produces his music.

When the mind is consciously occupied with a message the unconscious mind may be dealing with a different set of events. We have made some observations using a tachistoscope with the "all is vanity" illustration shown in Fig. 14.1. Even using a 1/150 of a second exposure, the skull is easily perceived. With repeated exposures at this speed people are unable to recognize the detail necessary to perceive the woman sitting at her vanity. Yet when subjects are asked to identify the sex of the skull, they overwhelmingly often answer that it is female. This "vanity" example is not offered in evidence, but rather as a suggestion for exploring more specifically the nature of the interdependent exchanges between the conscious and unconscious levels of the brain.

Concepts like "conscious v. unconscious" may be useful in helping us understand the variety around us. They become useless when our inquiry is limited by them, when we no longer conceive of, let alone try to examine underlying processes. Whereas the terms "conscious" and "unconscious" suggest boundaries, a more general organic view suggests the terms refer to similar and related processes. This difference is significant.

The Significance of the Blind Men and the Elephant

Five blind men encounter an elephant. One grasps the tail and thinks it is a rope. Another grasps the leg and thinks it is a tree. Still another grasps the tusk and thinks it is a spear. Yet another finds the body and thinks it a great boulder. The fifth grasps the trunk and thinks it is a great snake. When this story is heard some laugh at the blind men. But note that their effort is shared by all humans. We all have vision which is variously and variably impaired. The leg of the elephant can be thought to resemble a tree. A situation in which we fail to achieve our goal does appear to have some sort of breakdown.

Consider that the story does not in any way suggest that the elephant may have had some reaction to the situation. Perhaps, the point of view is omitted in the story because no one wished to suggest that reality could be conceptualized in any wholistic fashion. In the context of the story, the elephant may symbolize reality and the blindmen's ludicrous effort to categorize the various components of the elephant in isolation from each other would seem to be one of the obvious lessons the story may be thought to suggest to the hearer/reader. The elephant's point of view cannot be described, then, for that would propose that there exists the possibility of someone or something that understood—and understood in some rather complete way.

Our suggestion is that the elephant's point of view needs to be included. Though not easy, it is possible to understand the major variables in an array. It is possible to predict the behavior of individuals as well as population segments. The use of a systems terminology should not become in any way an excuse for shirking in the effort to comprehend.

A Note on Transition

At this juncture, we have been discussing some concepts relative to communication and other substantive areas of inquiry that, we feel, can be furthered with applications of more general systems style of thinking. We argue in favor of the adoption of a thought style that considers organisms from a more complete, organic perspective. This perspective leads us to consider communication in terms of the growth and development—a life cycle. This life cycle follows and is consistent with biological laws for growth and development.

The Life Cycle of a Communication System: Individual or Societal

Teilhard de Chardin[7] suggests that life begins as a chaotic state. From chaos, life proceeds through a series of organizational transformations of increasing complexity and returns to chaos. The second law of thermodynamics clearly governs in some measure the life cycle of non-organic matter. Control over this law is exerted only by the living organism though, perhaps, only so far as to delay or redistribute the rate of that decay. In this section, some of the general characteristics of living organizational processes are elaborated. While we focus on communication, the discussion is at a level of abstraction consistent with many levels of organization.

Assumptions

General systems is focused on discovery of concepts relevant or common to hierarchal levels of organization. It is also geared to discover how common concepts are tied from level to level. It is natural, for instance, to look upon mathematics as a reflection of human thought process. Yet, people do not generally view mathematical images as having much in common with biological or psychological ones. Mathematical systems and organic systems are, however, tied. G. Spencer Brown's[8] mathematical creations stem, according to him, as much from the study of biological process as from mathematical theory. Even mathematical systems, then, might be said to follow biological principles of growth and development. It is our purpose to show how by examining communication as a biological process (one with a life cycle) our understanding of the nature of communication can be enhanced. To achieve this purpose, we make three assumptions about the nature of biological systems and thus communication systems:

    a. Biological systems are open systems. This means that biological systems must be capable of exchange. The emphasis is upon throughput rather than feedback, though both are necessary.

b. The system tends toward coherency (i.e., the system is or soon becomes purposeful). As the system learns, its repertoire of possible behaviors is extended. The system must make choices among these behaviors and organize them in some coherent manner toward survival.

c. The paths of system exchange are parsimonious (This means that to the extent the purposes of both source and receiver are known, the law of parsimony is followed). The system will tend to become efficient in satisfying its goals or purposes.

Step One for the Life Cycle—Chaos

We begin with the chaos of Figure 14.2. To maintain the level of generality and abstraction at this point, we ignore the kinds of "stuff" in-

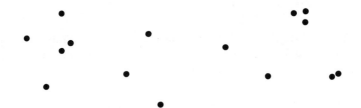

Fig. 14-2 This is: a) a medium; b) in which there are differentiated loci; c) which are randomly distributed through all dimensions of the medium

volved here (i.e.: the content of the loci, people, cells; the nature of the boundaries of the loci—skin, membranes; and the content of the space between the loci—atmosphere, fluids, etc). Through time, interconnections begin to form as in Figure 14.3. An interconnection is a connection (a link) over which the source and receiver have no control. All receivers are connected to the single input/output channel of each and every source (the exchange capacity/ability). Consider as an example a large group of strangers thrown together. The sources have no basis for selecting subsets of their receiver population for the transmission of specific messages. Nor do the receivers have any basis for sorting out a particular message and deciding not to receive it. A more direct example might be a roomful

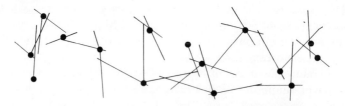

Fig. 14-3 Brownian movement, the formation of interconnections

of young children, strangers to one another and unattended. They have not yet learned to be selective. There is in one sense complete freedom or none. There is more order than there was in the chaotic condition in which there were no connections of any kind. But we are still a long way from having anything like a pattern with any medium degree of organization. How do we specify what we mean by organization? One way is implicit in the above. It is by having choices available, i.e., being able to identify and connect subsets of total sets, or populations: by increasing coherence.

Step Two for the Life Cycle—Increasing Coherence

At this stage there is an increase in the number of connections and a decrease in the number of interconnections as in Figure 14.3. In the first step, each locus of origin and termination of a transmission had one and only one channel which served both the transmission and the reception function. Order has not begun to develop and there is a complete lack of constraint upon choice. (For one thing we are talking at level of abstraction where each of the loci can be anything at all.) At this second step, the loci begin to group themselves and form connections. One may find, going back to the thrown-together-strangers, that groups of men, or of women, or of politicians have now begun to congregate. The movements are no longer the random ones of Figure 14.3, they are now the directed ones of Figure 14.4.

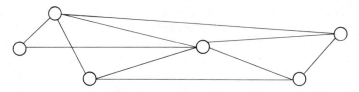

Fig. 14-4 Choices are being made, the dynamic is no longer Brownian or random

What we have here is the development of a process, the process of interconnection, which proceeds to a conclusion (step one). Then a new process, stemming from the termination of the former begins and tends toward its conclusion. This latter is the process of developing connections (step two). Its actual final state, or limiting state, is probably something other than its logically final state (i.e., a logically final state would be one of complete efficiency). The logically final state is one in which there are no interconnections and is given by the expression $n(n-1)/2$. This assumes that there are no redundant connections.

One of the things which is happening is that there are choices being exercised. To most of us the term "choice" implies some sort of teleological system, some value system in a human sense, is in operation. For the present argument, we use the notion of choice in a way that permits us to consider the variation in the course followed by a pinball as a matter of choices. A better illustration, perhaps, is that sometimes used to illustrate the way in which normal distributions are produced by a group of small balls which drop through a set of channels from a common point of origin at the center of the set of channels. Some of these small balls "choose" to always go to the right at every choice point and wind up in the channel which is farthest to the right. The fact that these are always few in number compared to those that "choose" to drop straight away is not relevant here.

The assumption is that there is a system of some kind operating, and the system, whether imposed by the observer or a function of the properties of the choice environment or of the properties of the chooser, gives a pattern to the choices. This pattern may be construed as an alteration, sometimes a reduction, in the number of choices which may yet be made. Sets of alternatives change with time and as the antecedents for their selection change. These antecedents are the consequences of prior choices. In other words, to have chosen is to have altered the nature of the choices available. It is not necessarily true that the number of choices is less, only that they are constrained by time. Except that if choices are, and they always are, part of a program designed to achieve *within* a certain time period a given goal, then the time pressures act to limit the number of alternatives that can be attended to as the deadline approaches. In this context, to choose is to use time, and as time, which is finite is exhausted, the parameters of choice diminish. To put it another way yet, as the loci of exchange, origin and reception, originate and receive they tend to develop what might be called preferences. That is, for whatever reason, through the operation of whatever system, they begin to establish regularities. This is what our earlier group of strangers has begun to do. This is a negative entropic function and the answer to the question: Why does it happen? It is also the answer to the question: What is life? As they develop these preferences, the manifestation of these preferences and the operational definition of them is the change in the mode of process from that of increasing the number of interconnections to that of decreasing the number of interconnections and increasing the number of connections.

The Third Step—Purpose

As this second process approaches whatever happens to be the limit in the particular situation since choices have been made, the effect, Figure 14.5, is to limit the number of alternatives among which the system can yet choose. This is the origin of *purpose* or *goals*.

Returning to our group of initial strangers we note they had congregated into groups according to preference. This congregating process serves to establish connections within some preference boundary—say a political one. The identification of a political boundary does not limit alternatives in any significant manner. So, whereas a boundary is

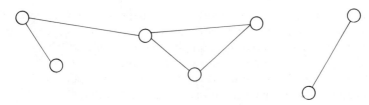

Fig. 14-5   Limiting the alternatives

established, there is as yet no differentiation of behavior. We have only a variety of preferences falling within a certain boundary. At the third state, a further differentiation is now produced. The loci, the people, begin to identify preferences for different kinds of political behavior. They choose to act upon or manipulate the environment in different ways to achieve their goals.

If we think of human systems some things start occurring to us now. One of them is really a set of post hoc errors. For example, we may say that our analysis of a situation in which humans are in communication among themselves shows that structure started to emerge before goals were recognized. We then attribute to the emerging structure the property of making goals recognizable. Or we may say that the emergence of structure occurs simultaneously with the recognition of goals and that there is no way to tell which comes first. Alternatively, one might argue that our analysis shows that it was not until and unless the loci, the people, recognized that there were shared goals that any structure emerged.

The Fourth Step: Emergence of Decision Bias

The fourth step involves a reduction in the number of connections as in Fig. 14.6.

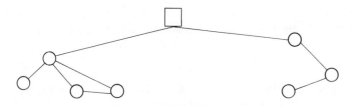

Fig. 14-6   Limiting number of connections and emergence of decision bias (A).

At this point it becomes possible to talk about formal and informal systems. Until now there was only the one system and it was *neither*! What happens now, in human systems, is that someone has taken unto himself, or been granted by the way the operation of the process turned out, the power/right/authority to decide what constitutes economy/efficiency as in Figure 14.8. This is the final step and leads back into Step 1.

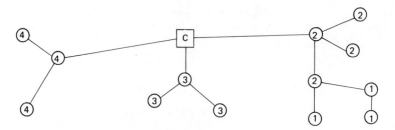

Fig. 14-7   Increasing Structure and Differentiation of Structure

What we have modeled here is a general, abstract, representation of the life cycle or growth cycles for communication systems (perhaps, any system). This effort to identify the growth nature of the structural system is a first step in examining, from a general system perspective, the dynamics of a system through time. A second step in this examination, then, is the identification of the "stuff" upon which communication systems operate. One of the more useful and general terms for this stuff is information.

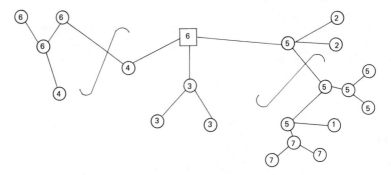

Fig. 14-8   System Fragmentation prior to renewal

The Importance of Information Generation/Creation by Humans

One characteristic which distinguishes the living organisms from non-living matter is the living organism's responsiveness to irritation from within or without. The capability for this responsiveness is inherent with the structure and function of nervous (and other) living tissue. This capability (the nervous one) permits living organisms to respond to and engage in exchange. Because the behaviors of living organisms are dependent/interdependent with neural structures, examination of the general operation of neural structures should permit determination of significant aspects of the communication process. Communication process is, after all, dependent upon operation of this neural circuitry. We raise the question, then, what is the stuff of communication which makes these circuits operate? In other words, "What is it about communication that irritates the circuitry?" What is the nature of this "stuff" such that when organisms exchange it results in communication?

Shannon [9] develops a measure reflecting a concept of information especially related to electro-mechanical communication systems. The utility of this concept and measure for study of human communication is frequently questioned. The questioning of the concept usually rests on a statement by Shannon to the effect that the question of semantics is not relevant for the engineering problem. This is clearly true. But this is not to say there is no relation between the information concept and the question of semantics. In fact, it may be, the semantic problem may overlay the technical one and both may be represented by the same concept and measure.

On the technical level for information relative to living organisms, we examine neural processing of electrochemical codes by the brain. On this level it is known that tissue is responsive to the statistical rarity (or lack of same) for stimulus signals.[10] It is also well known that neural nets exhibit a limited channel capacity for the processing of these signals.[11] These characteristics, response to statistical rarity and channel capacity, imply the relevance of Shannon's information concepts for study of neural events at least on a technical level.

Now, when dealing with a semantic level for information, the communication scientist is concerned with symbolic representations of all kinds. These include language, non-verbal symbols, objects which signify other objects or symbols, and so on. But whatever the problem of semantics refers to, the organism's response to these symbols is elaborated by its neural circuitry. If this is the case (and it must be) then semantic information processing should demonstrate a similar process character. Such seems to be the case. The statistical rarity of semantic signals produces effects similar to statistical rarity of neural signals in arousal of brain mechanisms. When a semantic signal lacks rarity, the organism is less aroused, less influenced. Semantic satiation occurs. As for notions of semantic channel capacity, this is also characteristic of human information processing. Note, here, we are not talking about limitations of a physiological nature at the technical level. Instead, we refer to what appear as limits for the processing of symbolic, semantic data, limits posed by the nature and structure of grammars for communication.

Human communication and human behavior are highly consistent with notions regarding information processing. Human systems become bored when faced with events and activities completely known or understood. Man seeks to understand and control those things that present him with statistical rarity (uncertainty). He becomes bored having understood and creates new events/systems to understand. Humans create information. That is one meaning of the statement that man is negentropic. No matter how voraciously he feeds on order from without, he is negentropic and an information generator.

As a living organism, man lives in extremely complex sensory environments. The capacity of man and living organisms, in general, is limited in so far as his processing of the rich array of stimuli with which he is bombarded. Because of these limitations and the capactiy for sensation, man is in a very real sense forced to form preferences, make choices, and decisions. He is in a sense forced by his sensitivity and limited capacity for information to proceed through the life cycle we have elaborated. The life cycle of a child for instance follows this very pattern. At birth, or shortly thereafter, he is bombarded by stimuli (Step 1). He then approaches the more preferred stimuli (information) and develops preferences for certain of them, the warmth of parents, for instance (Step 2). Choices are exercised and the child begins to develop a notion of purpose, say, in approaching the mother for feeding (a purposeful exchange, Step 3). The child then begins to attribute some kind of formal authority to the parental figures as he decides they can provide support in his movement through the environment (Step 4). He begins to recognize other stimuli like parents but different. He must differentiate them from parents, thus increasing the fine structure of his selections and perceptions (Step 5). And finally, as these other loci, systems—people—become too many, he must sever certain connections and maintain others as the complexity becomes too great (Step 6).

This we believe is the nature of organic systems, communication systems or any system resulting from organic development.

References and Notes

1. Ashby, Ross, "Editorial," *Behavioral Science*, Vol. 18, 1973, pp. 1-6.
2. Craik, Kenneth J. W., *The Nature of Explanation*, Cambridge: Cambridge University Press, 1943.
3. Beer, Strafford, "The World We Manage," *Behavioral Science*, Vol. 18, 1973, pp. 198-209.
4. Handler, Phillip, *Biology and the Future of Man*, London: Oxford University Press, 1971.
5. Broadbent, Donald, *Decision and Stress*, London: Academic Press, Inc., 1972.
6. Ackoff, Russell, and Fred Emery, *On Purposeful Systems*, Chicago: Aldine Atherton, Inc., 1972.
7. Chardin, Teilhard de, *The Phenomenon of Man*, New York: Harper & Row, Publishers, 1959.

8. Brown, Spencer G., *The Laws of Form,* New York: The Julian Press, Inc., 1972.

9. Shannon, Claude E., and Warren Weaver, *The Mathematical Theory of Communication,* Urbana, Ill.: University of Illinois Press, 1957.

10. Bekesy, Georg, *Sensory Inhibition,* Princeton, N.J.: Princeton University Press, 1967.

11. Jasper, Herbert, Arthur Ward, and Alfred Pope, *Basic Mechanisms of Epilepsies,* Boston: Little, Brown and Company, 1969.

Additional Sources

1. Arbib, Michael, *The Metaphorical Brain,* New York: Wiley-Interscience, 1972.

2. Attneave, Fred, *Applications of Information Theory to Psychology,* New York: Holt, Rinehart, and Winston, 1967.

3. Bar-Hillel, Yehoshus, *Language and Information,* London: Addison-Wesley, 1964.

4. Brillouin, L., "Mathematics, Physics, and Information," *Information and Control,* Vol. 1, 1957, pp. 1-5.

5. Buckley, Walter, *Modern Systems Research for the Behavioral Scientist,* Chicago: Aldine Publishing Company, 1968.

6. Burks, Arthur, *Essays on Cellular Automata,* Chicago: University of Illinois Press, 1970.

7. Fogel, Lawrence, *Human Information Processing,* Englewood Cliffs, N.J.: Prentice-Hall, Inc., 1967.

8. Hakes, D. T. and D. J. Foss, "Decision Processes During Sentence Comprehension: Effects of Surface Structure Reconsidered," *Perception and Psychophysics,* Vol. 8, 1970, pp. 413-416.

9. Hyman, L. M., and H. Kaufman, "Information and the Memory Span," *Perception and Psychophysics,* Vol. 1, 1966, pp. 135-137.

10. John, Roy E., *Mechanisms of Memory,* New York: Academic Press, Inc., 1967.

11. Kochen, M., and E. Galanter, "The Acquisition and Utilization of Information in Problem Solving and Thinking," *Information and Control,* Vol. 1, 1958, pp. 267-288.

12. Landahl, H. D., "Studies in the Mathematical Biophysics of Discrimination and Conditioning I," *Bulletin of Mathematical Biophysics,* Vol. 3, 1941, pp. 13-26.

13. Landahl, H. D., "Studies in the Mathematical Biophysics of Discrimination and Conditioning II: Special Case: Errors, Trials, and Number of Possible Responses," *Bulletin of Mathematical Biophysics,* Vol. 3, 1941, pp. 71-77.

14. Lenneberg, Eric H., "A Probabilistic Approach to Language Learning," *Behavioral Science,* Vol. 2, 1957, pp. 1-12.

15. Luria, A. R., "Speech Development and the Formation of Mental Processes," *A Handbook of Contemporary Soviet Psychology,* M. Cole and I. Maltzman, eds., New York: Basic Books, Inc., 1969.
16. Luria, A. R., *Higher Cortical Functions in Man,* New York: Basic Books, Inc., 1970.
17. MacKay, Donald M., *Information, Mechanism and Meaning,* Cambridge, Mass.: M.I.T. Press, 1969.
18. Malic, D., "Entropy and Philosophy," *Progress of Cybernetics,* Vol. 1, J. Rose, ed., London: Gordon and Breach, 1970, pp. 149-154.
19. McCulloch, Warren S., *Embodiments of Mind,* Cambridge, Mass.: M.I.T. Press, 1965.
20. Moss, D. E., and C. O. Neidt, "Applicability of Information Theory to Learning," *Psychological Reports,* Vol. 24, 1969, pp. 471-478.
21. Pribram, Karl, *Languages of the Brain,* Englewood Cliffs, N.J.: Prentice-Hall, Inc., 1972.
22. Pribram, Karl, and D. Broadbent, *Biology of Memory,* New York: Academic Press, Inc., 1970.
23. Procter, Lorne, *Biocybernetics of the Central Nervous System,* Boston: Little, Brown, and Company, 1969.
24. Rapoport, Anatol, "What Is Information," *Etc.,* Vol. 10, 1953, pp. 247-260.
25. Rapoport, Anatol, "On the Application of the Information Concept to Learning Theory," *Bulletin of Mathematical Biophysics,* Vol. 18, 1956, pp. 317-321.
26. Rapoport, Anatol, "A Derivation of a Rote Learning Curve from the Total Uncertainty of a Task," *Bulletin of Mathematical Biophysics,* Vol. 22, 1960, pp. 85-97.
27. Rapoport, Anatol, "The Perfect Learner," *Bulletin of Mathematical Biophysics,* Vol. 23, 1961, pp. 321-335.
28. Staniland, A. C., *Patterns of Redundancy: A Psychological Study,* Cambridge: Cambridge University Press, 1957.
29. Watanabe, Satosi, *Knowing and Guessing,* New York: Wiley-Interscience, 1969.
30. Zubek, John, *Sensory Deprivation: Fifteen Years of Research,* New York: Appleton-Century-Crofts, 1969.

15
Knowledge, Order, and Communication

LEE THAYER

"Then let us make a compact. I shall do everything to please you, and you must promise to do everything to please me."

"Tell me."

"Little things, Rima—none so hard as chasing you round a tree. Only to have you stand or sit by me and talk will make me happy. And to begin you must call me by my name—Abel."

"Is that your name? Oh, not your real name! Abel, Abel, what is that? It says nothing. I have called you by so many names—twenty, thirty—and no answer."

"Have you? But, dearest girl, every person has a name—one name he is called by. Your name, for instance, is Rima, is it not?"

"Rima! only Rima—to you? In the morning, in the evening . . . now in this place and in a little while where know I? . . . in the night when you awake and it is dark, dark, and you see me all the same. Only Rima—oh, how strange!"[1]

Man is the most plastic of all earth's creatures. Every new human comes into his world knowing literally nothing of what he will need to know eventually to function acceptably in a human society.

Whatever existence we have, as humans in human societies, hinges upon what we are able to comprehend of what others express, and what we are able to express that others will comprehend. Gibran is but one who has observed that it takes two to create a human truth: one to express it, another to believe it.[2] Because what *is*, and what is *true*, and what is *relevant*, and what is *right* and what is *wrong*, and what is *good* and what is *bad*, are not given in human genes, they must be first created and then maintained in social intercourse. Every human society, every human artifact, humanity itself, has its source, its coherence, and its destiny in what people can express, and what they can comprehend. This circumstance underpins the whole of the human condition, past, present, and future. It has pervasive implications for all who would study human behavior, or the social contexts which that behavior interlocks, regardless of approach or disciplinary persuasion.

1

The obvious point of departure is, of course, the individual.[3] The fact that no human is born into any human society knowing what he will need to know eventually to function acceptably as a member of that society means simply that he must be *in-formed*. Every new member of every human society must be less or more coercively in-formed with those knowledges and those ways of knowing that will enable him to comprehend what certain of his social fellows will say to him, and to express what they will be able to comprehend.

What a human is capable of comprehending of what others say to him, and what he is capable of expressing that will be comprehended by others, constitutes *social reality* for that individual. Each may experience his own toothache, of course. But that is a private experience, wholly inexpressible. What one may say about his own toothache may add dimensions to one's own or the other's experiences of *his* toothache, but no two may share the same toothache. As Lawrence Durrell observed (in *Balthazar)*, the "truth" of raw experience "disappears with the telling of it." What we must learn are ways of knowing about and talking about toothaches and wars and people and ideas and events which are comprehensible to certain of our social fellows, and of comprehending what they say of these things.

Knowledge is by definition social.[4] To know something which no one else knows, or to know it in a nonsanctioned way is, for the knower, asocial. To be able to express what no one else can comprehend, or to be able to comprehend what no one else can or will express, is asocial. To be a member of a human society, one must be able to express and to comprehend what *is*, what is *relevant,* what is true, and what is right and what is wrong for that society.

Socialization, then, is the process by which new members of a given human society are in-formed in such a way that they know what they will need to know, and the appropriate ways of knowing, in order to function acceptably in that society. To be socialized means that one has been informed to express what others will comprehend and to comprehend what others express in a way that maintains the order and the continuity of that society. The existence as well as the structure of every human society rests upon the social utility of what people can and cannot express, can and cannot comprehend.

2

Individual humans are therefore wholly dependent upon the societies into which they are born for the form or the structure of their social existences. We know what we know in virtue of the social utility which that knowing has for us as individuals. Whatever we know that has no social utility is utterly irrelevant to our social existence.

Because no human enters his social world pre-formed for existence in it but must be in-formed into it, what he knows and the ways in which he knows have no reality apart from his relations with his fellows. For the individual human, social reality is a process, the process by which the social utility of what he is capable of expressing and comprehending is created, confirmed, and assessed in continuous transactions with his fellows.

One need not, therefore, postulate a separate ''need'' for social order, or endow human societies with a teleology of their own. What is at stake is not human society as such, but individual human existence.

To be human is to be in social context. That which we can individually express and comprehend structures our consciousness; that consciousness upon which we can reflect constitutes our self-consciousness; and both together comprise our individual human existences. And consciousness implies continuity. Were the social context in which we exist as individual humans not reliable, not continuous, we could not emerge, or remain, human. We could not have human existence.

Social order is not *sui generis*. It is merely a function of the breadth and the degree of social utility which is what we know and our ways of knowing have for one another. We vest in social institutions the validity of what we know, in order to avoid the insufferable anxiety of confronting the precariousness and the arbitrariness of what we know, and in order to avoid starting all over again at every encounter. The surest knowledge we have is that which we can take for granted. What is true for large numbers of people are those truths which form and impel the social institutions to which they subscribe. For something to be and remain true for two or ten people, validation is a matter of direct and mutual validation. Love is re-affirmed in daily contact. But when daily contact is not possible, faith must be placed in the institution of marriage, or in institutionalized beliefs or myths about love. For something to be and remain true for hundreds or thousands of people, it is the institutions to which they subscribe that embody the affirmation they must have. Without direct or indirect affirmation of the validity of what we know, we could not have continuous human existence. Society is the means by which we achieve and confirm ✳ and maintain our existence as humans.

The condition of our birth places the center of the universe in every individual. Our ideologies, our institutions, are attempts to vest the center of the universe in some less precarious location, and one which transcends individual humans. Our human possibilities carry such terrible responsibilities that we fabricate what we can to avoid the one in order to escape the other.[5] In creating and maintaining social institutions, we play seriously at illusion-making on the grand scale. As Ernest Becker put it, ''The history of sociology is a series of attempts to overthrow fictional views of society in order to arrive at a truly fictional view of society.''[6]

Nothing would have meaning apart from social order. For Erich Kahler, "... order is the prerequisite of meaning."[7] The meanings that things have for us, and the meanings we have for ourselves and each other, hinge upon the ways in which we are ordered into one another. What *is*, what is *worthwhile*, what is *relevant*, what is right and what is wrong—all have their meaning in the individual and social order from which they emerge. Whatever we know that has social utility gives meaning to our lives, and orders the human societies in which we live those lives.

3

"No construction without destruction"; thus Kenneth Burke puts his view of a fundamental condition of life.[8] By it he means that the cost of constructing something is inevitably the destruction of something else. Life itself is had at the expense of other life, whether we eat meat or roots.

The form and the substance of individual human existence must be constructed. Whatever form and substance it takes on endows that individual with certain possibilities; the very emergence of a human existence from a biological capacity is clearly enabling. But whatever form and substance human existence takes on also clearly limits the alternative possibilities, not only for that individual, but for every other individual with whom that one is socially interlocked. The construction of a reliable identity requires the destruction of other possibilities, not only in oneself but in others, in much the same way that knowing something precludes the possibilities of learning something about it. Knowing requires the forfeiture of learning, knowledge the forfeiture of growth, being someone the forfeiture of being someone else.

Human societies are built upon the matching of questions and answers: it is out of bringing he who has the question into contact with him who has the answer that human society is constructed. The fewer the individuals who have unanswerable questions, and the fewer the individuals who have unasked-for answers, the more social order there will be. Society abhors an irrelevance; "no construction without destruction."

But it is not "society" that limits human possibilities.[9] Nor is it language as such that limits human possibilities. It is the price that we must pay for individual continuity that limits human possibilities.

There are no social "forces" which would persist if the people involved ceased to think, to talk, and to behave as they do. But we do not think and talk and behave for society's sake; we do so for our own sake. As humans, we have the sense of our existence in the continuity which links our individual futures to our individual pasts, through our individual presents. We depend ultimately upon others for confirmation of that continuity at every present moment. If what we can express in any present moment cannot be comprehended, or if what we can comprehend at that moment is not being expressed, our existence as humans is threatened. Every instance of nonconfirmation of the continuity of our individual existence is an instance of desocialization.

To be, we must be someone in some social context. To continue to be, we must continue to be that someone in that social context. Who we are is a process, and it is in that process that our human possibilities are both enabled and constrained.

Jean Anouilh put it this way: "Life has a way of setting things in order and leaving them be. Very tidy, is life.''[10] Yet any radical alteration or disintegration of the social order within which we have human existence is a threat to that existence. John Fowles wrote that "Our accepting what we are must always inhibit our being what we ought to be.''[11] Or what we might be. The paradox must be clear.

Nor is language the limiter it is sometimes presumed to be. While what we know is knowable only in the ways we have of expressing and of comprehending it, it is not language which constrains thought, but thought which constrains language. In telephone conversations, 50 common words account for 60% of all the words used.[12] Those who have nothing new to say do not feel constrained by their language. Those who do have something new to say recreate the language in the image of their thought. Wagner worked within the same constraints as his predecessors.

A major function of social order, into which our own thought is ordered, is to preclude the unexpected. Our fear of the unexpected in ourselves and in others ought not to be interpreted as an inadequacy of our language. We do indeed create our realities in the form of the words by which we name them. But those realities comprise a constraint only for those who do not participate in their creation, or who do not realize that human realities are means, not ends.

4

The more "civilized" a human society is, the more complex it is. A simple human society is one in which the knowledge required for membership is coherent and homogeneously distributed. A complex society is heterogeneous, where alternative knowledges compete and offer different paths to membership.

The more complex a human society, the less importance is attached to what one knows, and the more to the ways by which one comes to know what he knows. To function adequately in a complex, heterogeneous society, one needs to know more and more about less and less, yet less and less about more and more. Knowledges become specialized, and ways of knowing become specialized. One has his membership in one or more of the subsets of a complex society not only in virtue of whether he knows what he needs to know, but in virtue of whether he came to know what he knows in a way sanctioned by the other members of those subsets of the larger society to whose membership he aspires. As a practical matter, the most acceptable source of such knowledge is the other members of the same subset.

The social contexts in which our knowing and our ways of knowing have meaning and validity have been referred to as "epistemic communities,"[13] those subsets of complex societies in which we achieve and maintain our human existence. Within epistemic communities, we must believe in order to understand; between epistemic communities, we must understand in order to believe. Within epistemic communities, what we believe is the other person. Between epistemic communities, we must believe, if at all, not the other person, but what he says.

For two people who have formed a unique epistemic community comprised exclusively of themselves, the expression, "I love you," and the response, "I love you too," have some unique and exclusive meaning. To comprehend that unique and exclusive meaning, one would have to be one of those two persons. It is so with all epistemic communities: the unique and exclusive meaning of what is expressed and what is comprehended within epistemic communities does not depend upon understanding; it depends upon belief. To understand what "I love you" means in a specific instance, you must be the one who believes.[14] It is only between epistemic communities that we concern ourselves with what *words* mean. Within epistemic communities, the criterion is not what words mean, but what people mean.

The paradox emerges again. It is the incompatibilities of what we know and the ways we have of placing faith in what we know in different epistemic communities that lead us into conflict. Yet a homogeneous society, like an inbred and redundant gene pool, reduces our adaptability and our human possibilities.

Rationalism would have us eat our cake but keep it too. Rationalism would lead the true believer down the paths of righteousness and truth, with the "simple truth" as the goal. But human possibilities are not truth; they are born of inspiration and aspiration and imagination; and these are not matters of truth,[15] but of falsification.

Irrationalism throws the baby out with the bath water. To go my own way exclusively is to go no way. If I am to break away, I must break away from something. If the flight is from order to disorder, it is an abdication of human possibility. What gives way to a present order is not disorder, but a superior order.

It is one matter to recognize how one knows what one knows. But it is quite another matter to contemplate the further question: How do I know that what I know is what I need to know? The answer to that question is not given in nature, or even in society, but in the questioner.

Human societies not only provide answers to such questions, but comfortably preclude the need for asking such questions. Yet human possibilities ride on just such questions. It is having a question for which there is no social answer, having an answer for which there is no social question, that sets us free. Social bondage is having only questions for which others have ready answers, having only answers for which others have ready questions. What is the *human* answer to the question, How do I know that what *I* know is what *I* need to know?

5

This chapter explores some possible relationships between what we know, how we know what we know, and social order. In all of this, the role of communication has been left implicit.

In the recent past, we have typically asked, What are the functions of communication? It is the wrong question. We need to ask, not "What are the functions of communication that people make it so," but "What are the functions of people, that communication can make it so?"[16] To be "in communication" is to be interdependent; it is to be mutually dependent for purposes of that social enterprise. But there is nothing in the process that makes it imperative for that social enterprise to be base, or mean, or debilitating. If what one has to say reduces the human possibilities of both, is that to be called "effective" communication? There is no sense in which the reasons for the executioner's acquiescence to an order can be found in the order, any more than the reason for the reply "I love you too" can be found in the message, "I love you." It is not communication which has "effects," but people. To the extent we look for the causes and consequences of our actions in the one, we deny them in the other. Contrary to much popular rhetoric, man's existence is given not in his means but in his ends. The study of communication begins and ends in what people are for, not in what communication is for. It is not what he knows that dignifies man, but what he seeks.

To separate the process from the people is to sever the wings from the bird, the stem from the root. One does not study the rope to determine what can be—or should be—done with it.

References and Notes

1. Hudson, W. H., *Green Mansions,* New York: Random House, 1916, p. 116.
2. Among many others, one thinks here of writers as disparate as Samuel Butler, Ortega y Gasset, and R. G. Collingwood.
3. I mean not to raise the specious argument of which came first, or of which is more important. It is through socialization that a sense of individuality is achieved. There is no case in which the one exists without the other. It is simply this special condition of human birth that I take to be central to the present discussion.

4. *Cf.* "Knowledge and Society," *Inquiry into Inquiries: Essays in Social Theory* Chapter 1, A. F. Bentley, Boston: Beacon Press, 1954; cf. also "The Well-Informed Citizen: An Essay on the Social Distribution of Knowledge," Alfred Schutz, *Collected Papers II: Studies in Social Theory*, The Hague: Martinus Nijhoff, 1964.

5. A compelling argument is, of course, Erich Fromm's *Escape from Freedom*, New York: Holt, Rinehart, and Winston, 1941; cf. John F. A. Taylor, *The Masks of Society*, New York: Appleton-Century-Crofts, 1966. In the *Grand Inquisitor*, Dostoevski wrote: "Man is tormented by no greater anxiety than to find someone quickly to whom he can hand over that gift of freedom with which the ill-fated creature is born."

6. *Cf.* Wheelis, Allen, *The Illusionless Man*, New York: Norton, 1966; and G. W. Morgan, *The Human Predicament: Dissolution and Wholeness*, Providence, R.I.: Brown University Press, 1968. The Becker quote is from *Beyond Alienation*, New York: Braziller, 1967, p. 127.

7. Kahler, Erich, *The Meaning of History*, New York: Braziller, 1964, p. 193; cf. Ernest Becker, *The Birth and Death of Meaning*, New York: Free Press, 1962, particularly chapters 4 and 8. For more on the concept of order as a social phenomenon, *see* "Systems: Communication, Order, and Control," *Proceedings* of the 1st Brazilian Congress on Cybernetics and General Systems, Porto Alegre, November 1972.

8. Burke, Kenneth, "Communication and the Human Condition," *Communication*, Vol. 1, No. 2, Spring 1974.

9. For changing views on this issue, *see* John Plamenatz, *Man and Society*, 2 vols. New York: McGraw-Hill, 1963; cf. *The Quest for Self-Control*, ed. S. Z. Klausner, New York: Free Press, 1965.

10. Anouilh, Jean, *The Rehearsal*, tr. Lucienne Hill, London: Methuen, 1961.

11. Fowles, John, *The Magus*, Boston: Little, Brown, 1965, p. 27.

12. Carroll, John B., *Language and Thought*, Englewood Cliffs, N. J.: Prentice-Hall, 1964, p. 2. For a different perspective on the "linguistic-relativity hypothesis," *see* H. G. Furth, *Thinking Without Language*, New York: Free Press, 1966.

13. The term is Burkart Holtzner's—*Reality Construction in Society*, Cambridge, Mass.: Schenkman, 1968—but somewhat expanded here. "Communication: *sine qua non* of the Behavioral Sciences," *Vistas in Science*, 13th AFOSR Science Seminar, Albuquerque, N. M.: University of New Mexico Press, 1968.

14. St. Augustine's axiom, "To understand, you must believe," is just as relevant in this context. For a more thorough exploration of this issue, see my "Communication Systems," chapter 6 in *The Relevance of General Systems Theory*, ed. Ervin Laszlo, New York: Braziller, 1972.

15. In *The Concept of Nature*, Whitehead wrote that "the aim of science is to seek the simplest explanations of complex facts." But—"To me the truth is something which cannot be told in a few words, and those who simplify

the universe only reduce the expansions of its meaning" (Anais Nin, *The Diary of Anais Nin,* Winter 1931-32). William Blake wrote: "Nature hath no outline, but imagination has"; and Dostoevski: "Man needs the unfathomable and the infinite just as much as he does the small planet which he inhabits."

16. *Cf.* Kaplan, Abraham, "The Life of Dialogue," *Communication,* J. D. Roslansky ed., Amsterdam: North-Holland Publishing Co., 1969, p. 90ff. 90ff.

Selected Bibliography

ACKOFF, R. L., "Games, Decisions, and Organizations," *General Systems,* Vol. 4, 1959.

ACKOFF, R. L., "Systems, Organizations, and Interdisciplinary Research," *General Systems,* Vol. 5, 1960.

ACKOFF, RUSSELL, ed., *Systems and Management Science,* New York: Random House Annual, 1973.

ALLPORT, FLOYD H., *Theories of Perception and the Concept of Structure,* New York: Wiley, 1955.

ALLPORT, GORDON W., "The Open System in Personality Theory," *Journal of Abnormal Social Psychology,* Vol. 61, 1960.

ANGYAL, ANDRAS, "The Structure of Wholes," *Philosophy of Science,* Vol. 6, 1939.

ANGYAL, ANDRAS, "A Logic of Systems," *Systems Thinking,* F. E. Emery, ed., Baltimore, Md.: Penguin Books, 1969.

ASHBY, W. R., "Effect of Controls on Stability," *Nature,* Vol. 155, 1945.

ASHBY, W. ROSS, *Design for a Brain,* New York and London: Chapman & Hall, 1954.

✓ ASHBY, W. ROSS, *An Introduction to Cybernetics,* New York: Wiley, 1956.

ASHBY, W. ROSS, "General System Theory as a New Discipline," *General Systems,* Vol. 3, 1958.

BAKKE, E. WRIGHT, "Concept of the Social Organization," *Modern Organization Theory,* Mason Haire, ed., New York: Wiley, 1959.

BANATHY, BELA H., *A Systems View of Education,* Belmont, California: Fearon Publishers, 1973.

✓ BATESON, GREGORY, "Cybernetic Explanation," *American Behavioral Scientist,* Vol. 10, 1967.

BATESON, GREGORY, *Steps to an Ecology of Mind,* New York: Ballantine Books, 1972.

BEER, STAFFORD, *Cybernetics and Management,* London: English University Press, 1959

BEER, STAFFORD, "Below the Twilight Arch: A Mythology of Systems," *General Systems,* Vol. 5, 1960.

BEER, STAFFORD, *Decision and Control,* New York: Wiley, 1966.

BEISHON, JOHN and GEOFF PETERS, eds., *Systems Behavior,* New York: Harper & Row, 1973.

BERRIEN, KENNETH F., *General and Social Systems,* New Brunswick, N. J.: Rutgers University Press, 1968.

BERTALANFFY, LUDWIG von, and ANATOL RAPOPORT, eds., *General Systems,* Washington: Society for General Systems Research, 1956-1972.

BERTALANFFY, LUDWIG von, "An Outline of General System Theory," *British Journal of Philosophical Science,* Vol. 1, 1950.

BERTALANFFY, LUDWIG von, *Problems of Life: An Evaluation of Modern Biological Thought,* New York: Wiley, 1952.

BERTALANFFY, LUDWIG von, *Robots, Men and Minds,* New York: Braziller, 1967.

BERTALANFFY, LUDWIG von, *General System Theory,* New York: Braziller, 1968.

BOGUSLAW, ROBERT, *New Utopians: A Study of System Design and Social Change,* Englewood Cliffs, N. J.: Prentice-Hall, 1968.

BOULDING, KENNETH E., *The Organizational Revolution,* New York: Harper, 1953.

BOULDING, KENNETH E., "Toward a General Theory of Growth," *The Canadian Journal of Economics and Political Science,* Vol. 19, 1953.

BOULDING, KENNETH E., "General Systems Theory—Skeleton of Science," *Management Science,* Vol. 2, 1956.

BOULDING, KENNETH E., *The Image,* Ann Arbor: University of Michigan Press, 1956.

BOULDING, KENNETH E., "Political Implications of General Systems Research" *General Systems,* Vol. 6, 1961.

BRILLOUIN, LEON, "Life, Thermodynamics, and Cybernetics," *American Scientist,* Vol. 37, 1949.

BRILLOUIN, LEON, *Science and Information Theory,* New York: Academic Press, 1961.

BUCKLEY, WALTER, *Sociology and Modern Systems Theory,* Englewood Cliffs, N. J.: Prentice-Hall, 1967.

BUCKLEY, WALTER, ed., *Modern Systems Research for the Behavioral Scientist,* Chicago: Aldine, 1968.

CANNON, WALTER B., *The Wisdom of the Body,* New York: Norton, 1939.

CAWS, PETER, "Science and System," *General Systems,* Vol. 13, 1968.

CHURCHMAN, C. WEST, *The Systems Approach*, New York: Delacorte, 1968.

CONANT, JAMES B., *Science and Common Sense*, New Haven, Conn.: Yale University Press, 1951.

DERMERATH, N. J., and R. A. PETERSON, eds., *System, Change and Conflict*, New York: Free Press, 1967.

DEUTSCH, KARL W., "Mechanism, Organism, and Society," *Philosophy of Science*, Vol. 18, 1951.

DEUTSCH, KARL W., "On Social Communication and the Metropolis," *Daedalus*, Vol. 90, 1963.

DEUTSCH, KARL W., *The Nerves of Government*, New York: Free Press, 1963.

DUNCAN, HUGH D., *Symbols in Society*, New York: Oxford University Press, 1968.

DUNCAN, HUGH D., *Symbols and Social Theory*, New York: Oxford University Press, 1969.

EASTON, DAVID, *A Systems Analysis of Political Life*, New York: Wiley, 1965.

EMORY, F. E., *Systems Thinking*, London: Penguin Books, 1969.

FIRTH, RAYMOND, *Elements of Social Organization*, Boston: Beacon Press, 1963.

FITZGERALD, JOHN M. and ANDRA F. FITZGERALD, *The Fundamentals of Systems Analysis*, New York: Wiley, 1973.

FOERSTER, HEINZ von, and GEORGE W. ZOPF, Jr., eds., *Principles of Self-Organization: University of Illinois Symposium on Self-Organization, 1961*, New York: Pergamon Press, 1962.

GERARD, RALPH W., "Units and Concepts in Biology," *Science*, Vol. 125, 1957.

GLASSMAN, ROBERT, "Persistence and Loose Coupling in Living Systems," *Behavioral Science*, Vol. 18, No. 2 (March 1973).

GRAY, WILLIAM, F. D. DUHL, and N. D. RIZZO, eds., *General Systems Theory and Psychiatry*, Boston: Little, Brown & Co., 1969.

GRAY, W. and N. RIZZO, eds., *Unity Through Diversity* (4 volumes), New York: Gordon and Breach, 1971.

GRINKER, ROY R., *Toward a Unified Theory of Behavior*, New York: Basic Books, 1956.

HALL, EDWARD T., *The Hidden Dimension*, New York: Doubleday, 1966.

HANSON, NORWOOD R., *Patterns of Discovery: An Inquiry into the Conceptual Foundations of Science*, Cambridge: Cambridge University Press, 1958.

HAPP, H. H., ed., *Gabriel Kron and Systems Theory*, Syracuse, New York: Syracuse University Press, 1973.

HUXLEY, JULIAN, *Evolution in Action,* New York: Harper, 1953.

ITTELSON, WILLIAM, ed., *Environment and Cognition,* New York: Seminar Press, 1973.

KAST, F. E. and J. E. ROSENZWEIG, *Organization and Management: A Systems Approach,* New York: McGraw-Hill, 1970.

KIM, JOHN Y., "Feedback and Human Communication: Toward a Reconceptualization," an unpublished doctoral dissertation, University of Iowa, 1971.

KLIR, G. J., *An Approach to General Systems Theory,* New York: Van Nostrand Reinhold, 1969.

KLIR, G. J., "On the Relationship between Cybernetics and General Systems Theory," *Progress in Cybernetics,* J. Rose, ed., New York: Gordon and Breach, 1970.

KLIR, GEORGE J., ed., *Trends in General Systems Theory,* New York: Wiley Interscience Pub., 1972.

KOEHLER, W., "Closed and Open Systems," *Systems Thinking,* F. E. Emery, ed., Baltimore, Md.: Penguin Books, 1969.

KOESTLER, ARTHUR, and J. R. SMYTHIES, eds., *Beyond Reductionism: New Perspectives in the Life Sciences,* London and New York: Macmillan, 1969.

KUHN, ALFRED, "Toward a Uniform Language of Information and Knowledge," *Synthese,* Vol. 13, 1961.

KUHN, ALFRED, *The Study of Society: A Unified Approach,* Homewood, Ill.: Irwin, 1963.

KUHN, THOMAS S., *The Structure of Scientific Revolutions,* Chicago: University of Chicago Press, 1963.

LANGE, OSKAR, *Wholes and Parts: A General Theory of System Behavior,* New York: Pergamon, 1965.

LASZLO, C. A., M. D. LEVINE, and J. H. MILSUM, "A General Systems Framework for Social Systems," *Behavioral Science,* Vol. 19, No. 2, 1974.

LASZLO, ERVIN, *System, Structure, and Experience,* New York: Gordon and Breach, 1969.

LASZLO, ERVIN, *The Systems View of the World,* New York: Braziller, 1972.

LASZLO, ERVIN, *Introduction to Systems Philosophy,* New York: Gordon and Breach, 1972.

LASZLO, ERVIN, ed., *The Relevance of General Systems Theory,* New York: Braziller, 1972.

LASZLO, ERVIN, *The World System,* New York: Braziller, 1973.

LASZLO, ERVIN, "A Systems Philosophy of Human Values," *Behavioral Science,* Vol. 18, No. 4, 1973.

LATHI, BHAGAWANDAS P., *Signals, Systems and Communication*, New York: Wiley, 1965.

LEKTORSKY, V. A., and V. N. SADOVSKY, "On Principles of System Research," *General Systems*, Vol. 5, 1960. "O Printsipakh Issledovania Sistem," trans. by Anatol Rapoport, from Voprosy Filosofii, No. 8, 1960.

LYSLOFF, GEORGE O., "Semantic Categories and Hierarchy of Systems," *General Systems*, Vol. 14, 1969.

MARTENS, HINRICH and DON ALLEN, *Introduction to Systems Theory*, Columbus, Ohio: Merrill Pub., 1969.

MCCLELLAND, CHARLES A., "General Systems and the Social Sciences," *ETC*, Vol. 18, 1962.

MACKAY, DONALD M., "Towards an Information-Flow Model of Human Behavior," *British Journal of Psychology*, Vol. 47.

MACKAY, DONALD M., *Information, Mechanism and Meaning*, Cambridge, Mass.: M.I.T. Press, 1969.

MARUYAMA, MAGOROH, "The Second Cybernetics: Deviation Amplifying Mutual Causal Processes," *American Scientist*, Vol. 51, 1963.

MARUYAMA, MAGORAH, "Metaorganization of Information," *Cybernetica*, No. 4, 1965.

MASLOW, ABRAHAM H., ed., *New Knowledge and Human Values*, New York: Harper and Row, 1966.

MASLOW, ABRAHAM H., ed., *Motivation and Personality*, New York: Harper and Row, 1970.

MAURER, JOHN G., *Readings in Organization Theory*, New York: Random House, 1971.

MCCULLOCH, WARREN S., *Embodiments of Mind*, Cambridge, Mass.: Massachusetts Institute of Technology Press, 1965.

MEAD, GEORGE HERBERT, *Mind, Self, and Society*, Chicago: University of Chicago Press, 1934.

MENNINGER, K., M. MAYMAN, and P. PRUYSER, *The Vital Balance: The Life Process in Mental Health and Illness*, New York: Viking Press, 1963.

MESAROVIC, M. D., et. al., *Theory of Hierarchial, Multi-Level Systems*, New York: Academic Press, 1970.

MESAROVIC, M. D., *Views on General Systems Theory*, New York: Wiley & Sons, 1964.

MILES, RALPH F. Jr., ed., *Systems Concepts: Lectures on Approaches to Systems*, New York: Wiley, 1973.

MILLER, JAMES G., "Toward a General Theory for the Behavioral Sciences," *American Psychologist*, Vol. 10, 1955.

MILLER, JAMES G., "Living Systems: Basic Concepts; Structure and Process; Cross-Level Hypotheses," *Behavioral Science,* Vol. 10, 1965.

MILSUM, JOHN H. ed., *Positive Feedback,* London: Pergamon, 1968.

MONANE, JOSEPH H., *A Sociology of Human Systems,* New York: Appleton-Century-Crofts, 1967.

MORTENSEN, C. DAVID, *Communication,* New York: McGraw-Hill, 1972.

PADULO, LOUIS and MICHAEL A. ARBIB, *Systems Theory,* Philadelphia: W. B. Saunders Co., 1973.

PATTEE, HOWARD H., *Hierarchy Theory,* New York: Braziller, 1973.

PARSONS, TALCOTT, *Essays in Sociological Theory, Pure and Applied,* Glencoe, Ill.: Free Press, 1949.

PARSONS, TALCOTT, *The Social System,* New York: Free Press, 1957.

PARSONS, TALCOTT, E. A. SHILS, K. D. NAEGELE, and T. R. PITTS, eds., *Theories of Society,* New York: Free Press, 1961.

POPPER, KARL, R., *The Logic of Scientific Discovery,* New York: Harper, 1959.

POPPER, KARL R., *Conjectures and Refutations,* New York: Basic Books, 1962.

PRINGLE, J. W. S., "On the Parallel Between Learning and Evolution," *Behavior,* Vol. 3, 1951.

QUASTLER, H., *Information Theory in Biology,* Urbana: University of Illinois Press, 1953.

QUASTLER, H., *Information Theory in Psychology,* New York: Free Press, 1955.

RAMSOY, ODD, *Social Groups as System and Subsystem,* New York: Free Press, 1963.

RAPOPORT, ANATOL, "What is information?" *ETC,* Vol. 10, 1953.

RAPOPORT, ANATOL, *Operational Philosophy,* New York: Harper and Row, 1953.

RAPOPORT, ANATOL, "The Promise and Pitfalls of Information Theory," *Behavioral Science,* Vol. 1, 1956.

RAPOPORT, ANATOL and WILLIAM J. HORVATH, "Thoughts on Organization Theory" *General Systems,* Vol. 4, 1959.

RAPOPORT, ANATOL, "Methodology in the Physical Biological and Social Sciences," *General Systems,* Vol. 14, 1969.

RICE, CHARLES E., "A Model for the Empirical Study of a Large Social Organization," *General Systems,* Vol. 6, 1961.

RILEY, JOHN W. Jr. and MATILDA WHITE RILEY, "A Sociological Approach to Mass Communication," *Sociology Today,* Robert K. Merton, Leonard Broom and Leonard S. Cottrell, Jr., eds., New York: Basic Books, 1959.

RUBEN, BRENT D., "General System Theory: An Approach to Human Communication," *Approaches to Human Communication,* Richard W. Budd and Brent D. Ruben, eds., Rochelle Park, N. J.: Hayden Book Co. (Spartan) 1972.

ROSE, J., ed., *Progress of Cybernetics,* New York: Gordon and Breach, 1970.

ROSENBLUETH, ARTURO, *Mind and Brain: A Philosophy of Science,* Cambridge, Mass.: The Massachusetts Institute of Technology Press, 1970.

ROTHSTEIN, JEROME, *Communication, Organization and Science,* Indian Hills, Colo.: Falcon's Wing Press, 1958.

RUBIN, MILTON D., ed., *Man in Systems,* New York: Gordon and Breach, 1971.

RUESCH, JURGEN and GREGORY BATESON, *Communication: The Social Matrix of Society,* New York: Norton, 1951.

RUESCH, JURGEN, "The Observer and the Observed: Human Communication Theory," *Toward a Unified Theory of Human Behavior,* Roy R. Grinker, Sr., ed., New York: Basic Books, 1956.

SCHRODER, HAROLD M., MICHAEL J. DRIVER, and SIEGFRIED STREUFERT, *Human Information Processing,* New York: Holt, Rinehart and Winston, 1967.

SCHRODINGER, ERWIN, *What is Life?,* Cambridge: Cambridge University Press, 1945.

SHANDS, HARLEY, *Thinking and Psychotherapy,* Cambridge: Harvard University Press, 1960.

SHANNON, CLAUDE E. and WARREN WEAVER, *The Mathematical Theory of Communication,* Urbana: University of Illinois Press, 1949.

SIMON, HERBERT A., *Models of Man,* New York: Wiley, 1957.

SIMON, HERBERT A., "The Architecture of Complexity," *Proceedings of the American Philosophical Society,* Vol. 106.

SIMON, HERBERT A., *The Sciences of the Artificial,* Cambridge, Mass.: The Massachusetts Institute of Technology, 1969.

SINGH, JAGJIT, *Great Ideas in Information Theory, Language and Cybernetics,* New York: Dover Publications, 1966.

SMITH, ALFRED G., ed., *Communication and Culture,* New York: Holt, Rinehart and Winston, 1966.

SOMMERHOFF, G., "The Abstract Characteristics of Living Systems," *Systems Thinking,* F. E. Emery, ed., Baltimore, Md.: Penguin Books, 1969.

SPIEGEL, JOHN, *Transactions,* New York: Science House, 1971.

STANLEY-JONES, D., and K. STANLEY-JONES, *The Cybernetics of Natural Systems: A Study in Patterns of Control,* New York: Pergamon, 1960.

SUTHERLAND, JOHN W., *General Systems Philosophy for the Social and Behavioral Sciences,* New York: Braziller, 1973.

THAYER, LEE, "Communication and Organization Theory," *Human Communication Theory,* Frank E. X. Dance, ed., New York: Holt, Rinehart and Winston, 1967.

THAYER, LEE, *Communication and Communication Systems,* Homewood, Ill.: Irwin, 1968.

THAYER, LEE, "Communication: *Sine Qua Non* of the Behavioral Sciences," *Vistas in Science,* D. L. Arm, ed., Albuquerque: University of New Mexico Press, 1968.

THAYER, LEE, "Communication Systems," *The Relevance of General Systems Theory,* Ervin Laszlo, ed., New York: Braziller, 1972.

VICKERS, GEOFFREY, "Control, Stability, and Choice," *General Systems,* Vol. 2, 1957.

VICKERS, GEOFFREY, "A Classification of Systems," *General Systems,* Vol. 15, 1957.

VICKERS, GEOFFREY, "Is Adaptability Enough?", *Behavioral Science,* Vol. 4, 1959.

VICKERS, GEOFFREY, *Value Systems and Social Process,* New York: Basic Books, 1968.

VICKERS, GEOFFREY, *Freedom in a Rocking Boat,* London: Allen Lane, 1970.

WATZLAWICK, PAUL, JANET BEAVIN, and DON D. JACKSON, *Pragmatics of Human Communication,* New York: Norton, 1967.

WEISS, PAUL A., ed., *Hierarchically Organized Systems in Theory and Practice,* New York: Hafner Publishing Co., 1971.

WHITEHEAD, ALFRED NORTH, *The Concept of Nature,* Cambridge: Cambridge University Press, 1920.

WHITEHEAD, ALFRED NORTH, *Science and the Modern World,* New York: Macmillan, 1925.

WHITEHEAD, ALFRED NORTH, *Process and Reality,* New York: Macmillan, 1929.

WIENER, NORBERT, *The Human Use of Human Beings,* Garden City, N. Y.: Doubleday, 1954.

WIENER, NORBERT, *Cybernetics,* Cambridge: MIT Press, 1961.

YOUNG, O. R., "A Survey of General Systems Theory," *General Systems,* Vol. 8, 1963.

YOUNG, O. R., "The Impact of General Systems on Political Science," *General Systems,* Vol. 8, 1963.

Index

Index